# $S$ATELLITE IMAGE OF NORTH AMERICA

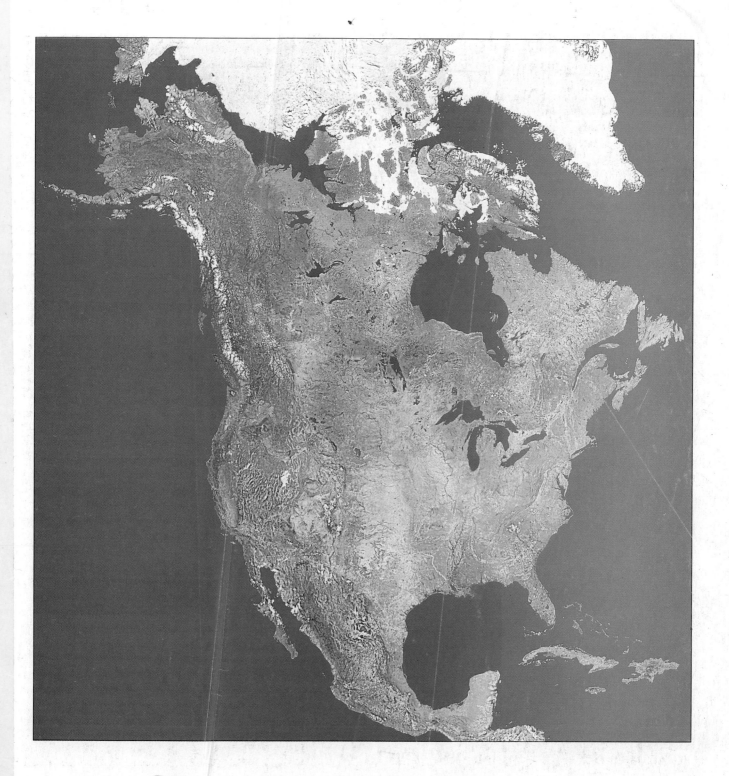

$A$ *picture of North America produced from a mosaic of Landsat satellite images.*
(*Source:* Worldsat International/Science Photo Library/Photo Researchers.)

*S*atellite images of the Earth at night, as recorded by the visible/infrared Operational Linescan System on board a Defense Meteorological Satellite Program (DMSP) spacecraft. The white patches indicate city lights, and thus the extent of urbanization around the world. Red areas indicate large-scale burning of vegetation (such as in tropical forest regions of equatorial Africa). Yellow areas are due to the burning of natural gas flares associated with oil fields (for instance, around the Persian Gulf). (*Sources:* Eastern Hemisphere (at left): NASA GSFC/Science Photo Library/Photo Researchers; Western Hemisphere (at right): NASA/Mark Marten/Science Photo Library/Photo Researchers.)

# ENVIRONMENTAL SCIENCE

## SYSTEMS AND SOLUTIONS

**MICHAEL L. McKINNEY**

UNIVERSITY OF TENNESSEE,

KNOXVILLE

**ROBERT M. SCHOCH**

BOSTON UNIVERSITY

**WEST PUBLISHING COMPANY**

MINNEAPOLIS/ST. PAUL

NEW YORK

LOS ANGELES

SAN FRANCISCO

## 𝒫RODUCTION CREDITS

COPYEDITING
Patricia Lewis

INTERIOR DESIGN
Diane Beasley

ARTWORK
*GRAPHS AND CHARTS*
John and Judy Waller, Scientific Illustrators

*MAPS*
Alice and Will Thiede, Carto-Graphics

*SCHEMATICS*
Precision Graphics

COMPOSITION
Parkwood Composition

INTERIOR ELECTRONIC PAGE LAYOUT
David J. Farr/ImageSmythe, Inc.

COVER DESIGN
Diane Beasley

COVER IMAGE
The Dolomiti Mountains of Veneto, Italy, copyright © 1995 by Koji Yamashita/Panoramic Images, Chicago. All rights reserved.

PRODUCTION, PREPRESS, PRINTING, AND BINDING
West Publishing Company

BRITISH LIBRARY CATALOGUING-IN-PUBLICATION DATA. A CATALOGUE RECORD FOR THIS BOOK IS AVAILABLE FROM THE BRITISH LIBRARY.

𝒞OPYRIGHT © 1996     BY WEST PUBLISHING COMPANY
                     610 OPPERMAN DRIVE
                     P.O. BOX 64526
                     ST. PAUL, MN  55164–0526

𝓛IBRARY OF CONGRESS CATALOGING-IN-PUBLICATION DATA

McKinney, Michael L.
    Environmental science: systems and solutions / Michael Lyle McKinney, Robert Milton Schoch.
      p. cm.
    Includes bibliographical references and index.
    ISBN 0–314–06401–X (alk. paper)
    1. Environmental sciences. 2. Pollution—Environmental aspects.
3. Environmentalism. I. Schoch, Robert M.  II. Title.
GE105.M39 1996
363.7—dc20                                                    95–25678
                                                             CIP

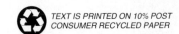

# WEST'S COMMITMENT TO THE ENVIRONMENT

In 1906, West Publishing Company began recycling materials left over from the production of books. This began a tradition of efficient and responsible use of resources. Today, 100% of our legal bound volumes are printed on acid-free, recycled paper consisting of 50% new paper pulp and 50% paper that has undergone a de-inking process. We also use vegetable-based inks to print all of our books. West recycles nearly 27,700,000 pounds of scrap paper annually—the equivalent of 229,300 trees. Since the 1960s, West has devised ways to capture and recycle waste inks, solvents, oils, and vapors created in the printing process. We also recycle plastics of all kinds, wood, glass, corrugated cardboard, and batteries, and have eliminated the use of polystyrene book packaging. We at West are proud of the longevity and the scope of our commitment to the environment.

West pocket parts and advance sheets are printed on recyclable paper and can be collected and recycled with newspapers. Staples do not have to be removed. Bound volumes can be recycled after removing the cover.

# ABOUT THE AUTHORS

**MICHAEL L. McKINNEY** is an associate professor in the Department of Geology and in the Department of Ecology and Evolutionary Biology at the University of Tennessee, Knoxville. Since 1985 he has taught a wide variety of courses, focusing especially on environmental science and biodiversity issues at the undergraduate level.

Dr. McKinney received his Ph.D. in geology and geophysics from Yale University in 1985. He is the author of the introductory text *Evolution of Life*, several technical books on ecology and evolution, and more than 40 technical articles. Many of these technical publications involve his research on extinction and biodiversity loss. He is also known for his work on how species evolve by changes in developmental stages, including the evolution of childhood. Dr. McKinney has received a number of teaching awards for establishing and teaching environmental science courses for nonscience majors at the University of Tennessee.

With Dr. Schoch, he shares the belief that environmental knowledge is only a first step toward what should follow next: informed and pragmatic environmental advocacy. Dr. McKinney is president of the Foundation for Global Sustainability, a "grassroots" environmental advocacy group in Knoxville that sponsors "eco-fairs" for children, runs a speaker's bureau, and operates many other activities to educate the general public about local environmental issues ranging from endangered species in the Smoky Mountains to water pollution in urban creeks.

**ROBERT M. SCHOCH** is an associate professor of science and mathematics at the College of General Studies, Boston University, where he has specialized since 1984 in teaching undergraduate science, including physical science, biology, geology, geography, and environmental science courses. Dr. Schoch always includes a strong environmental component in all of the courses he teaches. He is a recipient of his college's Peyton Richter Award for interdisciplinary teaching.

Dr. Schoch received his Ph.D. in geology and geophysics from Yale University in 1983 and is the author of several technical books and numerous articles on various aspects of paleontology and geology. In honor of his paleontological contributions, the fossil mammal genus *Schochia* was named after him in 1993. In some circles, however, Dr. Schoch is better known for his work in Egypt. Correlating ancient environmental changes with surface and underground weathering features, he concluded that the base of the Great Sphinx was initially carved more than two thousand years earlier than had been generally believed. This research has been the subject of many articles in the professional and popular archaeological and Egyptological literature and has also been featured in several television documentaries aired around the world. Understanding past environmental changes is important as we face future challenges.

Besides his academic and scholarly studies, Dr. Schoch is an active environmental advocate who stresses a pragmatic, hands-on approach. In this connection, he helped to found, and serves as president of, a local community land trust devoted to protecting land from harmful development. Likewise, Dr. Schoch takes an active part in "green" politics (in 1995 he was elected to the local city council).

Dr. Schoch lives in Attleboro, Massachusetts, with his wife, Cynthia, and their two sons, Nicholas and Edward.

# RIEF CONTENTS

*B*RIEF CONTENTS

# ONTENTS

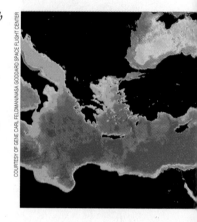

COURTESY OF GENE CARL FELDMAN/NASA GODDARD SPACE FLIGHT CENTER

NASA

CHAPTER 3

# $\mathcal{T}$HE BIOSPHERE  59

CHAPTER 4

# $\mathcal{E}$NVIRONMENT: AN INTEGRATED SYSTEM OF FOUR SPHERES  94

$\mathcal{C}$ONTENTS

# CHAPTER 5

## ⅅEMOGRAPHY   112

# CHAPTER 6

## ℘RINCIPLES OF RESOURCE MANAGEMENT   146

© HODSON/GREENPEACE

F. EDWORDS/VISUALS UNLIMITED

CHAPTER 9

# $\mathscr{A}$LTERNATIVE ENERGY SOURCES AND ENERGY CONSERVATION 226

U.S. DEPARTMENT OF ENERGY

CHAPTER 10

# $\mathscr{M}$INERAL RESOURCES 257

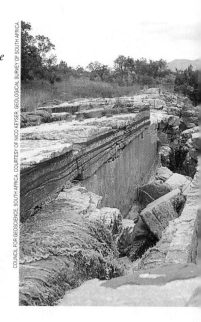
COUNCIL FOR GEOSCIENCE, SOUTH AFRICA. COURTESY OF NICO KEYSER, GEOLOGICAL SURVEY OF SOUTH AFRICA

## CHAPTER 13

# *F*EEDING THE WORLD  352

TED WHITTENKRAUS/
VISUALS UNLIMITED

SECTION  3    PROBLEMS OF ENVIRONMENTAL DEGRADATION                387

## CHAPTER 14

# *P*RINCIPLES OF POLLUTION CONTROL  388

DEAN DeCHAMBEAU

# CHAPTER 17

## ❰A❱IR POLLUTION: LOCAL AND REGIONAL  463

# CHAPTER 18

## ❰G❱LOBAL AIR POLLUTION: DESTRUCTION OF THE OZONE LAYER AND GLOBAL WARMING  493

CHAPTER 19

# $\mathcal{M}$ UNICIPAL SOLID WASTE AND HAZARDOUS WASTE  525

---

SECTION 4    SOCIAL SOLUTIONS    561

---

CHAPTER 20

# $\mathcal{E}$ NVIRONMENTAL ECONOMICS  562

CHAPTER 22

# $\mathcal{H}$ISTORICAL, SOCIAL, AND LEGAL ASPECTS OF THE CURRENT ENVIRONMENTAL CRISIS 606

# PREFACE

The critical importance of environmental science and environmental studies cannot be disputed as we enter the twenty-first century. Virtually everyone is aware of environmental issues—be they global warming, the depletion of the ozone layer, the controversy over nuclear power, or the continuing problems of water pollution and solid waste disposal. Politicians who once focused primarily on such issues as economic productivity and national security now increasingly acknowledge that environmental sustainability is a necessary prerequisite if we are to ensure our survival. The United Nations Conference on Environment and Development (popularly known as the "Earth Summit"), held in Rio de Janeiro in June 1992, was the largest international summit ever held, attracting delegates from over 175 countries including more than a hundred heads of state. No citizen of the Earth can afford to be ignorant of environmental issues.

We wrote this book to provide a comprehensive overview and synthesis of environmental science. *Environmental Science: Systems and Solutions* provides the reader with the basic factual data necessary to understand current environmental issues. But to know the raw facts is not enough. A well-informed person must understand how various aspects of the natural environment interconnect with each other and with human society. We thus use a systems approach as a means of organizing complex information in a way that highlights connections for the reader. The systems approach allows the reader to take in the information without feeling overwhelmed, as often happens when large amounts of information are presented in a disorganized fashion. With a subject as diverse as environmental science, it is easy to get lost in the details. We have always kept the "big picture" in mind.

All too often environmental discussions become bogged down in partisan rhetoric or "gloom and doom" tactics. Our intention is not to preach, but to inform. Accordingly, in approaching what is often an extremely controversial subject, we have adopted an objective and practical perspective that tries to highlight what is going right in dealing with modern environmental problems.

A key concept among modern environmentalists is sustainability. In this book we have adopted the sustainability paradigm: we focus on sustainable technologies and economic systems and the ways that sustainable development can be implemented around the world. Our emphasis is on specific examples that can give concrete meaning to the concept: sustainable technological and social solutions to environmental problems are discussed throughout the book. We hope to inspire the reader to move beyond simple awareness of current environmental problems to become an active promoter of sustainable solutions to those problems.

## ORGANIZATION

The book is divided into four basic sections. Section 1, *Environmental Principles* (Chapters 1–5), describes how natural systems work, including both physical systems (Chapter 2) and biological systems (Chapter 3). The systems approach is introduced in Chapter 1, reinforced in Chapter 4, and expanded throughout the rest of the book. The final chapter of the first section focuses on the increasing impact that the growing human population has had on all natural systems.

Section 2 (*Problems of Resource Depletion*) deals with issues surrounding the use of natural resources by human society. Chapter 6 introduces the broad principles of resource management. The following chapters address energy use, mineral use, water use, and the use of biological resources (including agriculture and soil resources). A major theme is that humans have been rapidly depleting many of these resources and that we must begin using them in a sustainable manner if we are to survive and flourish in the future.

Section 3 (*Problems of Environmental Degradation*) concentrates on various forms of pollution and waste—the results of dumping large amounts of the by-products of human society into the environment. Chapter 14 introduces the principles of pollution control while subsequent chapters deal with toxicology, pesticides, water pollution, air pollution, global warming and the destruction of the ozone layer, municipal solid waste, and hazardous waste. Every chapter includes discussions of how we can limit or mitigate the effects of excessive pollution, especially by limiting production of pollutants in the first place, as well as by increased efficiency, reuse, recycling, and substitutions.

A major emphasis of the book is on solutions to the current "environmental crisis." Woven throughout the text are discussions and examples of environmentally friendly technological, legal, and economic solutions. We firmly believe that sustainable and realistic solutions must be implemented and that the root causes of the environmental problems we now face must be addressed. Such problems cannot be solved using science and technology alone; the human aspect must also be taken into account. Therefore, even though this is primarily an environmental science text, we have devoted the final section (Section 4, Chapters 20–22) entirely to *Social Solutions*. This section includes explicit discussions of social, economic, legal, and ethical issues and solutions to current environmental problems.

# USING THIS BOOK FOR A COURSE IN ENVIRONMENTAL SCIENCE OR ENVIRONMENTAL STUDIES

This book was designed to be accessible to introductory non-major students, but it has enough depth and breadth to be used in a majors course. It can be adapted to either an environmental science course or an environmental studies course, and it can be utilized for either one or two semesters. Also, the book was designed so that the chapters need not necessarily be used in the order in which they appear. In particular, depending on the nature and emphasis of a particular course, an instructor may choose to use the social solutions chapters at either the beginning or end of the course or to omit certain chapters entirely.

Assuming a standard 15 full weeks for a semester (usually about a week is lost due to holidays, exams, and the like), the chapters of this text might be assigned according to one of the following schedules:

For a comprehensive environmental science and studies course:

- Week 1　Chapters 1 & 2
  Introduction and Physical Environment

- Week 2　Chapters 3 & 4
  Biosphere and Integration of the Physical and Biological Environments
- Week 3　Chapter 5
  Demography
- Week 4　Chapters 6 & 7
  Resource Management, Fossil Fuels, and Hydroelectric Power
- Week 5　Chapters 8 & 9
  Nuclear Energy, Alternative Energy Sources, and Energy Conservation
- Week 6　Chapters 10 & 11
  Mineral and Water Resources
- Week 7　Chapter 12
  Natural Biological Resources
- Week 8　Chapter 13
  Food and Agriculture
- Week 9　Chapters 14 & 15
  Pollution, Toxicology, and Pesticides
- Week 10　Chapter 16
  Water Pollution
- Week 11　Chapter 17
  Local and Regional Air Pollution
- Week 12　Chapter 18
  Global Warming and Destruction of the Ozone Layer
- Week 13　Chapter 19
  Municipal Solid Waste and Hazardous Waste
- Week 14　Chapters 20 & 21
  Environmental Economics and Ethics
- Week 15　Chapter 22
  Historical, Social, and Legal Aspects of Contemporary Environmentalism

For a basic environmental science course:

- Week 1　Chapters 1 & 4
  Introduction and Integration of the Physical and Biological Environments
- Week 2　Chapter 5
  Demography
- Week 3　Chapter 6
  Resource Management
- Week 4　Chapters 7 & 8
  Fossil Fuels, Hydroelectric Power, and Nuclear Energy
- Week 5　Chapter 9
  Alternative Energy Sources and Energy Conservation
- Week 6　Chapter 10
  Mineral Resources
- Week 7　Chapter 11
  Water Resources

- Week 8 Chapter 12
  Natural Biological Resources
- Week 9 Chapter 13
  Food and Agriculture
- Week 10 Chapter 14
  Pollution Control
- Week 11 Chapter 15
  Toxicology and Pesticides
- Week 12 Chapter 16
  Water Pollution
- Week 13 Chapter 17
  Local and Regional Air Pollution
- Week 14 Chapter 18
  Global Warming and Destruction of the
  Ozone Layer
- Week 15 Chapter 19
  Municipal Solid Waste and Hazardous Waste

For a general environmental studies course (emphasizing social and historical aspects):

- Week 1 Chapters 1 & 4
  Introduction and Integration of the Physical
  and Biological Environments
- Week 2 Chapter 21
  Environmental Ethics
- Week 3 Chapter 22
  Historical, Social, and Legal Aspects of
  Contemporary Environmentalism
- Week 4 Chapter 5
  Demography
- Week 5 Chapter 18
  Global Warming and Destruction of of the
  Ozone Layer—examples of the impact
  humans are having on the environment
- Week 6 Chapter 6
  Resource Management
- Week 7 Chapter 7
  Fossil Fuels and Hydroelectric Power
- Week 8 Chapters 8 & 9
  Nuclear Energy, Alternative Energy Sources,
  and Energy Conservation
- Week 9 Chapter 12
  Natural Biological Resources
- Week 10 Chapter 13
  Food and Agriculture
- Week 11 Chapters 14 & 15
  Pollution, Toxicology, and Pesticides
- Week 12 Chapter 16
  Water Pollution
- Week 13 Chapter 17
  Local and Regional Air Pollution

- Week 14 Chapter 19
  Municipal Solid Waste and Hazardous Waste
- Week 15 Chapter 20
  Environmental Economics

If this book is used for a two-semester course, some of the lengthier chapters should be used over a longer period than one week. In particular, we recommend that the following chapters be split as indicated and extended over two weeks:

- Chapter 2 General Physical Environment/
  Natural Hazards
- Chapter 7 Fundamentals of Energy/Fossil
  Fuels and Hydroelectric Power
- Chapter 9 Alternative Energy/Energy
  Conservation
- Chapter 12 Biodiversity/Public Lands
- Chapter 13 Food/Soil Resources
- Chapter 18 Destruction of the Ozone
  Layer/Global Warming
- Chapter 19 Municipal Solid Waste/
  Hazardous Waste
- Chapter 22 Historical and Social
  Perspectives/Environmental Law

If these chapters are used as suggested, then chapter or subchapter readings from the text will easily fit into a two-semester (approximately 30 full weeks) schedule.

## PEDAGOGICAL FEATURES

Each chapter uses the same basic organizational format. Following an opening photograph and an outline of the contents, the chapter begins with a Prologue that is intended to draw the reader into the subject matter of the chapter.

The text is written so as to be interesting and accessible to the average reader and is profusely illustrated with color diagrams demonstrating basic concepts and key ideas. Additionally, numerous charts, tables, drawings, and photographs enrich the basic text. Throughout the text key terms denoting important concepts are in boldface type. Each chapter contains a number of "Issues in Perspective" boxes that focus on current aspects and major controversies pertaining to the subject matter of the chapter. Most chapters feature "Case Studies" with thought-provoking questions to promote critical thinking.

The end-of-chapter material includes a comprehensive summary, a list of the chapter's key terms, and two kinds of questions. The Study Questions test objective knowledge and require fairly short answers; in most chapters the last two study questions include a quantitative component. Answers to the odd-numbered Study Questions are in Appendix F at the end of the book. The Essay Questions require more analytical and critical thinking skills. Finally, at the end of each chapter, a list of Suggested Readings directs the reader to recent, widely accessible books on related topics.

This book includes several special features. Inside the front cover is a map of North America showing the physical geography and political boundaries of all the states and provinces of the United States, Mexico, and Canada. Inside the back cover is a political map of the world. These maps will serve as handy reference guides for the reader when various states, provinces, and countries are mentioned in the text. It is increasingly important that everyone be familiar with basic global political geography.

The appendixes include discussions of common measures of energy and power, English/metric conversion tables (throughout the text we have used a dual system of English/metric units), selected major pieces of U.S. environmental legislation, selected pieces of international environmental legislation, a list of selected environmental organizations and government agencies, and finally the answers to odd-numbered Study Questions. These appendixes should be useful to students as they peruse the text or decide to delve deeper into environmental issues.

The book concludes with a glossary of key terms and a detailed index.

## ANCILLARY MATERIALS

To assist you in teaching this course and supplying your students with the best in teaching aids, West Publishing Company has prepared a complete supplemental package available to all adopters:

- The comprehensive instructor's manual and test bank, prepared by Robert Hollenbeck of Metropolitan State University, includes teaching ideas, chapter overviews, learning objectives, discussions of common student misconceptions, answers to the even-numbered Study Questions in the text, audiovisual and multimedia sources, Internet sources, and the test bank containing approximately 2,000 multiple-choice, true/false, fill-in-the-blank, matching, short-answer, analogy, and quantitative questions.

- The entire test bank is provided on diskette along with WESTEST, a computerized testing package. Using WESTEST 3.0, instructors can generate examinations containing questions they select or questions randomly generated by the computer. Instructors can also use the WESTEST 3.0 edit function to modify these questions, add new questions, or delete existing questions. Additionally, West's classroom management software allows student data to be recorded, stored, and used for various reports.

- An electronic slide presentation package using Persuasion, prepared by Charles Olmsted of the University of Northern Colorado, provides text outlines, graphs, artwork, and animations for each chapter of *Environmental Science*. The presentations are available for Macintosh and for Windows. Instructors with Persuasion software can customize the outlines, art, and order of presentation.

- West's Instructor's Reference CD-ROM, which contains all of the instructor's printed supplements, the electronic presentation package, and all of the art from the text, provides instructors with a single source for the supplements. The text's art has been converted to a visual format for computer projection in the classroom.

- A slide set and full-color transparency acetate set provide clear, effective illustrations of 150 of the most important pieces of artwork and maps from the text.

- *Readings in Environmental Literacy*, edited by Michael McKinney and Parri S. Shariff, is a collection of 50 current articles to supplement materials that students will encounter in their course work. *Canadian Issues in Environmental Science* by Paul West, director of the Environmental Science Program at the University of Victoria in British Columbia, Canada, is a collection of 55 current articles and readings from a Canadian perspective. The articles in both readers come from a variety of general interest and science magazines. West can make these supplements available with the text as a set, or they can be purchased separately.

- A collection of 60 case studies, prepared by Robert Schoch, explores controversial issues in environmental science. Each case study is followed by questions that emphasize critical examination of the issues and the impact poor ethical decisions can have on the environment. At the same time, the questions show that there are no easy answers to environmental issues. Each case study includes source references.

- An Internet activity book is available for students to investigate environmental resources on the Internet and conduct interesting research relevant to the topics covered in their class. The activities book will provide approximately 50 activities that use the Internet to access databases, find special interest groups, and interact with other students, experts, and even legislators.

- A study guide, written by Jim Blahnik of Lorain County Community College, is closely tied to the main text. The guide provides an overview of each chapter, learning objectives, exercises to test the students on key terms, chapter concept questions, table and graph interpretation exercises, quantitative exercises, and a practice exam consisting of multiple-choice, true/false, fill-in-the-blank, and matching questions. The study guide also includes resource material on "What You Can Do" in the form of specific suggestions, activities, resources available to students, and "green" career ideas that cover science and nonscience positions.

- A Student Note Taking Guide contains printed copies of all of the art that is used in the electronic slide presentation package. Bound with perforated, three-punched pages, it allows students to take notes as the slides are shown in lecture.

# ACKNOWLEDGMENTS

As authors, we are ultimately responsible for the content of this book, but dozens of people have provided help, encouragement, and advice. In particular, we are grateful for the advice of many teachers and practitioners of environmental science. Due to its depth and breadth, environmental science contains far more information than only two people can master, and we drew heavily on the expertise of people who have specialized in its many subfields. We therefore wish to express our deep appreciation to the reviewers of the book manuscript:

Clark E. Adams
Texas A & M University

David A. Adams
North Carolina University

John W. Adams
University of Texas, San Antonio

Michael Albert
University of Wisconsin, River Falls

Sara E. Alexander
Baylor University

Gary L. Anderson
Santa Rosa Junior College

Richard D. Bates
Rancho Santiago College

Mark C. Belk
Brigham Young University

Charles F. Bennett
University of California, Los Angeles

Keith Bildstein
Winthrop College

Gerald Collier
San Diego State University

Harold Cones
Christopher Newport University

Carl F. Chuey
Youngstown State University

Lorraine Doucet
University of New Hampshire, Manchester

Nicholas P. Dunning
University of Cincinnati

L. M. Ehrhart
University of Central Florida

George W. Hinman
Washington State University

Gary J. James
Orange Coast College

Robert L. Janiskee
University of South Carolina

Michael G. King
College of the Redwoods

Clifford B. Knight
East Carolina University

Cindy M. Lee
Clemson University

Jack Lutz
University of New Hampshire

Timothy F. Lyon
Ball State University

Theodore L. Maguder
St. Petersburg Junior College

Kenneth E. Mantai
SUNY, Fredonia

Heidi Marcum
Baylor University

Priscilla Mattson
Middlesex Community College

W. D. McBryde
Central Texas College

Richard L. Meyer
University of Kansas

Henry R. Mushinsky
University of South Florida

Muthena Naseri
Moorpark College

Arnold L. O'Brien
University of Massachusetts, Lowell

Charles E. Olmsted
University of Northern Colorado

Nancy Ostiguy
California State University, Sacramento

Richard A. Paull
University of Wisconsin, Milwaukee

Adrienne Peacock
Douglas College

Charles R. Peebles
Michigan State University

R. H. Pemble
Moorhead State University

Chris E. Petersen
College of DuPage

Dennis M. Richter
University of Wisconsin, Whitewater

Gordon C. Robinson
University of Manitoba

C. Lee Rockett
Bowling Green State University

Paul Rowland
Northern Arizona University

David B. Scott
Dalhousie University

Ray Sumner
Los Angeles Valley College

R. Bruce Sundrud
Harrisburg Area Community College

Peter G. Sutterlin
Wichita State University

S. Carl Tobin
Utah Valley State College

Jerry Towle
California State University, Fresno

Lee B. Waian
Saddleback College

Linda Wallace
University of Oklahoma

Joel Weintraub
California State University, Fullerton

Frank Williams
Langara College

Richard J. Wright
Valencia Community College

Craig ZumBrunnen
University of Washington

Very special thanks are due to Jerry Westby, college editorial manager for West Publishing Company. Jerry has played many key roles during this book's long years from conception to production. He has been a prime motivator, catalyst, and source of reason and understanding. West Publishing Company developmental editor Dean DeChambeau was also intimately involved with the development of this book and offered invaluable advice on making the information more "reader friendly." His hard work ranged from reading many revisions of the chapters to finding and even taking photographs for the book. Also, it would be very difficult to find better production editors than Barbara Fuller and Laura Nelson of West Publishing Company. They are consummate, dedicated professionals who greatly improved the final product; it was a pleasure working with them.

This book was initially conceptualized and begun by M. L. M., but given the magnitude of the undertaking, he invited R. M. S. to help him complete the book. In the final analysis, both authors are equally responsible for the entire book. Both pored over the manuscript many times, writing and rewriting so the book would speak with a single voice.

M. L. M. thanks Deb Tappan for her hard work in helping with the extensive retyping that was sometimes needed in a short time frame. Tina Rolan and Jane Ansley helped with reading, editing, and many production chores. Special thanks to Vickie McKinney for chasing down reluctant permission requests. Finally, thanks to my hundreds of students in environmental courses through the years. Your curiosity and interest inspire me.

R. M. S. thanks his wife, Cynthia, and sons, Nicholas and Edward, for their patience during the writing and production of this book. Furthermore, Cynthia often helped by reading and informally reviewing various chapters and sections. R. M. S. also extends his appreciation to his parents, Milton and Alicia Schoch, and his parents-in-law, Robert and Anne Pettit, who offered continued encouragement and support during this project.

*Michael L. McKinney, Knoxville, TN*
*Robert M. Schoch, Attleboro, MA*

# LEARNING GUIDE

Before you become absorbed in this textbook, take a moment to look over the next few pages. We've provided an overview of the built-in learning devices you'll find throughout the book. Becoming familiar with these unique features can make your navigation through the material much easier.

**GETTING STARTED**
**Chapter outlines will get you started with a quick overview of what topics you can expect to cover.**

**Prologues open each chapter. These interesting short stories provide a fascinating glimpse into a number of diverse subjects. Interesting and dynamic photos, such as the elephant you'll find opening Chapter 12, tie into the prologues.**

**PROLOGUE** *How Much Is That Ivory in the Window?*

In the contiguous United States, the bald eagle has rebounded from 400 nesting pairs in the 1960s to over 3000 pairs today. A flock of 20 whooping cranes has grown to 200. Bison have gone from just under 1100 to over 20,000. Even more important are success stories in tropical countries, which are the cradle for most of the world's biological diversity. But in these countries, which are beset by overpopulation and poverty, merely passing laws prohibiting killing does not work as well as it has in the United States. The most successful strategies in the tropics have fought extinction by removing economic incentives to kill species. An example is elephant survival.

Once home to millions of elephants, Africa had fewer than 700,000 by the late 1980s and was projected to have fewer than 25,000 by the early twenty-first century. Richard Leakey, son of the famed anthropologist and director of Kenya's Wildlife Services, had seen poachers reduce Kenya's elephant population by 70% in 10 years, killing them at the rate of three per day.

Leakey took action. Game wardens were issued new vehicles, automatic weapons, and surveillance aircraft, with orders to shoot poachers on sight. Within weeks, elephant killing dropped dramatically, from three per day to one per month. More importantly for the elephants' long-term survival, Leakey joined with many other conservationists in calling for a global ban on sales of ivory. In 1989, over 80 member nations of the Convention on International Trade in Endangered Species (CITES) agreed to this ban. It has been enormously successful. Before the ban, ivory in Africa sold for about $100 per pound. By 1990, the price had plummeted 20-fold to $5 per pound, and the elephant decline had slowed by 80%. Many bans had been instituted before, but the key difference here was the widespread resolve by people in many industrialized nations to stop buying ivory billiard balls, carved ivory, and other items. By removing the economic incentive to kill elephants, potential buyers of ivory did much more to stop the killing than armies of game wardens could accomplish.

But what of the poachers? Leakey realized that the local poverty would be magnified without the income formerly provided from ivory. He therefore turned to the growing market for "ecotourism," where tourists visit rainforests and go on safaris. By providing employment as hotel workers, guides, and many other local jobs, ecotourism provides incentives to maintain the pristine natural environment. (continued)

## BEAUTIFUL AND DYNAMIC

The text's illustration program and page layout were carefully developed to convey critical information in an attractive fashion. As you look through the text, you'll notice the consistent use of vibrant colors. Not only are the colors beautiful to look at, but they also make for clearer and more informative illustrations.

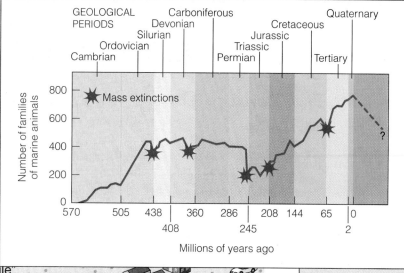

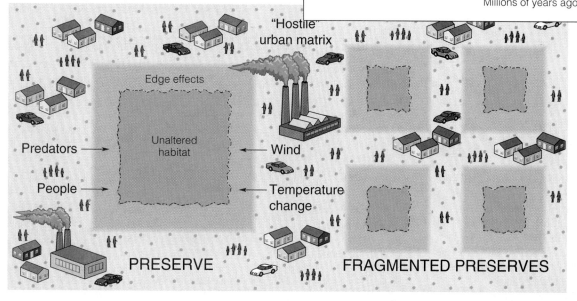

Buffer zones are another important preserve characteristic (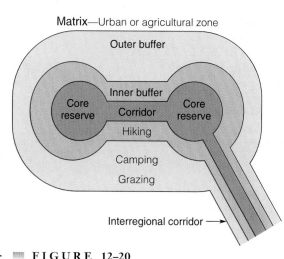 Fig. 12–20). Buffer zones are areas of moderately utilized land that provide a transition into the unmodified natural habitat in the core preserve where no human disturbance is allowed. For example, campgrounds and limited cattle grazing may be permitted in the outermost buffer zone, with hiking in the innermost buffer zone. Buffer zones are a major departure from traditional preserves that were viewed as "islands" of natural habitat in a hostile "matrix" of agricultural or urban landscape.

## NOW WHERE WAS I?

You just spent a few minutes studying an illustration and now you can't remember where you left off reading. This little gold box appears next to figure references within the text. It's a little feature, but a real time-saver.

**FIGURE 12–20**
Buffer zones can be used to support economic activities around a core of natural habitat. (*Source:* Modified from R. Noss and A. Cooperrider, *Saving Nature's Legacy* [Washington, D.C.: Island Press, 1994], p. 148.)

# The "Miner's Canary": Decline of Songbirds

In the 1980s, amateur birdwatchers began to notice a pronounced decline in the abundance of many different songbird species in North America. A number of statistical studies have confirmed the birdwatchers' observations. ● Table 1 shows the results of a study comparing bird sightings in the 1940s and in the 1980s in the Washington, D.C., area.

The loss of songbirds is alarming in many ways. One reason is the obvious reduction in quality of life to people who enjoy their beauty and singing. But more alarming to some is that songbirds are sensitive to many environmental changes. They are like the "miner's canary": these birds were kept in mines because they were more sensitive than people to bad air. A sick or dying bird was a warning.

Nor are songbirds declining only in North America. In 1994, the Worldwatch Institute reported that two-thirds of the songbird species of the world were experiencing a decline in abundance.

What is causing such declines? As usual, all the causes of extinction probably play at least some role: loss of food species and introduction of predators are clearly involved with some songbird losses. But John Terborgh of Duke University and many other bird experts have suggested that habitat loss and fragmentation are key factors in the decline. Indeed, songbirds are hit with a "one-two" punch of habitat loss. Many migrate from North America to the tropics, and they are losing habitat in both places. Species that spend winters in the tropics are declining faster than those that do not. One reason is that tropical defor-

**TABLE 1** *Sightings of Songbird Species in Rock Creek Park, District of Columbia*

| Species | MEAN NUMBER OF PAIRS SIGHTED | | Percentage Change |
|---|---|---|---|
| | In 1940s | In 1980s | |
| **Migrants** | | | |
| Red-eyed vireo | 41.5 | 5.8 | −86.0 |
| Ovenbird | 38.8 | 3.3 | −91.5 |
| Acadian flycatcher | 21.5 | 0.1 | −99.5 |
| Wood thrush | 16.3 | 3.9 | −76.1 |
| Yellow-throated vireo | 6.0 | 0.0 | −100.0 |
| Hooded warbler | 5.0 | 0.0 | −100.0 |
| Scarlet tanager | 7.3 | 3.5 | −52.1 |
| Black-and-white warbler | 3.0 | 0.0 | −100.0 |
| **Nonmigrants** | | | |
| Carolina chickadee | 5.0 | 4.3 | −14.0 |
| Tufted titmouse | 5.0 | 4.5 | −10.0 |
| Downy woodpecker | 3.5 | 3.0 | −14.3 |
| White-breasted nuthatch | 3.5 | 3.1 | −11.4 |

(*Source:* Reprinted by permission of the National Audubon Society.)

estation is removing their wintering sites.

But even songbirds that stay in North America all the time are declining. Here the reason is apparently habitat disruption in North America, especially from forest fragmentation. Investigations since the early 1980s have shown that fragmented forests can greatly hinder songbird reproduction because of edge effects. Nest predators, such as raccoons, opossums, and housecats, take a much greater toll where forest fragmentation produces edges that allow easier access to nests. Nests that are deep in the forest and thus less exposed are less preyed upon.

Furthermore, cowbirds destroy more eggs through nest parasitism when the forest is fragmented. Cowbirds lay eggs in songbird nests, and the songbirds raise cowbird chicks instead of their own. Cowbirds prefer disturbed farmland, so loss of forests promotes the spread of cowbirds and opens up songbird habitat to access by these nest parasites.

**ISSUES IN PERSPECTIVE**
These boxes provide more detailed discussions of interesting environmental science topics, applications, and positive environmental action. Interested in the global safe drinking water crisis? See Chapter 11. Want to know more about paper versus plastic? Turn to Chapter 19.

*L*EARNING GUIDE

## CASE STUDY

### *Are Habitat Conservation Plans the Answer? The California Gnatcatcher Example*

In 1982, Congress passed an amendment to the Endangered Species Act that was intended to meet some of the main criticisms of the original act. Opponents had charged that the act (1) interfered with economic growth, (2) emphasized saving species rather than whole ecosystems, and (3) waited until a species was on the verge of extinction before protecting it. The amendment created a new approach designed to make the act more flexible, reduce economic costs, and protect many species before they are near extinction.

The new approach is called a habitat conservation plan (HCP). Under an HCP, some of the habitat of an endangered species can be destroyed (called an "incidental take") as long as a plan is drawn up to reduce future losses. An HCP usually evolves as a compromise from discussions among landowners, developers, environmental groups, local governments, and the U.S. Fish and Wildlife Service, which eventually must approve the HCP. Ideally an HCP will protect all current or potentially endangered species in an area, while simultaneously permitting human use of nearby lands as deemed necessary by social consent.

By 1994, 7 HCPs had been approved and another 60 were under discussion from California to Key Largo, Florida. Each HCP is unique and some are more successful than others. California has the most HCPs to have been approved. The first was at San Bruno Mountain south of San Francisco, which emerged as a compromise between housing developers and environmentalists wanting to

■ **FIGURE 1**

The California gnatcatcher has generated national controversy. (*Source:* Anthony Mercieca/Photo Researchers.)

save the mission blue butterfly. In fact, this conflict at San Bruno led to the legislation creating the HCP concept.

A good example of the complexities an HCP can encounter involved the coastal sage scrub habitat of southern California. This habitat includes some of the nation's most expensive real estate in prime locations around Los Angeles, San Diego, and nearby areas. But it is also home to a rare songbird called the California gnatcatcher (■ Fig. 1). Only 2600 pairs remain, with 70–90% of the habitat already destroyed. In 1993, after three years of discussion among developers, environmentalists, and government officials, Interior Secretary Bruce Babbitt announced that the gnatcatcher would be listed as "threatened" instead of "endangered" as proposed by the U.S. Fish and Wildlife Service. The less urgent "threatened" status allows officials to work out the details of an HCP that may permit development on some of the remaining scrub habitat. But the HCP will also call for establishing up to 12 reserves that will benefit as many as 40 other coastal sage scrub species that are also in jeopardy from this disappearing habitat.

## Questions

1. Many environmentalists strongly dislike the HCP concept because they believe it is "giving away" species and habitat to development. Can you think of a better way to resolve habitat versus development conflicts? Explain.

2. Since "extinction is forever," why would anyone ever approve of the HCP concept? How could development ever be justified over the irreversible loss of species? Explain.

3. Would you approve of an HCP that permitted one species to go extinct, but allowed 5 other species to survive? If it allowed 10 others to survive? Twenty others? Explain your reasoning.

# KEY TERMS

biodiversity
biological impoverishment
bottom-up approach
buffer zones
charismatic species
chemical prospecting
clear-cutting
conservation biology
Convention on Biological Diversity (CBD)
Convention on International Trade in Endangered Species (CITES)
ecological extinction
ecosystem simplification
ecotourism
edge effects
Endangered Species Act
exotic species
extinction
extinction vortex
extirpation
genetic patent rights
habitat fragmentation
hot spots
indicator species
introduction
keystone species
marine protected areas
mass extinctions
minimum viable population (MVP)
multiple-use principle
National Marine Sanctuary
reintroduction
selective cutting
species-area curve
species richness
species triage
sustainable harvesting
taxonomists
umbrella species
unique species
Wilderness Act of 1964

# STUDY QUESTIONS

1. Is species richness at local scales related to species richness at regional scales? Explain and give an example.
2. What is the "bottom-up" approach? How are buffer zones, ecotourism, and sustainable harvesting related to this?
3. What is a species-area curve? What does it predict if 90% of a habitat is destroyed?
4. What is biological impoverishment? What causes it?
5. How many mass extinctions have occurred before now? What was the average extinction rate before humans? How much higher is the rate now?
6. Name and describe two key reasons why habitat fragmentation is one of the most destructive ways of disrupting habitat.
7. Name the four main causes of extinction.
8. Which are biological? Do most extinctions involve just one cause?
9. What is an extinction vortex? What are two basic causes of an extinction vortex? What is the minimum viable population?
10. Where are exotic species an especially important cause of extinction? Why? Give examples.
11. Are diverse communities more easily disturbed? Explain.
12. Are all species equally important? Give two major examples. Where do unique species fit in?
13. How are genetic patent rights important in promoting biodiversity conservation? Give specific examples. What is chemical prospecting?
14. What is a hot spot? How can hot spots be used in selecting the location of preserves?
15. What are two widely suggested solutions to the national park funding problem?
16. Compare and contrast selective cutting and clear-cutting.
17. If you estimate that 50 species per day are going extinct, how many species will be extinct in a year? In 100 years? What percentage of all species will be extinct in 100 years, if there are 10 million species on Earth?
18. If you estimate that 100 species per day are going extinct, how many species will be extinct in a year? In 100 years? What percentage of all species will be extinct in 100 years, if there are 10 million species on Earth?

# ESSAY QUESTIONS

1. Why is biodiversity important? Discuss some of its many values, and indicate the ones you favor the most.
2. What are the characteristics of a well-designed preserve? How are they related to "edge effects" and minimum viable population sizes?
3. What is "ecotourism"? Discuss its advantages and disadvantages in saving species.
4. Are marine species being threatened? By what? Discuss possible solutions.
5. Discuss the pros and cons of the U.S. Endangered Species Act. Is it a failure? A success? How should it be improved?
6. Discuss the problems of the U.S. Forest Service and those of the National Park Service. What differences and similarities do you see in the problems of the two agencies?

# SUGGESTED READINGS

Baker, R. 1993. *Environmental management in the tropics*. Boca Raton, Fla.: CRC Press.

Berger, J. J. 1990. *Environmental restoration*. Washington D.C.: Island Press.

Fiedler, P. L. and S. Jain, eds. 1992. *Conservation biology*. New York: Chapman & Hall.

Frome, M. 1992. *Regreening the national parks*. Tucson: University of Arizona Press.

Jacobs, L. 1992. *Waste of the West: Public lands ranching*. Tucson: Lynn Jacobs.

Jordan, C. F. 1995. *Conservation*. New York: Wiley.

Jordan, W. R., M. Gilpin, and J. Aber. 1987. *Restoration ecology*. Cambridge: Cambridge University Press.

Meffe, G. K., and C. R. Carroll. 1994. *Principles of conservation biology*. Sunderland, Mass.: Sinauer.

Norton, B. G., ed. 1986. *The preservation of species*. Princeton: Princeton University Press.

Noss, R., and A. Cooperrider. 1994. *Saving nature's legacy*. Washington, D.C.: Island Press.

O'Toole, R. 1987. *Reforming the forest service*. Covelo, Calif.: Island Press.

Primack, R. B. 1993. *Essentials of conservation biology*. Sunderland, Mass.: Sinauer.

Terborgh, J. 1992. *Diversity and the tropical rain forest*. New York: W. H. Freeman.

Tobin, R. J. 1990. *The expendable future: U.S. politics and the protection of biodiversity*. Durham, N.C.: Duke University Press.

Wilson, E. O. 1992, *The diversity of life*. Cambridge, Mass.: Harvard University Press.

**BUILT-IN STUDY AIDS**
Need a quick memory refresher for an upcoming exam? You'll find a chapter summary at the end of each chapter.

Extirpation? Ecotourism? Buffer zones? Important key terms are listed at the ends of each chapter. For more complete definitions, flip to the glossary in the back of the book. It's easy to find—there's a colored band on the edge of each glossary page so you can open right to it.

Study questions and essay questions are a great way to test your knowledge of the subject matter. They can really help you prepare for an upcoming exam.

Want to know more? A list of suggested readings tells you where you can find more information on a wide variety of environmental topics.

# ADDITIONAL RESOURCES FOR STUDENTS

We've put together a few additional resources that you may wish to purchase to help you in your environmental science class. They will also come in handy should you decide to pursue further environmental studies. Check with your college bookstore to see if any of these items are available.

## STUDENT STUDY AND ACTION GUIDE
This combination study and action guide provides study tips, environmental suggestions for your own life, and "green" career ideas for both science and nonscience majors. It also includes chapter overviews, learning objectives, quantitative exercises, table and graph exercises, concept questions, group learning exercises, and practice exams.

## STUDENT NOTE TAKING GUIDE
This guide includes copies of all electronic transparencies provided to instructors. They are printed on paper with space for you to take lecture notes. Saves you from having to copy everything off the transparencies.

## INTERNET ACTIVITY BOOK
This book contains approximately 50 activities that challenge you to locate and use a variety of Gopher, WWW, and other resources on the Internet.

## BOOK OF READINGS
*Readings in Environmental Literacy* contains approximately 50 articles. Each article begins with an introduction and ends with questions for discussion.

# ENVIRONMENTAL PRINCIPLES

*Science alone does not have and never will have solutions to the fundamental environmental problems of our time, which are religious in the largest sense of the word, dealing as they do with values and the human spirit. If we remember this at all times, our science will then be freed to play the part that is expected of it in the battle to save the life on this planet.*

DAVID EHRENFELD, biologist and writer

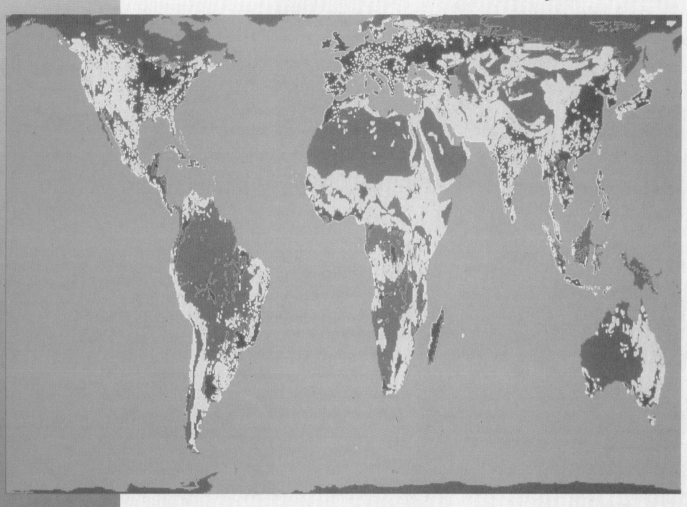

PHOTO    *Much of the world's land area has been disturbed by humans. In this photo, red indicates land that is greatly altered and yellow shows the partially altered land area. Only the green area remains in a relatively natural state, and it is disappearing rapidly.* (*Source:* Lee Hannah, Conservation International.)

# INTRODUCTION TO ENVIRONMENTAL SCIENCE

## PROLOGUE   *People Making a Difference*

One of the most common sayings in environmentalism is "think globally, act locally." Its key message is that while we should keep the "big picture" in mind, we should not become overwhelmed by the large scale of many environmental problems. Global warming, ozone deple-

PHOTO   *Norris McDonald has organized cleanups of the Anacostia River. (Source: © 1995 Robert Rathe.)*

tion, overpopulation, hazardous waste, extinctions, and many other problems are so great that we may conclude that individual actions cannot make a difference. But this is not true. Global environmental problems are the result of the local actions of many individuals, so the problems can only be solved if we change these many local actions. For example, the 7.7 to 8.8 billion tons (7 to 8 billion metric tons)* of carbon (the equivalent of 28.2 to 32.3 billion tons [25.6 to 29.3 billion metric tons] of $CO_2$, since carbon becomes carbon dioxide when combusted), added to the atmosphere each year are contributing to global warming. Much of this carbon comes from gasoline burned by individuals driving trillions of miles each year. Simple measures by each individual, such as car pooling or buying more fuel-efficient cars, could reduce the carbon addition by millions, even billions, of tons. Such local actions by each of us can save water, reduce pollution, reduce extinctions, and help solve many other environmental problems.

Working to solve these problems not only helps preserve the environment for future generations, it also makes you feel better. As this book will show, you yourself can do thousands of things that will make a difference. Indeed, you may already be doing so. Here are three examples of how individuals have made a difference.

With more than 2800 miles (4500 km) of shoreline to monitor, local officials lacked the funding to adequately enforce pollution laws around Puget Sound in Washington. As a result, levels of water pollution were increasing. Concerned citizens formed the Puget Sound Alliance, a watchdog coalition that formed volunteer groups to look for polluters. Led by former sailing ship skipper Ken Moser, some 200 volunteers now regularly patrol areas of Puget Sound in kayaks, small boats, and on foot. By 1994, these pollution fighters had stopped the flow of contamination from at least 12 industrial sites, with more than $150,000 in fines charged to polluters.

The Anacostia River of Washington, D.C., was labeled the city's "refuse pit" by the *New York Times* because it was rich in sewage, street pollution, and other refuse. Norris McDonald started a campaign to focus attention on the river and clean it up. McDonald organizes cleanup days, leads river walks, conducts water tests, and persuades businesses to "adopt" stretches of the fouled suburban streams that feed, and pollute, the river. McDonald's efforts are among the few devoted to solving the environmental problems of African Americans, who often live near the Anacostia River. McDonald also founded the Center for Environment, Commerce, and Energy, an environmental organization that focuses on a number of environmental problems affecting African Americans.

Ballona Lagoon in Los Angeles is one of the last remnants of a vast saltwater wetland system that once covered hundreds of acres along the coast of southern California. Although the lagoon contains only 16 acres (6.5 hectares), it provides valuable habitat for over 20 species of migratory waterfowl, shorebirds, and dozens of species of plants, fishes, crabs, and clams. When Iylene Weiss learned that a developer planned to dredge Ballona Lagoon into a boat marina, she organized a grassroots campaign to teach the local community about the ecological importance of the lagoon. The Ballona Lagoon Watch Society was able to use scientific information provided by the developer's environmental impact statement to defeat the developer's plan. Next, the society convinced the Coastal Commission and the U.S. Environmental Protection Agency (EPA) to provide more than $100,000 in grants toward restoring the lagoon to better health. Today, work is underway to improve the tidal circulation that flushes pollutants from the lagoonal waters, and Ballona Lagoon is once again alive with a variety of flowering native plants.

*Unless otherwise noted, *tons* refers to short tons (2000 pounds).

 NTRODUCTION

Concern about the environment is a worldwide phenomenon. The results of a recent poll, shown in ▀ Figure 1–1, reveal that most people in both industrialized and developing nations have at least some concern about environmental problems. As we will see throughout this book, environmental problems are global in scope because humans and our technology have become so widespread and so potent. Our planet has existed more than four billion years, yet never before has one species dominated the Earth and other species so completely (▀ Fig. 1–2). Few people doubt that humanity now stands at a unique crossroads. In all likelihood, the next few decades will drastically change the Earth and its inhabitants. It is up to individuals to try to influence the outcome so that the wel-

**FIGURE 1–1**

Percentages of respondents in different nations who express a "great deal" and a "fair amount" of concern about the environment. (*Source:* R. E. Dunlap, G. H. Gallup, Jr., and A. M. Gallup, *Health of the Planet* [Princeton, N. J.: George H. Gallup International Institute, 1993, p. 11]. Reprinted with permission from The George H. Gallup International Institute.)

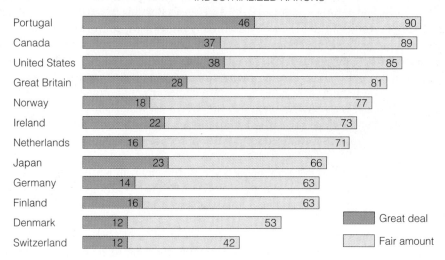

INDUSTRIALIZED NATIONS

| Nation | Great deal | Fair amount |
|---|---|---|
| Portugal | 46 | 90 |
| Canada | 37 | 89 |
| United States | 38 | 85 |
| Great Britain | 28 | 81 |
| Norway | 18 | 77 |
| Ireland | 22 | 73 |
| Netherlands | 16 | 71 |
| Japan | 23 | 66 |
| Germany | 14 | 63 |
| Finland | 16 | 63 |
| Denmark | 12 | 53 |
| Switzerland | 12 | 42 |

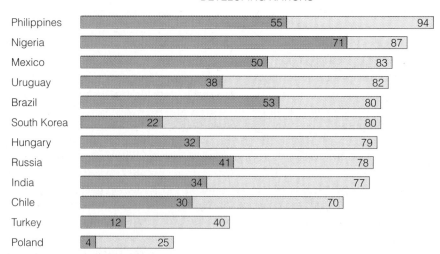

DEVELOPING NATIONS

| Nation | Great deal | Fair amount |
|---|---|---|
| Philippines | 55 | 94 |
| Nigeria | 71 | 87 |
| Mexico | 50 | 83 |
| Uruguay | 38 | 82 |
| Brazil | 53 | 80 |
| South Korea | 22 | 80 |
| Hungary | 32 | 79 |
| Russia | 41 | 78 |
| India | 34 | 77 |
| Chile | 30 | 70 |
| Turkey | 12 | 40 |
| Poland | 4 | 25 |

**FIGURE 1–2**

Even parts of Antarctica, shown here, have become dumping grounds for human waste. (*Source:* William E. Larose/Greenpeace.)

fare of both humans and the environment is best served.

While this book will present many important facts, it also has two larger goals. One is to help you sort through the huge amount of environmental information available and focus on important issues. The second goal is to show how this information can be used effectively to help society make the fundamental changes needed to build a world that can sustain many generations of people, with a decent standard of living, while minimizing human impact on the natural environment.

## Beyond "Information Overload": Environmental Wisdom

One of the challenges we face today is how to cope with information overload. Newspapers, radio, and television bombard us daily with data

*E*NVIRONMENTAL PRINCIPLES   SECTION 1

**FIGURE 1–3**
Henry David Thoreau was an early and articulate American naturalist. (*Source:* The Granger Collection, New York.)

and statistics. Feeling overwhelmed, most people react by "tuning out."

But rather than quit trying to assimilate this information, we might recall Henry David Thoreau's advice to "simplify! simplify!" Thoreau has become a hero to many environmentalists because he long ago predicted many of the problems that we now face (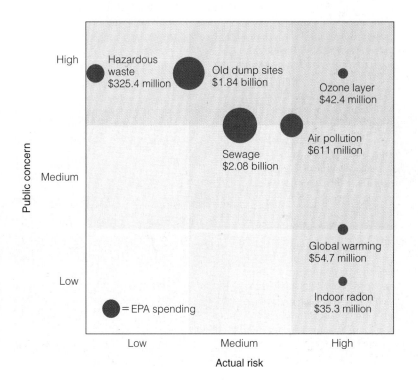 Fig. 1–3). His advice to simplify was a response to what he saw as a tendency for civilization to become increasingly more complex and removed from the natural world that nourished it. This, he said, led to anxieties and spiritual impoverishment despite material wealth.

We can heed Thoreau's advice by mentally stepping back and keeping our priorities set on what we think is important. In this way, we can focus on the information that we can use, instead of trying to learn it all (which no one can do). Ideally, we can strive to seek what might be called **environmental wisdom.** Wisdom is the ability to sort through facts and information to make correct decisions and plan long-term strategies. Wisdom is gained through education and practical experience, so environmental wisdom takes time to develop. Wisdom also means that we take a broad view in solving problems and weigh all kinds of information, social and economic as well as technical. Environmental science is often called **holistic,** meaning that it seeks connections among all aspects of a problem.

Lack of environmental wisdom is costly in many ways. It is costly to other species, to our quality of life, to future generations, and often to human happiness itself. But the most easily measured costs are economic. A good example is Figure 1–4, which shows that money is often poorly spent on environmental problems in the United States. Problems that pose substantial risks such as ozone depletion receive less money than hazardous wastes and other problems that are less threatening. Such spending inefficiencies occur because people often lack adequate information about the true risk of environmental problems. And when they do have this information, they fail to take a holistic approach and ignore such aspects as long-term global impacts. Lack of environmental wisdom also makes us, as individuals, susceptible to increasingly common "ecoscams" and "greenwashing" marketing that unscrupulously seek to profit from environmental concerns (see Issues in Perspective 1–1).

## Beyond Bumper Stickers: Building a Sustainable World

Many environmentalists now point out that past efforts have tended to be "Band-Aids," focusing on short-term, emergency actions rather than long-term solutions. Examples of this approach include cleanup of wastes and pollution after they are produced (Fig. 1–5) and trying to save species only when they are nearly gone. Besides being less effective, such piecemeal, late-acting remedial solutions are almost always the most expensive way to solve environmental problems.

**FIGURE 1–4**
The actual risk of a hazard compared to the amount of public concern about that risk. There is often little correlation between the risk and the concern. As a result, large amounts of money (size of "dot") are spent on small risks while large risks, such as global warming, get less money. (*Source:* Environmental Protection Agency.)

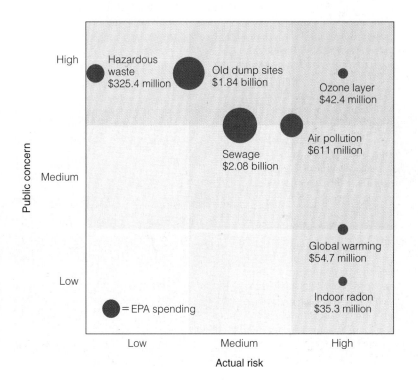

# Environmental Insanity and Pseudoscience: Perils of Ignorance

One of the paradoxes of modern life is that technology permits people to live in unprecedented comfort while remaining in unprecedented ignorance of the natural physical and biological systems that support their lifestyles. Many modern citizens, preoccupied with their daily concerns, have become mentally isolated from the natural environment that supports them ( Fig. 1). Some writers and social scientists consider this isolation to be a form of insanity. Science historian Gerald Holton, for example, says: ". . . persons living in this modern world who do not know the basic facts that determine their very existence, functioning, and surrounding, are living in a dream world. Such persons are, in a very real sense, *not sane.*"

This ignorance of natural science has greatly impaired society's ability to solve the growing number of environmental problems. When people lack even a basic understanding of science, they can be easily swayed by politicians, interest groups, and many others who use "scientific" data to influence public opinion for their own purposes. For example, the late Dixy Lee Ray wrote two books, *Trashing the Planet* (1990) and *Environmental Overkill* (1993), arguing that public debate on environmental issues is dominated by unqualified alarmists. Many environmental groups and certain political groups, she argued, have used such issues as global warming to further their own agendas. Moreover, these groups allegedly use dubious data and poorly trained "experts" to scare an unknowing public.

Ironically, Dr. Ray was herself a well-known politician of strong convictions. Her own books have subsequently been criticized as being highly biased in their selective use of scientific data and poorly qualified "experts" to argue against various environmentalist claims. Nevertheless, Ray's main point is certainly valid: an ignorant public will always remain at the mercy of people who use scientific claims to influence them. Such people include not only politicians seeking votes, but also businesses. "Greenwashing" is a new fad in marketing that seeks to sell products by making environmental claims. Often, these claims are greatly exaggerated; gullible consumers spend extra money, but the environment does not benefit.

Aside from such marketing scams, environmental ignorance causes money to be wasted in another way: spending priorities for environmental problems may be distorted. Consider how the U.S. Environmental Protection Agency (EPA) spent its nearly $7 billion 1993 budget. As Figure 1–4 shows, the EPA often spent the least money on environmental problems that pose the highest risk: ozone depletion, global warming, and indoor radon. The agency spent the most money on problems that have much lower risk, such as old dump sites and sewage, which kill far fewer people each year.

Why does such inefficient spending occur? Much of the reason is that the EPA's spending priorities simply reflect the concerns of the taxpaying public it serves. As the graph illustrates, the public is more worried about sewage and old dump sites than about indoor radon and global warming. The implication is that if the public were better educated about the environment, money would be spent more wisely.

What can be done? Two actions need to be taken to solve the problem of public ignorance. First, citizens must try to become better informed about basic science, especially environmental sciences, by taking a college course in the subject or similar measures. But the educational process continues throughout life, so everyone must also keep up with environmental news in newspapers, magazines, and books. It is important to focus on the factual information available and reach your own conclusions, instead of relying only on opinions of others.

Second, more scientists should actively participate in the public debates on environmental issues. Traditionally, scientists have avoided the public arena for many reasons: (1) professional scientific organizations reward time spent on research and offer no recognition (or even chastisement) for public service; (2) the frustration of dealing with biased ideologues; (3) the difficulty of communicating complex arguments in an era of "sound bites" and information oversaturation; and (4) the inability of science to resolve questions of social values, which are the cause of many environmental disputes. Nevertheless, valid scientific information is desperately needed, so reluctant scientists must be persuaded to join the debate.

**FIGURE 1**

City-dwellers throughout the world often live in little or no contact with the natural environment. (*Source:* Francois Perri/Gamma Liaison.)

**FIGURE 1–5**
Cleaning up toxic waste is an expensive "band-aid" approach. It is much cheaper to design methods that produce less waste. (*Source:* Paul Bierman/Visuals Unlimited.)

The United States has spent more than $1 trillion on pollution cleanup since 1970.

In the last few years, the rising cost and inefficiency of cleaning up pollution after it is produced have led to a search for better approaches to solving environmental problems. Generally, holistic approaches have been able to solve problems more cheaply and efficiently. By examining society and the environment as an interconnected system, we can often solve many problems at once. As Figure 1–6 shows, environmental problems arise from (1) resource depletion and (2) pollution. Past efforts at pollution control were largely "end-of-pipe" solutions, cleaning up waste after it was produced. But as the figure shows, pollution can also be controlled by reducing the flow of material through society. Such **input reduction,** which conserves resources and reduces pollution at the same time, is now widely accepted by environmental economists (Chapter 20) and others as a better solution to most environmental problems. Input reduction illustrates the kind of fundamental change needed to build a society that can be maintained for many years without degrading the environment.

Figure 1–6 also identifies the two basic causes of environmental problems, population and traditional industrial technology. Both need to be addressed if long-term solutions are to be achieved. Population and traditional industrial technology have both led to increased resource consumption and pollution. Two key solutions are therefore to reduce population growth and develop environmentally "friendly" technologies. Many newer technologies, such as solar and wind power, are much less harmful to the environment than the traditional, resource-intensive, highly polluting technologies of the industrial age.

Fossil fuels, for example, are a rapidly disappearing, nonrenewable resource and a major cause of most forms of air pollution. The World Bank estimates that building a world economy based on

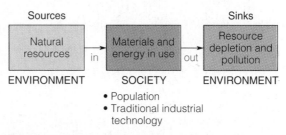

**FIGURE 1–6**

Environment is a source and a sink for matter and energy that flow through society. Population and traditional industrial technology accelerate the flow, leading to resource depletion and pollution. (*Source:* Modified from D. H. Meadows, D. L. Meadows, and J. Randers, *Beyond the Limits* [Post Mills, VT.: Chelsea Green, 1992, p. 7]. Reprinted from *Beyond the Limits*, Copyright © 1992 by Meadows, Meadows, and Randers. With permission from Chelsea Green Publishing Company, White River Junction, Vermont.)

solar, wind, and other renewable, less-polluting fuels would cost about $20 trillion, or about twice the amount of money spent by the United States and the former Soviet Union on the Cold War. To put it another way, the cost is almost equal to the $21 trillion gross world product, the goods and services produced by the world economy in one year. The United States could switch away from fossil fuels for an estimated $2 trillion, which is the amount we spend on the military in eight years.

## What Is Environmental Science?

**Environmental science** is the application of all fields of natural science toward solving environmental problems. Biology, geology, chemistry, physics, meteorology, and many other disciplines are included in a basic environmental science text such as this. In addition to presenting scientific concepts, the book also discusses social solutions to environmental problems. These are included because many of us who teach environmental courses have found that people (understandably) become discouraged and pessimistic if we talk only about problems. Laws, ethics, economics, and other aspects of human behavior will play a key role in solving environmental problems.

Environmental science courses at both the basic and the advanced level are the most rapidly growing courses at many colleges in the United States and in many other nations. Individual disciplines are developing environmental chemistry, environmental biology, environmental geology, and many similar courses to address society's changing needs. Many colleges now recognize majors in environmental science, and some schools are even establishing departments of environmental science.

## $\mathcal{H}$ ISTORY OF ENVIRONMENTAL IMPACT AND ENVIRONMENTAL MOVEMENTS

Considering the age of the Earth and even the human species, the massive environmental impact of humans is a very recent development. Indeed, our relationship with the environment has evolved as we and our technology have evolved.

Environmental historians often identify five basic stages in this evolution, as shown in ▬ Figure 1–7. These stages are largely determined by the economic activity in which humans engage

using the technologies available. This activity, in turn, affects how humans impact the environment.

1. *Hunting and gathering.* Early humans were largely at the mercy of their environment, so they generally viewed it in adversarial terms. Weather, predators, food shortages, and disease were constant threats.

2. *Agriculture and conservationism.* The shift from hunting and gathering to cultivating food is one of the most profound milestones in human evolution. It allowed a great increase in population size and permitted people to settle down in large towns and cities. But agriculture also had a major impact on the environment. People began to view land as a resource to be exploited wherever needed. As land was cleared and cultivated, however, the wilderness vanished. Toward the end of the agricultural stage, the loss of wilderness became so great that alarmed citizens began conservation movements to set up preserves for the remaining wilderness. In the United States, this happened in the late nineteenth century and is often associated with President Theodore Roosevelt (▬ Fig. 1–8). Today many developing countries still have agricultural economies, and their vanishing wilderness, especially tropical rainforests, has stimulated the growth of conservationism.

3. *Industry and environmentalism.* The Industrial Revolution began in England around 1800. As nations industrialize, population grows faster, and the environment is perceived more and more as a place to dispose of the concentrated waste by-products of industry. The result is a rapid increase in air and water pollution, as well as problems with solid and hazardous waste disposal. Toward the end of this stage, pollution becomes so widespread that antipollution social movements emerge. In the United States, these social movements began in the early 1960s and peaked in the 1970s. When people talk about "environmentalism," this antipollution movement is often what they mean. Several early books heralded this new awareness including *Silent Spring* (1962) by Rachel Carson, which warned of pesticide pollution; *The Population Bomb* (1986) by Paul Ehrlich; and *The Limits to Growth* (1972) by Donella H. Meadows and others. As ● Table 1–1 shows, the antipollution movement added litigation and citizen activism to the lobbying tactics used by the conservationists. These efforts and rising public concern led to the passage of landmark environmental legislation by the U.S. Congress:

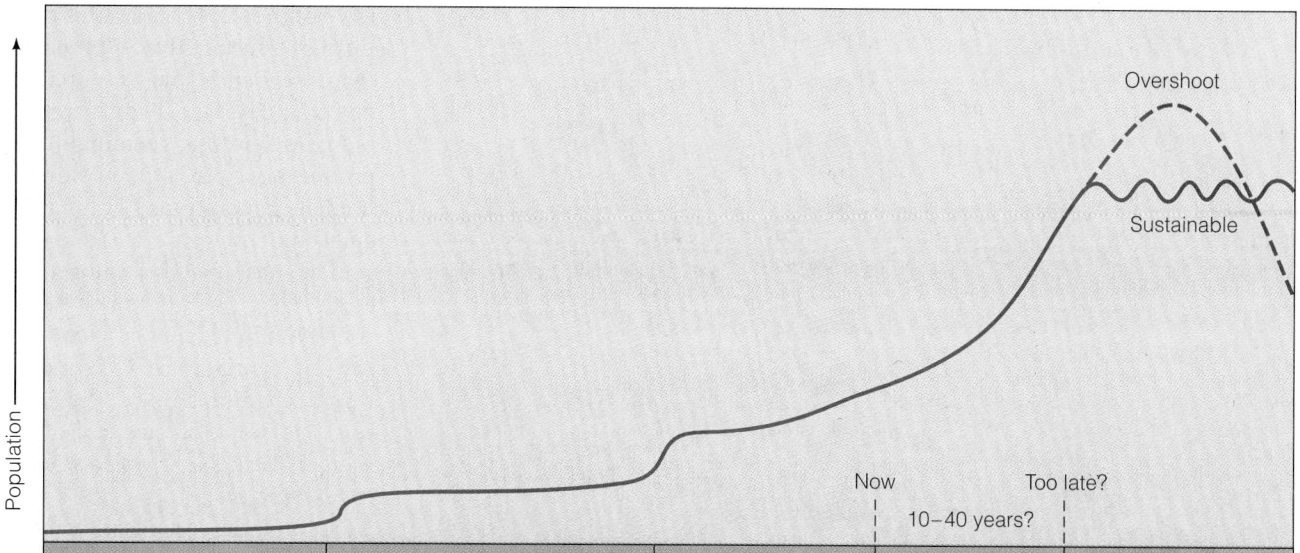

**Population** (vertical axis)

Overshoot

Sustainable

Now | Too late?
10–40 years?

| | Hunting and gathering | Agriculture | Industry | Transition | Postindustrial |
|---|---|---|---|---|---|
| Economic activity | Hunting and gathering | Agriculture | Industry | Transition | Postindustrial |
| Perception of environment | Adversary | Resource | Dumping ground | Awareness of limits | Spaceship or wasteland |
| Environmental impact | Minimal | Vanishing wilderness | Pollution | Widespread degradation | Minimal or massive |
| Environmentalist response | — | Conservation movement | Environmental movement | Sustainability movement | — |
| Examples | — | Game preserves, parks | Clean Air, Water, Waste Acts of 1970s | Market-based incentives | — |

Time ⟶

- 1970 NEPA: National Environmental Policy Act requires environmental impact studies before land development projects.

  EPA: Environmental Protection Agency created.

  CAAA: Clean Air Act Amendments.

- 1972 CWA: Clean Water Act reduces pollution of lakes and rivers.

  CZMA: Coastal Zone Management Act begins cleanup of coastal ocean waters.

- 1973 ESA: Endangered Species Act enacted to preserve endangered species.

- 1974 SDWA: Safe Drinking Water Act requires EPA to set and enforce drinking water standards.

- 1976 TSCA: Toxic Substances Control Act helps limit the amount of poisonous chemicals made and sold in the United States.

- 1980 CERCLA: Comprehensive Environmental Response, Compensation, and Liability Act, or "Superfund," began systematic cleanup of large waste sites.

Many more federal, state, and local laws and amendments have been passed since these. The United States now spends about $115 billion per year, over 2% of the gross national product (GNP), to clean up pollution. This figure is expected to rise to $170 billion (or 2.6% of GNP) by the year 2000. The efforts to clean up pollution have been highly successful in some areas, including lakes and rivers, toxic waste dumps, and ocean dumping.

4. *Transition and sustainability.* Although some forms of pollution have been reduced, many other environmental problems have increased. In the United States, for example, species of wildlife are becoming imperiled at increasing rates as habitat is destroyed. Groundwater contamination has worsened, and there are many thousands of hazardous and radioactive waste sites that will likely not be cleaned up for centuries. Despite recycling and precycling efforts, the amount of solid waste produced per person continues to climb. Globally, the EPA has cited global warming, ozone depletion, and increasing species extinction as the greatest

**FIGURE 1–7**
Population and traditional industrial technology have increased the human impact on the environment in exponential fashion. Environmentalists have responded with the conservation movement, the environmental movement, and the current sustainability movement. Many people believe that we are currently in a transition stage and that humans have 10–40 years to prevent "overshoot" and attain sustainability.

**FIGURE 1–8**
Theodore Roosevelt (left) and
John Muir in Yosemite. (*Source:*
Theodore Roosevelt Collection/
Harvard College Library.)

environmental threats to future generations. These problems are caused in large part by rapidly increasing population in developing countries, which also leads to local food shortages and the loss of billions of tons of soil to erosion each year.

We are currently in this fourth stage—the transition. Environmental problems have become so widespread that they demand large-scale solutions that involve many aspects of society. Beginning in the early 1980s, a sustainability movement has emerged to try to deal with these problems. Unlike the conservation and antipollution movements of the past, which emphasized specific problems, this movement seeks long-term coexistence with the environment. **Sustainability** means meeting the needs of today without reducing the quality of life for future generations. This includes not reducing the quality of the future

environment. Sustainability is achieved through sustainable ("green") technologies that use renewable resources such as solar power and recycle many materials. These technologies allow a **sustainable economy** that produces wealth and provides jobs for many human generations without degrading the environment.

The sustainability movement uses three approaches not attempted by previous environmental movements. First, it focuses explicitly on trying to reduce society's use of all resources. Emphasis is thus on input reduction, as opposed to end-of-pipe solutions. *Waste is viewed as a symptom, not a cause, of the environmental crisis.*

Second, the sustainability movement is more holistic. It realizes the necessity of addressing the social, and especially economic, causes of environmental degradation. This has led to an increasing appreciation of the role of poverty and other economic factors that cause people to deplete resources and pollute. Market-based solutions are becoming more popular, and less emphasis is placed on the legal solutions used in the past. For example, many experts now agree that it is often more effective and cheaper for society to tax coal, gasoline, and other polluting substances than to pass laws specifying how much pollution may be emitted. The higher gasoline prices encourage people to drive less or buy fuel-efficient cars, for instance. Such economic approaches acknowledge that, far from being anti-environmental, business can greatly benefit the environment. It is what people produce and sell that can cause environmental problems, not the acts of producing and selling in themselves. Producing and selling furniture made from tropical rainforest timber will harm the environment whereas brazil nuts, rubber, and many other rainforest products may be extracted and sold with little or no long-term damage.

Third, the sustainability movement has encouraged the growth of thousands of local community action groups, as opposed to the national groups that dominated the conservationism and environmentalism periods. As Table 1–1 shows, most of the major environmental organizations arose before 1980, during the conservationism and environmentalism periods. Since the Love Canal toxic dump (1978) and the Three Mile Island nuclear accident (1979), residents of communities have become increasingly active in addressing local environmental problems. Vocal debates over

**TABLE 1–1** *Major Environmental Organizations in the United States*

| LOBBYING ORGANIZATIONS | | | | NONLOBBYING ORGANIZATIONS | | | |
|---|---|---|---|---|---|---|---|
| Era/Organization | Year Founded | 1990 Membership[a] (Thousands) | 1990 Budget ($ Million) | Type/Organization | Year Founded | 1990 Membership[a] (Thousands) | ($ Mill |
| **Progressive era** | | | | **Direct action** | | | |
| Sierra Club | 1892 | 560 | 35.2 | Greenpeace USA[b] | 1971 | 2300 | 50.2 |
| National Audubon Society | 1905 | 600 | 35.0 | Sea Shepherd Conservation | | | |
| National Parks and | | | | Society | 1977 | 15 | 0.5 |
| Conservation Association | 1919 | 100 | 3.4 | Earth First! | 1980 | (15) | 0.2 |
| **Between the wars** | | | | **Land and wildlife preservation** | | | |
| Izaak Walton League | 1922 | 50 | 1.4 | Nature Conservancy | 1951 | 600 | 156.1 |
| The Wilderness Society | 1935 | 370 | 17.3 | World Wildlife Fund | 1961 | 940 | 35.5 |
| National Wildlife Federation | 1936 | 975 | 87.2 | Rainforest Action Network | 1985 | 30 | 0.9 |
| | | | | Rainforest Alliance | 1986 | 18 | 0.8 |
| **Post–World War II** | | | | Conservation International | 1987 | 55 | 4.6 |
| Defenders of Wildlife | 1947 | 80 | 4.6 | | | | |
| | | | | **Toxic waste** | | | |
| **Environmental era** | | | | Citizens' Clearinghouse | | | |
| Environmental Defense Fund | 1967 | 150 | 12.9 | for Hazardous Waste | 1981 | 7 | 0.7 |
| Friends of the Earth | 1969 | 30 | 3.1 | National Toxics Campaign | 1984 | 100 | 1.5 |
| Natural Resources Defense | | | | | | | |
| Council | 1970 | 168 | 16.0 | **Other major organizations** | | | |
| Environmental Action | 1970 | 20 | 1.2 | League of Conservation | | | |
| Environmental Policy Institute | 1972 | NA[c] | NA | Voters | 1970 | 55 | 1.4 |
| | | | | Sierra Club Legal Defense | | | |
| | | | | Fund | 1971 | 120 | 6.7 |
| | | | | Cousteau Society | 1973 | 264 | 16.3 |
| | | | | Earth Island Institute | 1982 | 32 | 1.1 |

[a]Membership data are for individual members. Data in parentheses are estimates.
[b]Greenpeace created a sister lobbying organization, Greenpeace Action, in 1988. Membership overlaps considerably between the two organizations.
[c]Not a membership group.
(*Source:* "Major Environmental Organizations in the U.S.," from *Encyclopedia of the Environment*, edited by Ruth A. Eblen and William R. Eblen. Copyright © 1994 by Houghton Mifflin Company. Reprinted with permission of Houghton Mifflin Company. All rights reserved.)

incinerators, landfills, land development, and many other environmental issues now often dominate the local news (■ Fig. 1–9). Such local participation is often called **grassroots activism.** Recently, grassroots groups with common interests have begun to network by establishing regional and national newsletters and computer nets. By the mid-1990s, many of the national organizations listed in Table 1–1 had begun to experience a decline in membership. Although some people suggest that this decline means environmental interest is waning in the United States, others argue that it simply reflects the transfer of environmental allegiance from national to grassroots organizations.

All three characteristics of the sustainability movement arose from the desire to find better ways to solve widespread environmental problems. Grassroots activism is often the best way to deal with local issues. The rise of input

reduction and economic approaches reflects the need to reduce social costs. While litigation and lobbying are still used, the sustainability movement also uses direct action and lifestyle changes. In keeping with its more holistic approach, this movement is also ecocentric ("environment-centered") instead of anthropocentric. In other words, the sustain-

**FIGURE 1–9**
Citizen protest is an effective and growing way to promote local environmental sustainability. (*Source:* Reuters/Bettmann.)

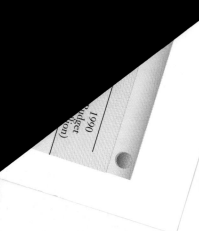

...y movement seeks to preserve nature for ...ons beyond simply improving the quality ...human life. Nature is viewed as having a ...gh "intrinsic" value that is not related to ...uman needs.

*Postindustrial stage—sustainability or overshoot?* The current stage is called the transition because it will almost certainly determine the long-term fate of the environment for many future generations. Environmental degradation is now occurring so fast and on such a large scale that, according to most estimates, the Earth will reach the fifth, or postindustrial, stage, when the outcome will be irreversible, in 10 to 40 years.

As Figure 1–7 shows, this outcome will be one of two possible alternatives. One is a sustainable future, where population stabilizes and technology becomes less environmentally harmful. The second alternative is **overshoot,** where population climbs so high and technology is so harmful that the environment is degraded to the point that relatively few people can be supported, at least with a decent standard of living.

What can be done to avoid overshoot at this critical transition time? Let us begin by taking a closer look at what is meant by "environmental impact," and why humans cause it.

# *W* HAT IS
# ENVIRONMENTAL IMPACT?

Environmental impact refers to the alteration of the natural environment by human activity ( Fig. 1–10). Figure 1–6 identified two basic types of environmental impact: resource depletion and pollution. In other words, there is too much input (resources) and too much output (pollution). Input reduction seeks to slow both depletion and pollution, while output reduction just slows pollution.

Figure 1–6 also showed that population and traditional industrial technology are the two main forces accelerating resource depletion and pollution. The following equation is a simple way to remember this:

$$\text{Impact} = \text{population} \times \text{technology, or}$$

$$I = PT$$

It is easy to see why the number of people affects impact. Traditional industrial technology has historically tended to increase the effect of each person. For example, a baby born in the United States has many times the impact of a baby born in a developing country because over a lifetime the U.S. baby has historically consumed many more resources, such as fossil fuels, and produced much more pollution.

Both population and traditional industrial technology have been increasing very rapidly worldwide. This has led to an extremely rapid increase in environmental impact. This section briefly examines both of these factors.

## Exponential Growth of Human Population

The world population is currently 5.8 billion. For millions of years, relatively few humans were on Earth at any given time. As technology improved, so did human control over the environment. Fossils show that humans began to hunt larger game animals and migrated from Africa into other parts of the world over 500,000 years ago. Both inhabiting new environments and exploiting new foods such as larger game allowed human populations to increase. Nevertheless, the total human population on Earth remained quite low until the development of agriculture. Even then, population growth did not become explosive until the 1900s when it was aided by the global spread of industry and modern medicine, especially the great reduction in infant deaths. Each year the world population experiences a net gain of about 95 million people, the equivalent of about one-third of the population of the United States.

### *Exponential Growth*

Exponential growth of any kind is caused by multiplicative processes. It occurs in population growth because biological reproduction is inherently multiplicative: by producing offspring, we "multiply." Exponential growth usually has an initial "lag phase" of slow growth followed by a period of increasingly accelerated growth (see Fig. 1–7). This pattern occurs because, initially, small numbers are being multiplied together; as larger numbers are multiplied, the rate of growth increases "explosively." Consider, for example, a pond where the algae cover starts from a single algal cell and doubles in size each day. For a long time, you would see nothing happening. Once larger areas were covered, however, the algae would spread extremely fast: one day, the pond would be only half covered; the next day, it would be completely covered.

How long will human population growth continue before it encounters environmental limitations? The answer depends on how many people the Earth can support, a question that is much

(a)

(b)

 **FIGURE 1–10**

Human impact on the Catskill Mountains is seen in these paintings by Thomas Cole, created just six years apart. Note the deforestation between 1837 (a) and 1843 (b). (*Sources:* (a) Thomas Cole, *View on the Catskill, Early Autumn* (1837). The Met-

ropolitan Museum of Art, Gift in memory of Jonathan Sturges by his children, 1895. Copyright © 1979/80 by the Metropolitan Museum of Art. (b) Thomas Cole, *River in the Catskills* (1843). Gift of Mrs. Maxim Karolik for the M. and M. Karolik Collection of American Paintings, 1815–1865. Courtesy of Museum of Fine Arts, Boston.)

debated, in part, because the answer depends on how high a standard of living one assumes. However, many estimates predict that the Earth can adequately and sustainably support between 6 and 8 billion people (Chapters 5 and 13). If true, population growth clearly must decline very soon if overshot is to be avoided. Unfortunately, almost all population projections by the United Nations, the World Bank, and other organizations indicate that world population will probably not stabilize until it exceeds 11 billion, sometime in the middle to late twenty-first century.

## Exponential Growth of Technology

The second basic factor in our impact equation, $I = PT$, is technology. Traditional industrial technology has increased the overall environmental impact by increasing the impact per person:

$$\text{Overall impact} = \text{population} \times \text{technology}$$
$$= \text{number of individuals} \times$$
$$(\text{impact/individual})$$

As ▓ Figure 1–11 shows, this impact per person occurs through an increase in both resource depletion and pollution.

Traditional industrial technology has tended to increase per capita resource use and pollution for many types of resources and pollutants. ▓ Figure 1–12a illustrates the fact that solid waste output has grown dramatically in the United States in the last few decades.

But technology need not have this harmful effect. Traditional industrial technologies, such as

the internal combustion engine, were developed during a period of rapid industrial growth, when resources were abundant and pollution was of little concern. As we see later in the chapter, many new sustainable or "green" technologies are being developed that can greatly reduce individual impact. More efficient technologies, such as fuel-efficient cars, use fewer resources and produce less pollution when an individual uses them. Alternative technologies can eliminate many impacts altogether. Replacing coal-burning machines with solar-powered machines conserves nonrenewable fossil fuels and eliminates many air pollutants released by burning coal. Many people are reducing their reliance on any kind of modern technology and learning the benefits of "living more simply." Examples include using fewer household appliances and fewer chemical pesticides and fertilizers on lawns.

▓ **FIGURE 1–11**

Traditional industrial technology (T) has increased the throughput per person. This is multiplied by the number of people (population or P) to obtain the total resource depletion and pollution produced by a society.

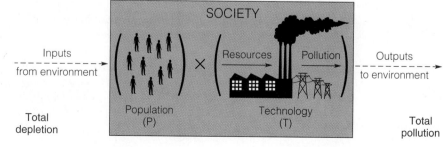

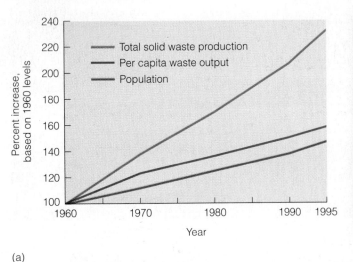

(a)

(b)

**FIGURE 1–12**
(a) Trends in U.S. total solid waste production, output per person, and population.
(b) Greenpeace protesters on a New York garbage barge. (*Sources:* (a) Based on data from the U.S. Environmental Protection Agency and the U.S. Bureau of the Census. (b) Dennis Capolongo/Greenpeace.)

## Exponential Growth of Environmental Impact

The exponential increase of population and traditional industrial technology have caused an exponential increase in environmental impact, I. For example, Figure 1–12a shows how the overall impact of municipal solid waste of U.S. society has grown as a result of both increased population and increased waste per person.

The increase in total solid waste in Figure 1–12a is typical of the pattern seen in many other kinds of pollution. A society that produces such waste is likely to be consuming many resources that ultimately generate the waste. For example, global consumption of fossil fuel has risen exponentially due to the growing world population and the spread of technologies that use fossil fuels (increasing per capita use of fuels). As more fossil fuels are burned, not only are resources depleted but more pollution is generated, including the carbon that contributes to global warming. Figure 1–13 illustrates this correlation between depletion and pollution. As technology and population grow, more materials and energy move through society. This accelerates the depletion of environmental resources. In addition, the materials and energy that move through society must have somewhere to go when society is finished with them. Solid waste, air and water pollution, and other outputs usually end up in the environment. The movement

of materials and energy through society is often called **throughput.** Environmental resources are referred to as **sources** of throughput, and environmental reservoirs that receive throughput are called **sinks.** This "throughput" model is the basis for many "systems approaches" that attempt to link social systems such as the economy to natural systems. For instance, it is the basis for many important concepts in environmental economics (Chapter 20). The throughput model is discussed in a number of important books such as *Beyond the Limits* (1992) by Donella Meadows and others. In the fossil fuel example, fossil fuels are the sources showing consumption impact, and the atmosphere is the sink showing pollution impacts of carbon, leading to global warming. Carbon is the material whose throughput is being accelerated by growing population and technology.

Acceleration of throughput to increase both depletion and pollution in industrialized societies is evident by almost any measure:

1. Developed nations have only 22% of the world's population, but consume 88% of the world's natural resources and 73% of the world's energy.
2. The United States consumes far more meat, fossil fuels, and pesticides per person than the vast majority of other nations, while producing more solid waste per person than almost any other nation.

**FIGURE 1–13**
Throughput of matter and energy depletes and pollutes the environment. (*Source:* Modified from D. H. Meadows, D. L. Meadows, and J. Randers, *Beyond the Limits* [Post Mills, Vt.: Chelsea Green, 1992, p. 7]. Reprinted from *Beyond the Limits.* Copyright © 1992 by Meadows, Meadows, and Randers. With permission from Chelsea Green Publishing Company, White River Junction, Vermont.)

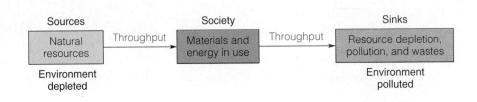

# Is Human Impact on the Environment the Same as Cancer?

*M*any observers have described the human species as a kind of planetary disease, namely, cancer. They see the growth of civilization as a malignancy that is destroying the global ecosystem. Although this analogy may seem preposterous at first, it is remarkably accurate in a number of ways. If we consider humans to be the cancer and the environment healthy tissue, the history of human activities exhibits all four major characteristics of a malignant process.

1. Rapid, uncontrolled growth
2. Invasion and destruction of adjacent tissue (environment)
3. Metastasis (colonization and urbanization)
4. Undifferentiation (homogenization of global culture)

Furthermore, mathematical models show that the details of the spread of civilization are strikingly similar to the spread of cancer. ■ Figure 1 shows the growth of London from 1880 to 1955, but you can find similar pictures in medical texts that illustrate the growth of cancer cells.

The cancer analogy even fits well with the impact equation, $I = PT$. The growth of civilization has witnessed both an increase in the number of people and the growth of technologies that have increased T, the rate of depletion and pollution per person. Similarly, many kinds of cancer cells use more nutrients and produce more waste than slower-growing normal cells.

Let us hope that the analogy with cancer does not extend to its final trait: The ultimate fate of all cancer cells is to die when they kill their host. Cancer cells obviously cannot think, and we can hope that humans can find a way to build a soci-

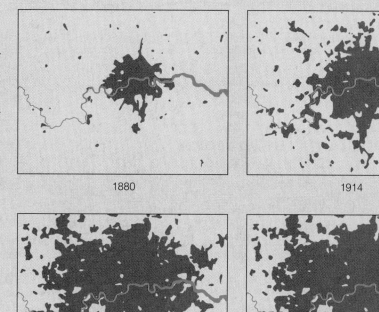

■ **FIGURE 1**

The growth of London from 1880 to 1955. (*Source:* Reprinted with permission from James H. Johnson, *Urban Geography* (1967), p. 124.)

ety that more closely resembles healthy tissue, which has no net growth and less-wasteful cells. We could accomplish this in two ways:

1. Reducing P. We could replace uncontrolled population growth with replacement turnover (each cell is replaced as it dies) so there is no net growth.
2. Reducing T. We could replace resource-consumptive and highly polluting technologies with efficient ones that use fewer (and renewable) resources and pollute less. This reduces per capita impact.

3. The United States has about 5% of the world's population but produces nearly 20% of the world's greenhouse gas pollution (and many other air and water pollutants) and between 33% and 50% of the world's solid waste (estimates vary).

In summary, there are two basic kinds of environmental impacts, depletion and pollution. Both have increased because growing consumption of resources increases pollution as throughput is accelerated. The main causes of increased throughput have been the growth of (1) population and (2) traditional "industrial" technology. This human impact on the environment has even been compared to cancer (see Issues in Perspective 1–2).

## WHY DO PEOPLE DEPLETE AND POLLUTE? THE ENVIRONMENT AS A COMMONS

In 1968, the biologist Garrett Hardin wrote a famous essay called "The Tragedy of the Commons." He argued that property held in common by many people will be destroyed or at least overused until it deteriorates. He gave the example of a pasture where each herdsman in the village can keep his cattle. The herdsman who overgrazes the most will also benefit the most. Each cow added by a herdsman will benefit the owner, but the community as a whole will bear the cost of overgrazing. Because the benefit of adding another cow goes to the individual and the cost of overgrazing goes to the community, the "rational" choice of each individual is to add cows. The commons thus rewards behaviors that lead to deterioration, such as overgrazing, and punishes individuals who show restraint. Those who add fewer

**FIGURE 1–14**
A computer-enhanced image of pollution in the Mediterranean Sea. Red, yellow, and orange areas are concentrations of plankton growth promoted by discharge of raw sewage. (Blue indicates clear water.) Most coastal cities lack sewage treatment. (*Source:* Courtesy of Gene Carl Feldman/NASA Goddard Space Flight Center.)

cows will simply obtain fewer benefits while the commons itself deteriorates anyway because of the individuals who continue to add cows. This problem with common property was known long before Hardin's eloquent essay. For instance, the ancient Greek philosopher Aristotle noted that "what is common to the greatest number has the least care bestowed upon it."

Hardin's pasture exemplifies the problems that arise when any part of our natural environment is treated as common property. Unless there is some kind of regulation, overexploitation will likely occur via both input and output impacts:

1. Commonly held resources, such as the pasture, will become depleted through excessive consumption.
2. Commonly held environmental sinks will be overwhelmed by pollution.

Many local, regional, and global environmental problems illustrate this view of the commons as a source or a sink:

|  | PROBLEM |
| --- | --- |
| ■ Atmosphere as global common sink | Global warming, ozone lost |
| ■ Atmosphere as regional common sink | Acid rain |
| ■ Atmosphere as local common sink | Urban smog |
| ■ Ocean as global common sink | Ocean pollution |
| ■ Ocean as global common resource | Many fish species overfished |
| ■ Rainforest as common sink | Global warming promoted by deforestation |
| ■ Rainforest as common resource | Biodiversity reduced by deforestation |

Notice that some of these commons are shared by many nations. The international nature of many environmental problems adds greatly to the complexity of solving them because international agreements are required. Consider the Mediterranean Sea. A confined shallow ocean basin surrounded by many nations, this sea is one of the most overfished and polluted large bodies of water on Earth (■ Fig. 1–14).

## SAVING THE COMMONS: REDUCING THROUGHPUT BY PAYING TRUE COSTS

If we are to save the environmental commons, the throughput of matter and energy through all soci-

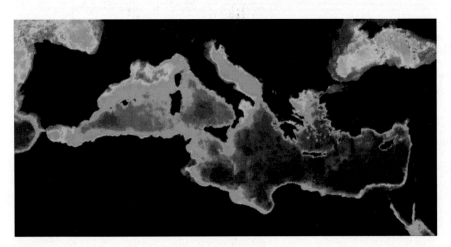

*ENVIRONMENTAL PRINCIPLES*   SECTION 1

eties must be reduced. This will slow both depletion and pollution. Increased impact (I) has been
driven by increasing population (P) and traditional industrial technology (T), so their growth
must be reduced.

The economic forces that promote population
growth and the use of environmentally harmful
technology have arisen because the environment
has been *undervalued* in the past. The true costs of
using the environment as both a source and a sink
have not been incorporated into global economic
activity. Traditional economics has considered the
environment as a "free" commodity, such as the
atmospheric sink, or a source of very cheap materials, such as cheap timber or ores. This view has
led to technologies that are inefficient, wasteful,
and highly polluting. It has also contributed
greatly to the rapid population growth of developing nations. Poverty is strongly correlated with
high population growth rates, and people in
resource-rich tropical developing nations are
often underpaid for their resources (as compared
to prices in many developed nations) ( Fig.
1–15).

**FIGURE 1–15**
People in tropical countries are
often greatly underpaid for
their resources. This Honduran
picking coffee beans will
receive only a tiny fraction of
the price the beans will eventually bring in the supermarket.
(*Source:* © Daemmrich/Stock,
Boston.)

## Reducing Technological Impact: Defusing the Bomb of the North

Rapid population growth is often described as a
"time bomb" that will greatly degrade the environment in coming years. While population
growth is especially rapid in the Southern Hemisphere, the industrialized nations of the Northern
Hemisphere are also contributing to environmental degradation through their widespread use of
traditional industrial technologies developed during a time of abundant resources. Traditional
industrial technologies are not only wasteful and
polluting, but they also tend to rely on nonrenewable resources. Thus, technology impact may be
viewed as the environmental "time bomb" of the
North. The solution is to reduce technological
impact, or T in the impact equation I = PT.

There are two basic ways to reduce technological impact. Neither needs to involve painful self-
sacrifice and a lower quality of life. To the con-
trary, both methods of technology reduction can
improve quality of life in many ways by improving
human health and the environment.

- *Use less technology.* One way to reduce technology impact (T) is simply to try and use less
  technology. Long before Thoreau, many people observed that machines can have detrimental effects on humans. Riding bicycles to work
  (instead of cars), buying products with fewer

artificial chemicals, and using fewer appliances
are but a few ways that people have reduced
their reliance on technology.

- *Use sustainable technology.* The second way to
  reduce technology impact is to use technologies that are much more "environmentally
  friendly" than the fossil fuel–based, industrial
  technologies of the past. **Sustainable technology** permits humans to meet their needs with
  minimum impact on the environment. It produces a sustainable economy that provides jobs
  for many generations without degrading the
  environment.

There are many kinds of sustainable technologies, ranging from direct solar and wind power to
recycling. While advances in pollution cleanup
technologies are often heralded, true sustainability results from input reduction: slowing resource
depletion also slows pollution. Figure 1–16
illustrates the three basic ways that sustainable
technologies achieve input reduction, or conservation: (1) efficiency improvements, (2) reuse and
recycle, and (3) substitution.

**Efficiency improvements** reduce the flow of
throughput by decreasing the per capita resource
use. The United States, more than almost any
other country, uses technologies developed during
times of abundant resources. As a result, it generates much waste, providing enormous opportunities to save many resources by relatively simple
changes in existing technologies. The amount of
waste is so great that, in many cases, the large

amount of resources saved will more than compensate for the cost of investment to make the change.

Let us again use the example of energy, which drives all economies. Each year, the United States spends about 10–11% of its national wealth to pay for the energy needed to produce that wealth. In contrast, Japan spends only about 5–6% of its national wealth on energy because it uses energy about twice as efficiently as the United States. For example, more efficient machines, often designed to be lighter and smaller, perform the same tasks but use less energy. It is estimated that changes in U.S. technology, ranging from high-mileage cars to superefficient heating and cooling systems to new lighting technologies could reduce overall energy consumption by up to 80%. A simple illustration of the amount of waste is the widely used incandescent lightbulb that wastes 95% of the electricity used by converting it to heat instead of light.

Many other resources in the United States could also be utilized much more efficiently. To list just a couple of examples:

1. *Wood.* The United States converts only about 50% of raw timber directly into furniture and other refined timber products, compared to 70% in Japan.
2. *Water.* The United States uses over twice as much water per person as most other nations on Earth. The average U.S. farmer could easily cut water use by more than half by adopting water conservation measures such as microirrigation that pipes water to crops instead of using evaporation-prone irrigation ditches.

Reuse and recycling are the second best way to accomplish input reduction (Fig. 1–16). **Reuse** refers to using the same resource over and over in the same form. An example would be soda bottles that are returned, sanitized, and refilled. **Recycling** refers to using the same resource over and over, but in modified form. The soda bottles, for instance, could be melted to produce new glass bottles. Wastewater, paper, plastics, and many other resources can also be recycled. In general, reuse is less costly than recy-

**FIGURE 1–16**
Three ways to reduce inputs are efficiency improvements, reusing and recycling, and substitution. Three ways to manage outputs are "end-of-pipe" removal, remediation, and restoration.

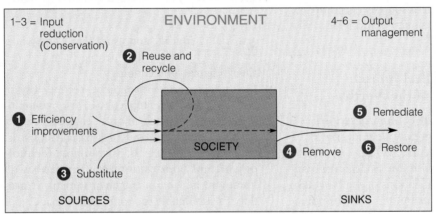

Simply switching to compact fluorescent bulbs, which are much more efficient, would allow the United States to shut down all the nuclear power plants in the nation. This example shows how conservation can reduce environmental damage.

In addition to reducing environmental damage, efficiency improvements have two immediate economic advantages. First, as noted, the improvement usually pays for itself. The cost of a technological change that increases efficiency is usually recovered within a few years, and sometimes almost immediately. A 1993 study by the Aluminum Corporation of America found, for instance, that reducing the weight of aluminum cans by just 1% will save about $20 million per year in aluminum. Also, increased efficiency tends to produce many more jobs than wasteful technologies. The energy industry, such as oil, coal, and nuclear, is much less labor-intensive than the energy conservation industry that designs and maintains many kinds of energy conservation equipment.

cling because the resource is not modified. Both measures are often less costly than extracting "virgin" resources, such as aluminum ore or cutting trees for paper, because they usually consume less energy and fewer natural resources than making products from virgin materials. Recycling aluminum cans, for example, can save up to 95% of the energy cost of cans from newly mined aluminum. Recycling and reuse are thus less costly in both economic and environmental terms than using natural raw materials.

Reuse and recycling are also labor-intensive so they create many new jobs. Increasing the recycling rate of aluminum in the United States from 30% to 75% would create an estimated 350,000 new jobs. For every 15,000 tons (13,600 metric tons) of solid waste recycled, nine jobs are created; incinerating that waste creates two jobs.

**Substitution** of one resource for another can benefit the environment in a number of ways. A renewable resource can be substituted for a nonrenewable one, or a less-polluting resource can

*E*NVIRONMENTAL PRINCIPLES    SECTION 1

substitute for a highly polluting resource. Often the newly substituted resource provides both benefits. Substituting renewable, cleaner alternative fuels such as solar and wind energy for fossil fuels is an example. Another example is making products from paper instead of plastics, which are made from fossil fuels and last longer in the environment. Like conservation, reuse, and recycling, substitution also often yields economic benefits. Studies routinely show that substitution of solar and wind power technologies for the fossil fuel energy now consumed in the United States would produce three to five times as many jobs as now exist in fossil fuel industries.

### Promoting Sustainable Technology: Paying True Costs

Some people are surprised to learn that many sustainable technologies were invented centuries ago. Wind and water power are examples. The solar cell was invented in the 1950s. These technologies have failed to become widespread largely for social and economic reasons, not technical ones. When nonrenewable resources are cheap, they will be wasted because people have no incentive to increase efficiency, recycle/reuse, and substitute renewable resources. ▬ Figure 1–17a shows the situation when resources are cheap and sinks are free and are treated as "commons." Note that there is much throughput, which leads to high rates of resource depletion and pollution.

For instance, many private and government studies show that the price of gasoline is at least $3.50 per gallon when all environmental costs are included. These environmental costs include smog and other urban air pollutants, global warming, contamination of groundwater by leaking underground oil tanks, oil spills, and many other well-known impacts of gasoline use. Yet the price of gasoline in the United States has remained far below $3.50 (averaging less than $1.50 per gallon), although most other industrial nations have higher prices.

When market prices do not reflect all the true costs of a product or service, economists call this a **market failure** (also called an "externality"; see Chapter 20). Many environmental problems can ultimately be traced to market failures. To list just a couple of examples:

1. Electricity from nuclear energy does not include the cost of disposing of nuclear waste; electricity produced by coal burning omits the cost of most air pollution.
2. Water used by many U.S. farmers does not reflect the fact that the groundwater is being depleted much faster than it is being replenished by rainfall.

Most economists suggest society can correct market failures by adjusting the costs of products and services to include environmental costs. Figure 1–17b shows how fees can be imposed at many locations of throughput to make these adjustments. Such fees are often called **green fees.** Fees that increase the price of a resource are particularly effective because they promote conservation of the resource and also reduce pollution by reducing throughput. For example, higher user fees on federal land for timber and ore deposits would encourage more efficient use of those

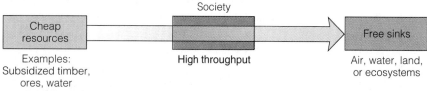

(a) Environmental costs excluded

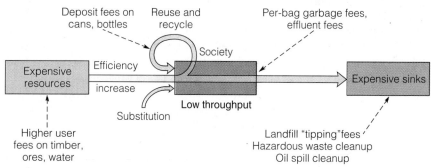

(b) Environmental costs included

resources and reduce solid waste. Similarly, fossil fuels taxes, such as a "gas tax" or "carbon tax" covering all fossil fuels, would encourage reduced and more efficient use of these fuels.

Other green fees include deposits, such as on cans or bottles, to encourage recycling (Fig. 1–17b). Charging for garbage by the bag and effluent (pollution) fees on factories are other examples. These fees motivate people to reduce the waste they produce. Other fees can be imposed for using sinks, such as "tipping fees" for landfill use or making polluters pay for cleanup (Fig. 1–17b).

Another benefit of green fees is that they may improve the environment at lower monetary costs than simply passing regulations and arresting violators. ▬ Figure 1–18 compares the effect of regulatory efforts to reduce carbon emissions with two different carbon (fossil fuel) taxes, one phased in slowly, the other phased in rapidly. All three

▬ **FIGURE 1–17**
(a) Excluding environmental costs by allowing cheap resources and free sinks promotes high throughput (and therefore much depletion and pollution). (b) Including environmental costs by imposing user fees and deposit fees promotes an increase in efficiency, recycling, and all other forms of input reduction.

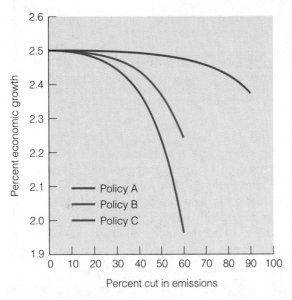

**FIGURE 1–18**
Effects on economic growth of three methods of cutting greenhouse gas emissions. Under Policy A, international carbon taxes are phased in slowly. Policy B also uses taxes, but they are phased in rapidly. Policy C relies on government regulations phased in rapidly. (*Source: The Economist*, July 7, 1990, p. 22. Copyright © 1990 The Economist Newspaper Group, Inc. Reprinted with permission. Further reproduction prohibited.)

policies reduce greenhouse gas emissions, but carbon taxes, especially when phased in slowly, may have less negative impact on economic growth.

Although the United States is the world's largest resource consumer and polluter (by most measures), it unfortunately lags far behind most of the industrialized world in the use of green fees and other economic incentives to conserve resources and reduce pollution. The general trend has been the continuation of cheap resources and free sinks. In fact, in many cases the United States actively discourages conservation and encourages pollution by subsidies that reward these activities (as opposed to green taxes that discourage them). A 1993 study by the Alliance to Save Energy found that 58% ($21 billion) of federal energy subsidies went to fossil fuels and 30% ($11 billion) to nuclear energy; only 3% went to energy efficiency projects and 2% to renewable energy projects.

Figure 1–19 shows an example of great importance, the cheap cost of oil in the United States since the early 1980s, which has led to a reversal of the previous trend toward more fuel-efficient cars. Nevertheless, many observers think that a "greener" economy is inevitable because of

**FIGURE 1–19**
Price of oil per barrel in the United States (in 1994 dollars). (*Source:* U.S. Department of Energy.)

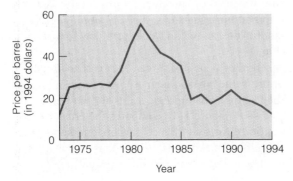

consumer demand for environmental quality and the economic benefits of sustainable technologies such as increased efficiency, reduced resource imports, and more jobs. As Issues in Perspective 1–3 describes, there are many signs that U.S. business is indeed becoming greener. This trend has been accompanied by increased discussion of green fees and the removal of government subsidies on timber, grazing lands, ore deposits, and oil companies (Chapters 6, 20, 22).

## Reducing Population: Defusing the Bomb of the South

Over 90% of world population growth occurs in developing nations. Most developing nations are in the Southern Hemisphere, so this cause of throughput is especially important there. To defuse this so-called **population bomb,** we must address its central causes, which are often economic. Figure 1–20 shows how population growth is often driven by poverty. Poor people tend to have more offspring for a variety of reasons, including lack of education about birth control, lack of economic opportunities for women, and the need for children to perform chores and care for the aged (see Chapter 5). The result is a "vicious circle" in which population growth leads to poverty because too many people reduce the standard of living. Furthermore, the growing population reduces the amount of money available for investment in education, equipment, and other needs for economic growth.

Can this "poverty-population-environment cycle" of human misery and environmental destruction be broken? Decades of experience show that the economic causes of this cycle must be addressed. Poor people often have little interest in such abstract ideas as global warming or animal rights because they are trying to survive. Many people still subscribe to the **fallacy of enlightenment,** or the idea that education will solve the problem. But education is not enough; realistic solutions that remove the root causes of the problem must be found. Attempting to protect the environment by legal means, such as creating game reserves, is often not effective either because desperate people will break laws. Eliminating poverty will not only reduce many causes of population growth, but it will reduce environmental degradation as well.

### *Reducing Population Growth by Paying True Costs*

It has long been known that the economic woes of the developing nations must be solved. In 1961,

# Business Is Green: The Jobs versus Environment Myth

In his book *The Environmental Economic Revolution* (1993), economist Michael Silverstein discusses how widespread interest in environmental quality is radically changing both the world economy and the discipline of economics. The rapid growth of the environmental cleanup and antipollution industries are the most obvious indicators. The United States alone will spend between $1.2 to $1.5 trillion on waste cleanup in the 1990s; worldwide, the estimate is $3–4 trillion. Antipollution and cleanup technologies have been among the fastest growing industries.

Silverstein argues, however, that the environmental revolution is affecting much more than the cleanup and antipollution industries. He contends that virtually all sectors of the U.S. and world economy are becoming "greener," and often profiting from it. His examples include:

1. *Travel industry.* The rapid growth of "eco-tours" that promote appreciation of nature (but must be done correctly to minimize harm).
2. *Recycling industry.* The rapid growth of recycling of many materials, from wood products to metals to plastics.
3. *Efficiency design industries.* The rapid growth of industries that design more efficient technologies that use fewer resources to accomplish the same task: low-flush toilets, energy-efficient machinery and cars, and so on ( Fig. 1).
4. *Chemical industry.* The rapid growth of research into and production of chemicals that are less toxic and less persistent in the environment.

**FIGURE 1**

The low-flush toilet is just one of many new products that benefit the environment and the economy. (*Source:* Burrows/Gamma Liaison.)

Silverstein identifies two forces that are driving these changes in industrialized nations. One is public demand for goods and services that are less environmentally harmful. The other is that increased competition in the global economy demands that companies become efficient and

**FIGURE 2**

Energy use in socialist versus capitalist economies. (*Source:* From *Resources, Environment, and Population: Present Knowledge, Future Options,* edited by Kingsley Davis and Mikhail S. Bernstam. Copyright © 1991 by the Population Council, Inc. Reprinted by permission of Oxford University Press, Inc.)

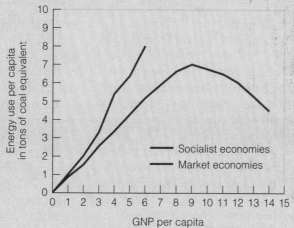

reduce waste. U.S. companies have traditionally been very wasteful of energy and materials.

As a result of this ongoing environmental economic revolution both the economy and the environment are benefiting. Economic benefits include increasing profits for "green" companies both because consumers prefer their products and because such companies are more efficient. Also, as discussed in the text, "green" activities tend to create more jobs than depleting or polluting activities. In part, this is because recycling, making solar cells, installing insulation, and other environmentally friendly activities rely more on human labor than on machines. But it is also because these activities sustain the resources they rely on and therefore employ people for longer times. Loggers and miners, for example, often find themselves unemployed when the local trees or ore deposits are gone.

Most economists think that moderately free market economies are better at promoting environmentally friendly economic growth than socialist, or planned, economies. Poland, and many of the other formerly communist countries, are among the most polluted in the world. Socialist economies are much less energy efficient than market economies and therefore produce much more waste and depletion, as shown in Figure 2. The reason is that free markets tend to provide incentives for individuals to do the right things, and property rights help reduce abuse of an environmental commons. But, as noted in the text, a completely free market can lead to environmental degradation, too. Green taxes, laws, and other forms of regulation are then used to correct such market failures.

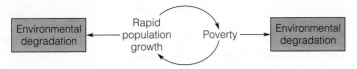

Poverty-population-environment cycle

the United Nations General Assembly pledged that developed nations would donate 1% of their gross national product (GNP) to developing nations. The model was the U.S. Marshall Plan, which provided money to help rebuild Europe and Japan after World War II. But instead of improving, the economies of most developing Southern Hemisphere nations have declined. Indeed, the gap in wealth between the developed and developing nations has widened at an increasing rate (Chapter 20). By the early 1990s, per capita wealth was nearly 20 times greater in high-income countries such as those of western Europe than in the developing countries.

This gap continues to grow because developing countries now pay a huge amount of interest on money that was lent to them many years ago. Developing countries now owe over $1.3 trillion. As a result of interest on this debt, the *net flow of money has been from South to North* since 1982. Rich countries now receive more money from poor countries (over $50 billion per year) than they transfer to them. This is sometimes called the **debt bomb.**

Some people argue that the solution to the debt bomb is increased foreign aid. They note that the 1% of GNP pledged in 1961 to developing nations has never been achieved. In 1994, the United States spent about $10 billion on foreign aid, which is about 0.17% GNP or slightly more than is annually spent on lawn care in the United States. It is also much less than the approximately $270 billion spent on national defense even though refugees from developing nations may be a bigger threat to national security than large-scale warfare.

Some economists argue that foreign aid to poor countries should not be viewed as charity. They note that these poor but resource-rich nations would not need charity if they were paid the true costs for their resources. This view is becoming increasingly common among the people living in the Southern Hemisphere. They maintain that if people in the developed Northern Hemisphere wish to save rainforests, they should pay for the environmental goods and services the forests produce. This would mean paying much higher prices for tropical forest products (such as fruits) and services such as the trees' absorption of carbon dioxide to slow global warming. Although it is very difficult to estimate the true environmental costs in most cases, nearly all estimates indicate that developing nations are greatly underpaid for their resources (Chapters 6 and 20).

Appropriate payment for environmental goods and services could help eliminate poverty, probably much more effectively than foreign aid donations. These payments would break the vicious cycle and reduce population growth as well. A key necessity is that this increased wealth be used to buy sustainable technologies that focus on efficiency, recycling/reuse, and renewable resources. This proposal contrasts with older views that saw "modernization" of developing countries following the same developmental pathway as Europe, North America, and Japan.

## THE ROLE OF THE INDIVIDUAL

The writer Wendell Berry said that the roots of all environmental problems ultimately lie in the values of the individuals who comprise society. Or, as the writer Paul Hawken put it, the environment is not being degraded by corporate presidents; it is being degraded by popular demand. By this he means that companies only produce things that people buy, and they cause depletion and pollution only as long as society permits such behavior to be profitable. For example, we have just seen how green fees, such as a carbon tax, could be used to correct the market failures that cause pollution. Yet these strategies are rarely applied in practice. People have generally voted down proposals to add green taxes, even where income and other taxes would be reduced to compensate.

A good example is the "gas tax." In the early 1990s, the Clinton administration initially conceived of a gasoline tax of up to a few dollars per gallon. As gasoline was only about a dollar per gallon, this would have raised gasoline costs close to the estimated true environmental cost of $3.50 per gallon. The goal of the tax was to promote fuel conservation and alternative fuels and reduce air pollution including carbon dioxide. The United States signed an international agreement, pledging to reduce carbon dioxide to slow greenhouse gas emissions (the United States produces nearly 20% of such emissions). But after extensive congressional debate, a gas tax of only about four cents was imposed rather than the two or three dollars originally conceived.

environ
people
be disas
used an
people

Assu
precaut
mental
rest of
But you
1–2, wh
tal risks
guished
Enviror
table li
species
climate
because
descenc
pollutar
lems, f
probler
collecti
ment o
But it
about p

**Visual**

Recall t
of toda
future
many o
sustain
discuss
major
society
the hu
ple. Se
religior
nomic
are aff
ultimat
the co
values
ized,
system

The
reflect
scienc
almost
from t
nomic
flow o
of dep
on the

## Values on the Here and Now: Why We Avoid True Costs

Why do individuals have values that lead to environmental degradation by "popular demand"? Many writers have argued that most large-scale problems arise because individuals are not good at dealing with problems beyond their own immediate situation. We tend to focus on the "here and now" of current time and local space. We think most about things we can see around us and things that have just recently happened to us or will soon happen to us.

This focus on the "here and now" is why people have been reluctant, especially in the United States, to pay true costs for goods and services that deplete or pollute the environment. Economists call this "discounting the future" and "discounting by distance." **Discounting the future** results from focusing on the "now": Environmental costs of our actions on future generations are not fully paid. Cheap gasoline and minerals, for instance, lead to rapid depletion of these nonrenewable resources making them unavailable to future generations. These resources are cheap because their current cost does not incorporate their value to future generations. Nor does the cost include the future effects of their use, such as global warming or other pollution hazards. **Discounting by distance** results from focusing on the "here": Environmental costs of our actions on people living in another area are not fully paid. Cheap ivory, imported animals, and tropical timber, for instance, lead to rapid depletion of those tropical resources, thereby degrading the environment for the people who live there. These resources are so cheap because their cost does not incorporate their full value to their local environment.

From an individual viewpoint, being preoccupied with immediate concerns has been a good survival trait. In our evolutionary and historical past, individuals needed to be aware of activity in their immediate vicinity to avoid predators and other dangers. However, modern technologies have led to problems that occur on far larger scales of time and space; their effects are global and last many centuries. Such problems require long-range planning that will span many generations and involve international cooperation. In their book *New World, New Mind* (1989), Robert Ornstein and Paul Ehrlich state that they believe our minds have a "putting out fires" approach to problems; another term might be "Band-Aid" approach. They indicate that only recently, with the sustainability movement, has there been widespread interest in addressing the systematic causes that underlie these problems.

## A Solution: Values beyond the Self

It can be argued that the single greatest obstacle to building a sustainable society is this tendency of the human mind to focus on the here and now. It limits our ability to make the systemic social changes needed to solve regional and global problems. This is why David Ehrenfeld, in *The Arrogance of Humanism* (1981), warns that history shows that humans have never successfully managed anything for very long. How can we expect to solve global environmental problems with such limitations?

Figure 1–21 shows how people can extend their sphere of concern, beginning with close relatives and progressing through other social groupings to include all people. Ultimately, all living things can be included, as in the well-developed philosophy of "deep ecology" (Chapter 21). All of us initially begin with the self because infants and young children are preoccupied with their own needs. Some people remain very selfish throughout life, while other people develop some or all of the spheres of concern in Figure 1–21. If we are to place a higher value on the environment of the future and in other parts of the world, such extended spheres of concern are needed. If many people adopt this view, society will be more willing to pay green taxes, vote for politicians who favor sustainable lifestyles, and, in general, promote the solutions outlined here that require looking beyond the here and now.

Most sociologists believe that the trend has been in the opposite direction until now. The growth of modern civilization has promoted individualism that has progressively shrunk the sphere of

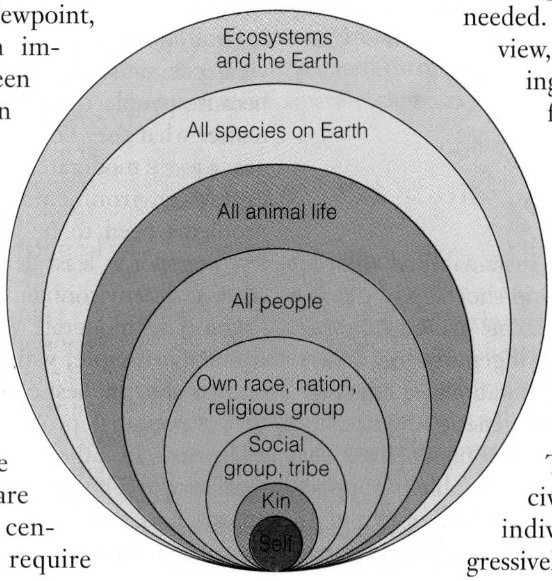

Ecosystems and the Earth
All species on Earth
All animal life
All people
Own race, nation, religious group
Social group, tribe
Kin
Self

**FIGURE 1-21**
An ethical sequence in which the individual concerns extend outward beyond self to progressively more inclusive levels. (*Source:* R. Noss, "Essay: Issues of Scale," in P. L. Fiedler and S. Jain, eds., *Conservation Biology* [Chapman & Hall, 1992, p. 240]. Reprinted by permission of Chapman & Hall.)

Because the environment is a "commons," a commodity possessed by all, it is subject to the "tragedy of the commons." Commonly held resources are depleted through over-consumption, and commonly held environmental sinks are overwhelmed by pollution. The growth of both population and traditional industrial technology must be reduced in order to save environmental commons.

Environmental economists contend that in the past, the environment has been undervalued, giving rise to economic forces that promote increased population and environmental impact. In the Northern Hemisphere, the location of the majority of developed nations, the increase in harmful traditional industrial technologies is the greatest threat to the environment. However, by promoting efficiency improvements, reuse, recycling, and substitution, "green" or sustainable technology can reduce depletion and pollution. Economic incentives such as green fees can also be used to reduce throughput. By paying the true environmental costs of resources and sinks, exploitation and pollution can be discouraged. Until now, the opposite has been true in the United States, which has undervalued resources and used environmental sinks for waste disposal at little or no cost.

The Southern Hemisphere, which contains most of the developing nations, is responsible for 90% of the world's population growth. A vicious cycle exists in which population growth leads to poverty, which leads to environmental degradation. This cycle can be broken by building sustainable economies with sustainable technologies.

Industrial society has traditionally had values that lead to environmental degradation because they focus mainly on the "here and now." These values may be the single greatest obstacle to building a sustainable society. Whether society will succeed in building a sustainable world is highly debatable. Some people take the deeply pessimistic "cassandran" view while others take the other extreme, the blindly optimistic "cornucopian" view. Many people have more moderate views, such as those embodied in the "precautionary principle," which assumes that we are "better safe than sorry." People who hold this principle acknowledge that environmental problems are real, and seek long-term realistic solutions without being overly pessimistic or optimistic.

## KEY TERMS

cassandras
cornucopians
debt bomb
discounting by distance
discounting the future
efficiency improvements
environmental science
environmental wisdom

fallacy of enlightenment
grassroots activism
green fees
holistic
input reduction
market failure
overshoot
population bomb
precautionary principle

recycling
reuse
sinks
sources
substitution
sustainable economy
sustainable technology
sustainability
throughput

## STUDY QUESTIONS

1. Name several costs of a lack of environmental wisdom.
2. What is the most expensive way to solve environmental problems?
3. What is throughput?
4. Why is input reduction a good solution to many environmental problems?
5. Name the two basic causes of environmental problems.
6. Why was the cultivation of food such an important development in human technological evolution?
7. Name three pieces of landmark environmental legislation enacted by Congress and briefly describe each.
8. Define *sustainable technology* and a *sustainable economy*.
9. What is the difference between conservation movements of the past and the movements of the current transition stage?
10. What is a green fee? The "debt bomb"?
11. What is "discounting the future"?
12. How do environmental problems illustrate the tragedy of the commons?
13. What percentage of GNP did the United States pledge to developing nations in 1961? How much did the United States spend on foreign aid in 1994?
14. If the current world population is 5.8 billion, what will it be if it increases by 75% in 50 years?
15. If the current world population is 5.8 billion, what will it be if it increases by 50% in 50 years?

# ESSAY QUESTIONS

1. Identify and describe the fourth stage of human and technological evolution. How does the environmental movement that emerged during this stage differ from previous environmental movements?

2. What is environmental impact? Identify two basic types of environmental impact and explain their causes.

3. Name and describe the three ways technological improvements can achieve input reduction, thereby decreasing environmental damage.

4. Describe the difference between the environmentalism of the 1970s and current environmentalism. What problems were associated with early environmentalism?

5. Why is the economic gap between the developed and developing countries increasing?

# SUGGESTED READINGS

Brown, L., *et al.* Published annually. *Vital signs.* New York: W. W. Norton.

————Published annually. *State of the world.* New York: W. W. Norton.

Eblen, R., and W. Eblen, eds. 1994. *The encyclopedia of the environment.* Boston: Houghton Mifflin.

Harrison, P. 1992. *The third revolution.* New York: I. B. Tauris.

Meadows, D. H., D. L. Meadows, and J. Randers. 1992. *Beyond the limits.* Post Mills, Vt.: Chelsea Green.

Piel, G. 1992. *Only one world.* New York: W. H. Freeman.

World Resources Institute, 1994. *The 1994 information please environmental almanac.* Boston: Houghton Mifflin.

# THE PHYSICAL ENVIRONMENT

## PROLOGUE    *The Year without a Summer*

In New England 1816 was known as "the year without a summer." During June of that year average temperatures were 7 degrees Fahrenheit (F) below normal, ranging from a chilly 35°F (1.7° Celsius, or C) to a high of 88°F (31°C). Typical temperatures that summer were in the low 60s°F. Many crops failed and their prices rose. Since there was no feed for the hogs and cattle, livestock was sold off at record rates, causing the meat markets to collapse.

But the problems were not limited to New England; the story was the same in many parts of the world. Western Europe experienced similar cold weather, resulting in crop failures, food shortages, and famines. There were even food riots; armed bands raided and looted farms, bakeries, and grain warehouses looking for anything to eat. Europe suffered a typhus epidemic in 1816–1819, perhaps fostered by the widespread famine that left many people in a weakened state.

PHOTO   *The 1993 floods along the Mississippi and Missouri Rivers brought devastation to many areas, including Portage Des Sioux, Missouri, as can be seen in this photograph. (Source: Robert Visser, Greenpeace.)*

The year of 1816 was also a time of natural wonders. The Sun seemed to rise and set through a red cloud or veil of dust and vapor. Snows were very strange—they were colored. Brown, blue, and red snows fell in Maryland, brown snow in Hungary, and red and yellow snows in Taranto in southern Italy. In Taranto any snow is unusual, but red and yellow snow was actually alarming.

The strange weather of 1816, and its consequences, are attributed to a simple geological event: a volcanic eruption that had occurred the previous spring and summer (April through July 1815) at the mountain of Tambora on the island of Sumbawa in Indonesia. Tambora is the largest volcanic eruption recorded in modern historical times, and one of the largest in the past 10,000 years. An estimated 24 cubic miles (100 km$^3$) of rock and debris were ejected from the volcano. Sulfur dioxide and small dust particles entered the stratosphere and blocked the light from the Sun, causing cold temperatures worldwide. The sound of the explosion could be heard a thousand miles away. Reportedly, only 26 of Sumbawa's 12,000 inhabitants survived. Forests and settlements were leveled in the tremendous explosion; lava covered the island and poured into the sea.

Tambora was a huge volcanic explosion by human standards, but geologically there have been much larger ones—even in the relatively recent past. Another eruption in Indonesia, which goes by the name of Toba, ejected an estimated 240 cubic miles (1000 km$^3$) of rock and debris (10 times the volume of Tambora) in about 73,000 B.C. Our physical Earth is still a young and evolving planet. We, as small creatures crawling on the surface of the globe, are still subject to the mercies of nature in many respects even as we tamper with the global ecological balance. We must never forget we cannot totally isolate ourselves from our physical surroundings on this small world.

# INTRODUCTION

The environment is everything that surrounds you, including the air, the land, the oceans, and all living things. For convenience; the **natural environment** can be subdivided into two parts: (1) the **physical environment**, which includes non-living things, and (2) **the biological environment**, which includes all life-forms. The physical environment can be further subdivided into the three basic states of physical matter: solid, liquid, and gas. This division creates four "spheres" that compose the natural environment. The three physical spheres are called the **lithosphere** ("lithos" = rock), **hydrosphere** ("hydro" = water), and **atmosphere** ("atmos" = vapor). The biological environment is called the **biosphere** ("bios" = life).

 Figure 2–1 shows how the four spheres form the outermost layers of the planet Earth. They are underlain by a very thick molten layer of rock belonging to the **mantle** and a heavy metallic **core**.

Three major points about Figure 2–1 should be stressed. First, these four spheres make the Earth a dynamic planet. The lithosphere creates rocks as hot magma, generated by the "internal heat engine" of radioactive minerals. Sometimes this magma erupts onto the surface in the form of volcanoes such as Tambora. The atmosphere erodes the rocks with chemically reactive gases. The hy-drosphere also erodes rocks as well as transporting them as sediments that are often ultimately deposited in ocean basins. The moving lithosphere then carries these sediments to great depth where they are reheated and remelted into magma, beginning the cycle anew. The life of the biosphere inhabits parts of the other spheres, relying on the cycling of chemicals through all of the spheres. Life also effects the other spheres by altering the cycling of chemicals, such as oxygen. Many rocks (for instance, most limestones) are the result of direct biological activity, and recent studies have discovered anaerobic bacteria living in rocks over 9000 feet (2740 m) below the Earth's surface.

Second, the figure illustrates that the spheres closely interact with one another. Matter is transported both within and between the spheres in various kinds of cycles. For instance, gases are expelled from the lithosphere (by volcanoes) and the biosphere (by plants and animals) into the atmosphere. Similarly, water vapor moves from the oceans to the atmosphere and back again. Moreover, there are also numerous cycles within each sphere. For example, new rocks are now being created in the lithosphere while simultaneously older rocks are being eroded away (the "rock cycle," discussed later). Thus, the Earth is an active, integrated system, with many cycles that

## FIGURE 2–1

Spheres of the environment. The dates given in billions of years ago (bya) are approximate times when each of the major spheres of the environment originated: lithosphere 4.0 bya, atmosphere and hydrosphere 3.8 bya, and biosphere 3.5 bya. Note that the Earth is a dynamic planet and that all of the spheres have evolved and changed since its origin.

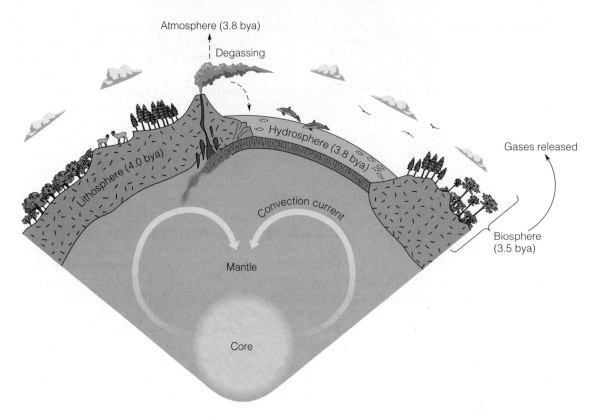

constantly transport matter both within and between the spheres at various rates.

Third, these dynamic and interactive spheres have evolved through time. Figure 2–1 depicts the environment as it exists today, but the Earth is about 4.6 billion years old. The current lithosphere, forming from a molten layer on the hot, young Earth, probably originated some 4 billion years ago. The oceans and atmosphere date back to at least 3.8 billion years ago, and the earliest known fossils (single-celled microbes) representing the biosphere are at least 3.5 billion years old. The evolution of the four spheres is discussed in this chapter (physical environment) and Chapter 3 (biosphere).

The Earth has evolved from a relatively homogeneous collection of particles (cosmic dust) to form a well-differentiated, complex, dynamic, recycling machine. Our planet may seem eternal and unchanging, yet it was very different 4 billion years ago, and it will continue to evolve and change. From a human perspective, such changes are slow and gradual, taking hundreds of millions of years. We must have a clear understanding of the delicate, and in many ways fortuitous, development of the present state of the Earth to fully comprehend just how fragile our environment really is.

## WORKINGS OF PLANET EARTH TODAY

### Earth and Its Neighboring Planets

Earth is the third planet out from the center of the solar system, but it is very different from the other planets.* Unlike its two immediate neighbors, Venus and Mars, which both have atmospheres that are 95–97% carbon dioxide, Earth has an atmosphere composed of about 78.1% nitrogen, 20.9% oxygen, and only 0.03% carbon dioxide. As a result, much of the sunlight and heat reaching the Earth is scattered back into space, and Earth has an average surface temperature of 59°F (15° Celsius, or C). At this temperature water can exist in a liquid state (water quickly evaporates on the hot surface of Venus and remains frozen on Mars), making it possible for life to be maintained on Earth. As far as we are aware, no other planet has anything resembling life.

The gases surrounding the Earth ( Fig. 2–2) and the liquids (primarily water) on its surface are continually swirling and moving, causing the degradation, erosion, and destruction of

_____

*Moving out from the Sun, the planets are: Mercury, Venus, Earth, Mars, Jupiter, Saturn, Uranus, Neptune, and Pluto.

topographic highs such as mountains. The surface of our Moon is pockmarked with craters (Fig. 2–2) due to the lack of an atmosphere to weather them away. There are very few craters on Earth because they quickly erode away. Why then does the Earth's surface have any relief at all? The reason is that the Earth has an "internal engine."

The Earth's interior is seething and churning. Rocks slide and move plastically around one another. The interior is very hot, and at breaks and cracks, molten rock erupts at the surface as volcanoes. In other areas ancient rock is dragged back toward the center of Earth only to be reheated, melted, and rejuvenated. The vast majority of the Earth's surface is relatively young rock. In comparison, some of Earth's close neighbors—the Moon, Mercury, and Mars—are relatively inactive. The Moon and Mars show no evidence of plate tectonic activity, and their surfaces are covered with very ancient rocks, dating back more than 3 billion years. Mars has large volcanoes, including Olympus Mons, which rises 17 miles (27 km) high and is 340 miles (550 km) in diameter at the base, but shows no evidence of true plate tectonic activity. Of the planets close to Earth, only Venus shows some evidence of limited crustal movements comparable to the plate tectonics seen on Earth. But any tectonic movement on Venus appears to have been relatively limited; most of that planet's geological activity seems to be in the form of active volcanoes situated over stationary "hot spots" where molten rock wells up from the interior.

## Present-Day Deep Structure of the Earth

In order to understand natural processes on the surface of the Earth, we must have a clear understanding of the structure of the Earth. The internal make-up of the Earth accounts for volcanoes and earthquakes. It even affects the composition of the atmosphere, oceans, and ultimately the nature of life on the Earth.

If we could cut a slice through the Earth, we would see that it is formed of concentric rings of differing constitutions—similar to the layers of an onion ( Fig. 2–3). From the outside, the first

major layer is the Earth's gaseous envelope or atmosphere. It extends in rarefied form for hundreds of miles above the Earth's surface, although almost the total mass is contained within the bottom 12 to 13 miles (20 km). The Earth's surface is covered with seawater or dry land (including land that contains freshwater lakes or ice patches) in a ratio of about 7 to 3. If all water were removed from the surface, we would observe two basic terranes: ocean basins, which average about 3 miles (5 km) depth below sea level and are floored with basaltic-type rocks, and continents and continental islands, which on average rise several hundred feet (a few hundred meters) above sea level, and are founded on granitic-type rocks. Actual ocean basins cover only about two-thirds of Earth's surface; in places the oceans lap onto the shallow continental margins.

The thin crust under the oceans averages only about 3 miles (5 km) thick. It is composed of about 50% (by weight) silicon dioxide (perhaps most familiar as the mineral quartz) and contains higher amounts of iron, magnesium, and calcium

## FIGURE 2–2

The Earth seen from the Moon. The Earth is a "living planet" with an active atmosphere and an internal heat engine driving many geological processes. In contrast, the Moon is a "dead planet" (our Moon is larger than Pluto and nearly as large as Mercury) with virtually no atmosphere or active geological processes on its surface. As a result, the Moon's surface is pockmarked with craters that have not eroded away. (*Source:* NASA.)

## FIGURE 2–3

Schematic section through the Earth.

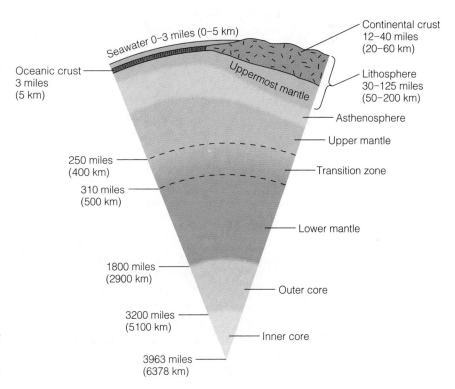

Seawater 0–3 miles (0–5 km)

Continental crust 12–40 miles (20–60 km)

Oceanic crust 3 miles (5 km)

Uppermost mantle

Lithosphere 30–125 miles (50–200 km)

Asthenosphere

Upper mantle

250 miles (400 km)

310 miles (500 km)

Transition zone

Lower mantle

1800 miles (2900 km)

Outer core

3200 miles (5100 km)

Inner core

3963 miles (6378 km)

than are generally seen in continental crust. The continental crust, ranging from about 12 miles to 40 miles (20 km to 60 km) thick, is about two-thirds silicon dioxide.

Below the crust, extending to a depth of about 1800 miles (2900 km), is the mantle, which is composed of about 45% silicon dioxide and 38% magnesium oxide. The relatively rigid upper layer of the mantle with its attached crust is known as the lithosphere. The lithosphere is the major unit of movement in plate tectonics (discussed below). Below the lithosphere lies another layer of the mantle, the relatively weak and soft **asthenosphere** (literally, weak or glassy sphere; see Fig. 2–3).

Beneath the mantle is the Earth's core. The outer core extends from a depth of about 1800 to 3200 miles (2900 to 5100 km) and consists of a liquid iron-nickel (mostly iron) alloy. Movements within the outer core probably are responsible for generating the Earth's magnetic field. The inner core, extending from a depth of about 3200 miles (5100 km) to the Earth's center (3963 miles [6378 km] deep), is composed of a solid iron-nickel alloy.

## Plate Tectonics

If you look carefully at a map and imagine that the continents are pieces of a jigsaw puzzle, you will notice that the east coasts of North and South America appear to fit into the west coasts of Europe and Africa. This simple observation, and a wealth of other data, led to the hypothesis of drifting continents, first proposed by the German scientist Alfred Wegener in about 1912. Today a variation of the theory of continental drift, known as **plate tectonics**, is accepted by virtually all earth scientists. Indeed, plate tectonics forms the unifying theory for most of the geological structures observed on the surface of the planet. It is the active process of plate tectonics that not only moves continents, but also raises mountains, creates new sea floor, destroys and recycles old sea floor, and causes volcanoes to erupt and earthquakes to occur. Plate tectonics plays a major role in natural biogeochemical cycles on Earth—cycles which are now being disrupted by human activities (Chapter 4).

Today the Earth's lithosphere is divided into about eight major tectonic plates and numerous

**■ FIGURE 2–4**
The Earth's tectonic plates. The plates are in continuous motion relative to one another. Notice the relationship between plate boundaries, intense earthquakes, and major volcanic eruptions.

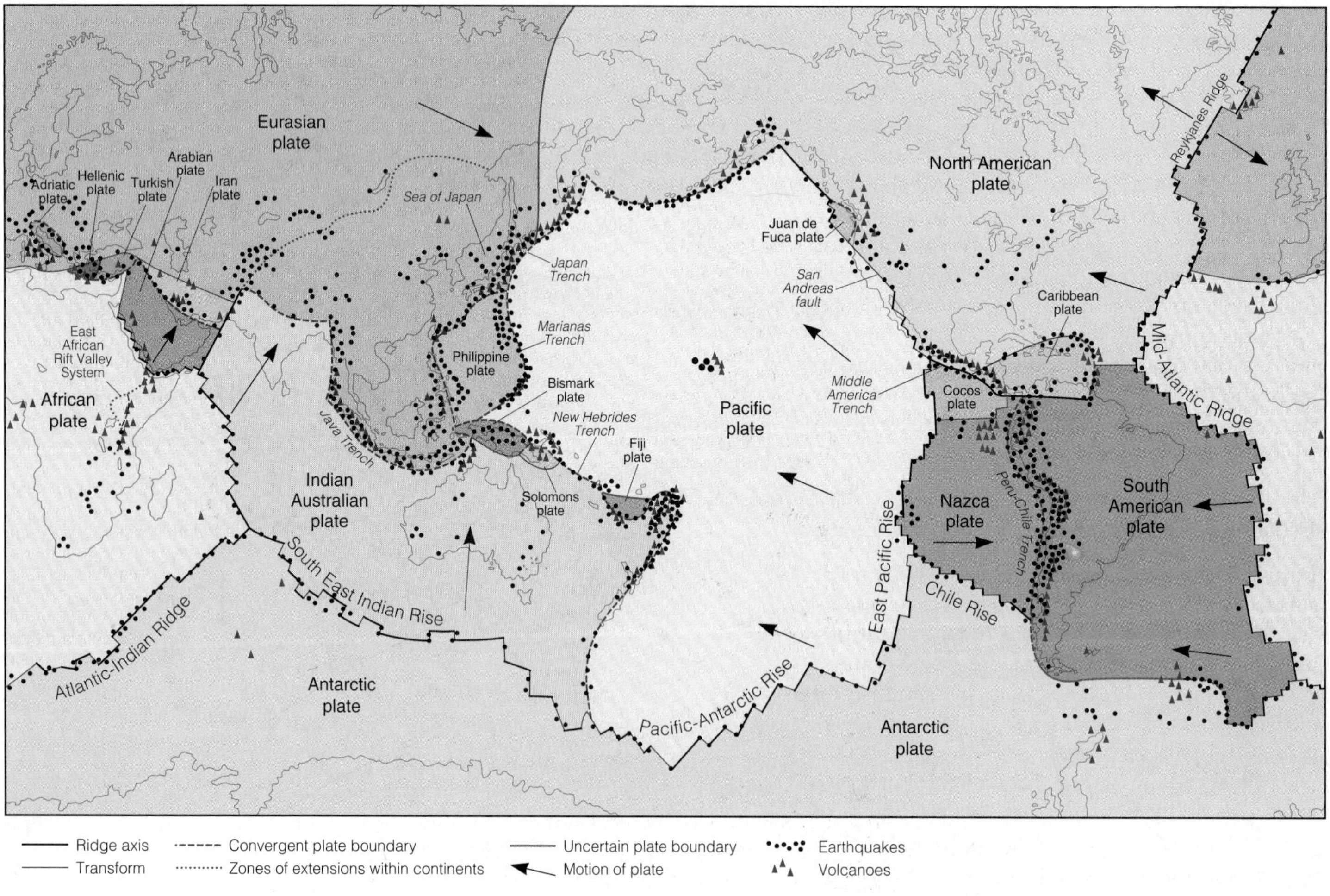

Ridge axis — Transform — Convergent plate boundary ----- Zones of extensions within continents ·········· Uncertain plate boundary — Motion of plate ← Earthquakes •••••• Volcanoes ▲▲

smaller ones (▬ Fig. 2–4). These plates are in continuous motion, sliding past one another, colliding, or pulling apart from each other. Essentially, the continents are carried on the tops of the plates. The plates do not move very fast from a human perspective, about 0.8 to 12 inches (2 to 30 cm) a year, but this is fast enough to have caused major changes in the positions of the continents over the last few hundred million years (▬ Fig. 2–5).

Prior to about 2.5 billion years ago, the Earth's surface was probably covered by small, rapidly moving "platelets," which slowly coalesced into larger, thicker plates. Only in the last 800 million years has the crust been characterized by modern-style, large, thick plates. About 240 million years ago, all of the continental landmass formed a single supercontinent, Pangaea, which has since split up into the present-day continents.

What causes the plates to move? This has been a topic of heated discussion over a number of years. Today most scientists believe that convection currents in the molten mantle move the lithospheric plates (▬ Fig. 2–6). Heat continually flows out from the hot center of the Earth. As in a pot of cooking soup, the hot liquid rises to the surface and flows there for some distance; as the liquid cools, it sinks below the surface, only to be heated up and start the cycle once again. This is known as a **convection cell**. Giant convection cells are believed to exist in the liquid mantle, and as they cycle, the flowing mantle drags the overlying, rigid lithosphere plates along. As the Earth cools over time, the rates of motion of the plates are decreasing, and they are continuing to enlarge and thicken.

At divergent plate boundaries, places where two lithospheric plates are moving away from each other, a gap or void is left in the solid crust (▬ Fig. 2–7). Initially, the rock in this area may start to collapse, forming a rift valley, but as the plates move apart, hot molten rock from the mantle wells up to fill the void and form new oceanic crust. This process is often referred to as sea-floor spreading. The classic example of a divergent plate boundary is the Mid-Atlantic Ridge, which runs roughly north-

south through the Atlantic Ocean.

Along deep-sea rift zones, hot water (about 660°F, or 350°C) emanates from hydrothermal vents. These vents often support unique ecological communities that are based on geothermal energy rather than the solar energy most ecosystems require (▬ Fig. 2–8). Bacteria use the energy found in hydrogen sulfide ($H_2S$) and similar

(a)

(b)

(c)

▬ **FIGURE 2–5**
Continental movements over the last 240 million years. (a) The Earth about 240 million years ago. (b) The Earth about 70 million years ago. (c) The modern Earth.

chemicals emanating from the vents to produce organic molecules from inorganic molecules. Crabs, clams, tube worms, and fishes then feed on the bacteria. Thus these vents dramatically illustrate the interrelationships between geological processes and living organisms.

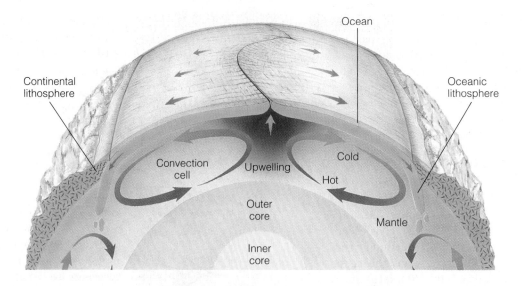

In some places, convergent plate boundaries occur where two lithospheric plates converge or collide (see Fig. 2–7). If the colliding edges of the two plates both bear oceanic crust, either plate may be forced, or subducted, under the other plate. A subduction zone is formed under the leading edge of the plate that remains on top. On the surface, where the plates are downwarped, a deep trench forms. As the subducted plate moves down into the hot mantle, it melts, and the lighter rock components rise to the surface, forming volcanoes. New continental crustal material, formed from the recycled oceanic crust, collects behind the trench. The northern and western edges of the Pacific Ocean (known as the "ring of fire" for their numerous volcanoes) are lined with convergent plate boundaries (see Fig. 2–4).

If the leading edge of one colliding plate contains continental crust and the leading edge of the other plate contains heavier oceanic crust, the plate with oceanic crust will always be subducted under the plate bearing lighter continental crust, which "floats" on top. If leading edges of colliding lithospheric plates both contain continental crust, neither can be subducted because they are both relatively light. Instead, the continents crash into one another, crumple, and deform, often raising imposing mountain ranges. The mighty Himalayas are the result of two continental landmasses crashing into one another. Eventually, the plates lock and relative motion between them stops.

Finally, two plates may slide past one another; their edges grind and slip against each other along what are commonly termed transform

■ **F I G U R E   2–7**
Principal types of plate boundaries.

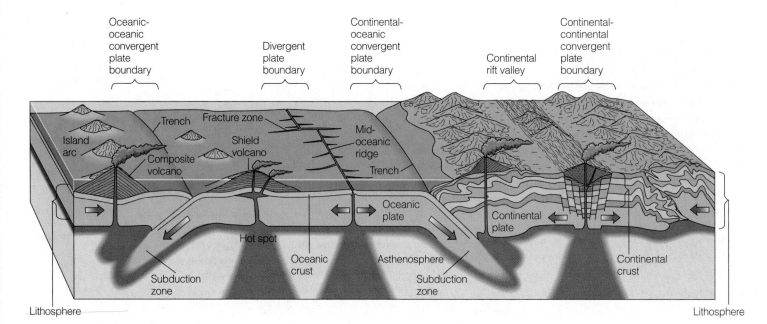

faults. This is the least dramatic type of relative plate motion in that it usually does not involve either volcanoes or mountain building. Earthquakes are common along transform faults, however, as is well known by residents of California, where the Pacific plate slides north past the North American plate. The surficial rocks do not flow past one another slowly and smoothly, but tend to "hang up." Pressure builds, and then is suddenly released—the rock "jumps" and an earthquake occurs.

## The Composition of Matter on the Earth

Rocks are by far the most common substances on the Earth's surface. Indeed, everything is rock or made primarily of materials that were once components of rocks. A clear understanding of rocks and the rock cycle (discussed later) are necessary in order to understand the cycling of matter through the environment (Chapters 1 and 4). Rocks themselves are composed of minerals, which in turn are composed of elements.

**Minerals** are naturally occurring, inorganic solids that have a regular internal structure and composition—they are said to be crystalline. Some well known minerals include quartz, diamond, garnet, and pyrite. In all, over two thousand different minerals are known. Minerals are composed of combinations of atoms of elements.

The **elements** such as iron, hydrogen, oxygen, mercury, and gold are the fundamental substances of our world. An element cannot be broken down chemically into other elements. There are close to 90 naturally occurring elements found in measurable amounts on Earth today, and additional elements have been artificially synthesized under laboratory conditions.

Atoms are the smallest units of an element that retain the physical and chemical properties of the element. When combined together, substances composed of different elements can take on new properties. Water, for instance, is a **compound** composed of atoms of the elements hydrogen and oxygen. Atoms themselves are divisible into even smaller particles. In the center of each atom is a nucleus composed of protons and neutrons ( Fig. 2–9). Protons carry positive charges and neutrons are electrically neutral. Most of an atom's mass is contained in its nucleus, where the number of protons determines to what element the atom belongs. For example, all atoms of hydrogen have only one proton in their nucleus, whereas all atoms of gold have 79 protons in their nucleus. The number of protons in the nucleus is referred to as the atom's atomic number and is characteristic of the atoms of a particular element.

The number of protons and neutrons in the nucleus is the atom's atomic mass number. Atoms of the same element can have varying numbers of neutrons in their nucleus. In nature one can find carbon atoms with atomic mass numbers of 12, 13, or 14. These variants are known as isotopes of the element carbon. Some isotopes are unstable and undergo radioactive decay by emitting particles spontaneously so as to change into a more stable form of atom (see Chapter 8).

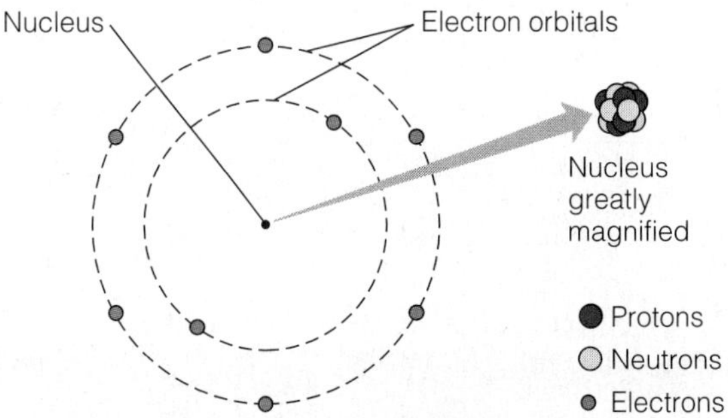

**FIGURE 2–8**
A deep-sea hydrothermal vent and its unique biotic community, which is based on geothermal energy rather than the solar energy most systems require. Bacteria use the energy found in hydrogen sulfide and similar chemicals to produce organic molecules. Crabs, clams, giant tube worms, and fishes then feed on the bacteria. (*Source:* Science VU–WHOI, D. Foster/Visuals Unlimited.)

**FIGURE 2–9**
The basic structure of an atom.

Nucleus — Electron orbitals

Nucleus greatly magnified

● Protons
○ Neutrons
• Electrons

Properties of Atomic Particles

| Particle | Charge | Mass | Location | Symbol |
| --- | --- | --- | --- | --- |
| Proton | Positive | $1.673 \times 10^{-24}$g | Nucleus | $p$ |
| Neutron | Neutral | $1.675 \times 10^{-24}$g | Nucleus | $n$ |
| Electron | Negative | $9.110 \times 10^{-28}$g | Orbitals | $e$ |

Orbiting around the protons and neutrons of the atom's nucleus are electrons (Fig. 2–9), small negatively charged particles that electrically balance the protons in an electrically neutral atom. If an atom has more electrons than protons, it will be a negatively charged ion. If it has fewer electrons than protons, it will be a positively charged ion.

Single atoms are much too small for us to perceive in isolation. Substances that we are familiar with are composed of tremendous numbers of atoms, which are almost always bonded together in various arrangements. Depending on how the atoms are arranged, we refer to states of matter composed of atoms as solids, liquids, or gases.

## Rocks—Their Origin and the Rock Cycle

Most rocks are composed primarily of minerals and are classified into three basic categories: igneous, sedimentary, and metamorphic ( Fig. 2–10).

**Igneous rocks** formed, or crystallized, from extremely hot molten rock known as magma

("igneous" = fire-rock). The lava that flows out of a volcano and hardens into rock is a well-known type of igneous rock. Igneous rocks that formed from lava flows or volcanic ash ejected from a volcano are known as extrusive igneous rocks. Most igneous rocks, however, form deep underground as liquid magma slowly cools and crystallizes; such rocks are known as intrusive igneous rocks. Typical intrusive igneous rocks include basalt, gabbro, and granite. Igneous rocks are the most common rocks, forming the vast bulk of the Earth's crust and all of its rocky inside (where it is not molten). On the surface of the Earth, however, igneous rocks are often covered by a blanket of sediments or sedimentary rocks.

Having formed deep inside the Earth, most igneous rocks are inherently unstable at the surface. Over time, the rocks weather, broken down by both mechanical (running water, ice, or wind) and chemical agents (such as acids and solvents found in nature—for instance, the ubiquitous carbonic acid of rainwater), and disintegrate into fragments. These fragments are known as sediments;

 **FIGURE 2–10**
The three basic types of rocks—igneous, sedimentary, and metamorphic—and the rock cycle.

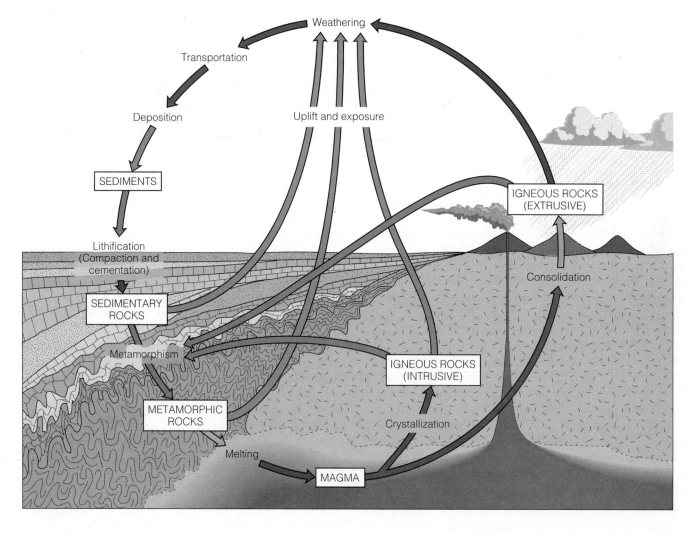

*Environmental Principles*   SECTION 1

they generally consist of either small pieces of rock or single mineral grains, and come in various sizes—such as gravel, sand, silt, or mud. The sediments are physically transported from higher to lower elevations by running water, wind, or ice flows (glaciers), until they are deposited in a resting place. As piles of sediments accumulate, they become compacted and cemented together, or even crystallized. Minerals may precipitate between the sediment grains, binding them tightly together to form a **sedimentary rock** (Fig. 2–10). Sedimentary rocks cover approximately 75% of Earth's surface. Among the most common sedimentary rocks are sandstones and shales.

Not all sedimentary rocks are formed from the weathered remains of other rocks. Many limestones, for example, are formed from sediment that consists entirely of the old calcium carbonate shells or skeletons of sea organisms. Fossils, the remains of ancient organisms, are almost always found encapsulated in sedimentary rocks such as limestones, sandstones, and shales. Peats, coals, oils, and other fossil fuels, formed of the fragments of many plants and other organisms, are components of some sedimentary rock layers. Other types of sedimentary rocks are formed from the precipitation, or "sedimentation," of substances out of an aqueous solution, perhaps as it evaporates. For instance, large deposits of rock salt (halite) often form in this way.

Like igneous rocks, sedimentary rocks weather and break down. The sediments formed from sedimentary rocks can then be recycled to form other sedimentary rocks. The next generation of rocks may weather and the resulting fragments be recycled again, with the pattern occurring over and over.

The remaining class is **metamorphic rocks** ("metamorphic" = change of form). Metamorphic rocks are made when rock—igneous, sedimentary, or in some cases another metamorphic rock—is subjected to great temperature (but not hot enough to completely melt the rock) or pressure, or both (Fig. 2–10). The rock undergoes some combination of mineralogical changes (certain minerals are turned into other minerals) and/or textural changes (mineral grains may grow in size). In some cases the metamorphic rock may be produced by hot fluids released at the edge of a molten rock body that penetrates preexisting rock. Some common metamorphic rocks include slate (produced from the metamorphism of shale or mudstone), marble (produced from limestone), quartzite (produced from quartz sandstone), and various schists and gneisses (produced by the extreme metamorphism of various other types of igneous, sedimentary, and metamorphic rocks).

Geologists often refer to the **rock cycle** (Fig. 2–10). Effectively, all rock/earth material on the Earth's surface begins as igneous rock. Initial crystallization takes place at a rift zone where two lithospheric plates diverge. This new rock may weather directly into sediments or become metamorphosed, but perhaps most often it gets carried to a subduction zone where it is remelted, rises toward the surface, and eventually is added to the continental crust. From here it may be metamorphosed or remelted again, or it may be weathered at the surface, with the fragments eventually forming sedimentary rocks. The sedimentary rock may be weathered, broken into fragments, and made into other sedimentary rocks, or more sediments may be piled on top of it, until it is buried deep below the surface. With increasing temperatures and pressures, the sediments may be metamorphosed and eventually find themselves in a setting where they actually melt. If so, they will form genuine igneous rocks upon cooling and crystallization, thus continuing the rock cycle.

By human standards, the rock cycle is very slow, taking on the order of millions to hundreds of millions of years. Furthermore, it is not a complete or closed cycle. Once continental (granitic type) material is formed, it remains continental material, even if it cycles from igneous to sedimentary, to metamorphic, back to igneous, and so on. As described in the section on plate tectonics, continental material is too light to be subducted back into the mantle; thus, it is not recycled in that sense. More continental crustal material is in existence today than ever before in Earth history.

## The Surface of the Earth: Hydrologic and Atmospheric Cycles; Climate and Weather

The Earth's surface is almost entirely covered with water—not just the seas and oceans, but numerous lakes, ponds, swamps, and even morning dew on the "dry" land. It is enveloped in an atmosphere composed predominantly of nitrogen, or $N_2$ (78.1%), and oxygen, or $O_2$ (20.9%). It is also bathed in radiation—energy in the form of heat (infrared radiation) and light—from the Sun. All of these components work together to make the surface conditions of our planet very active and constantly changing.

The Earth's atmospheric envelope is divided into layers, distinguished mainly by the changing temperature gradient encountered as one moves up into the atmosphere ( Fig. 2–11): the troposphere, stratosphere, mesosphere, and ther-

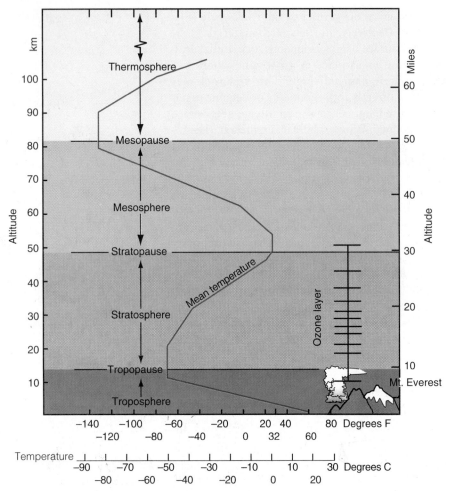

**FIGURE 2–11**
The structure of the Earth's atmosphere. The tropopause, stratopause, and mesopause are the boundaries between the troposphere and stratosphere, stratosphere and mesosphere, and mesosphere and thermosphere respectively.

mosphere. The changing temperature gradient is the result of the interplay of the energy received directly from the Sun, the gaseous constitution and density of the atmosphere at different levels, and the distance the energy (heat) reflected and emitted from the Earth's surface reaches into the atmosphere.

The density of the atmosphere decreases exponentially going away from the Earth's surface. An estimated 80 to 85% of the mass of the atmosphere is in the troposphere; 99% is found in the troposphere and stratosphere combined. Except for water vapor and ozone ($O_3$), the gross composition of the atmosphere (78.1% $N_2$ and 20.9% $O_2$, along with trace gases) is fairly constant up into the bottom of the thermosphere. Virtually all the water in the atmosphere is found in the troposphere, the region of the phenomena we call weather.

In terms of energy flow, the Earth's surface is an open system: it constantly receives energy from the Sun, and it continuously loses most of this energy to space. Approximately 30% of the incoming solar energy that reaches the upper atmosphere is immediately reflected back to space, and another 20% is absorbed by water vapor in the atmosphere, so only about 50% reaches Earth's surface. Very little (less than 1%) of the Sun's energy that reaches Earth goes into photosynthesis, and thus the direct support of living organisms. The vast majority of the energy that reaches Earth goes into evaporating surface waters; it thus reenters the atmosphere and is eventually dissipated into space as heat (electromagnetic radiation in the infrared range).

The movement of water about the surface of Earth, driven by energy from the Sun, constitutes the **hydrologic cycle** ( Fig. 2–12). Approximately 97.4% of the water on or near the Earth's surface is found in the seas and oceans, 1.98% is bound up as ice (primarily in the polar ice caps), 0.59% is stored temporarily as groundwater, only 0.014% is found in freshwater lakes and streams, and a mere 0.001% takes the form of atmospheric water vapor at any one point in time. The shifting of water over the globe through the hydrologic cycle redistributes heat and generally makes for more equitable climates. The hydrologic cycle also plays a prominent role in the rock cycle through the weathering and decomposition of rocks. Together with the atmospheric cycles, the hydrologic cycle is also responsible for **weather**, or the short-term, daily perturbations in the atmospheric/hydrologic cycles. **Climate** is the average weather over time ranges of decades to millennia to hundreds of millions of years.

Based on large-scale **atmospheric cycles**, the Earth's surface is divided into several major climatic belts that roughly correspond to latitudinal changes (north and south). Working out from the equator, one finds the rainforest belt (centered about the equator), the desert belts (centered about 30° north and south), the temperate regions, and the polar regions.

Convection cells form in the atmosphere similar to those believed to occur in the mantle. The rays of the Sun fall most directly on the equator, making the equatorial regions hotter than the rest of the Earth's surface. The hot air rises, carrying with it large quantities of water vapor (warm air can hold more moisture than cool air). The rising air leaves a relative void, and cooler, drier air closer to the surface flows in from the north and south to fill the void ( Fig. 2–13). This new cool air heats up, picks up moisture, and then itself rises from the equator. The rising air quickly cools, however, and loses its capacity to hold moisture. Consequently, vast quantities of water are released in the vicinity of the equator producing the tropical rainforests. As the air con-

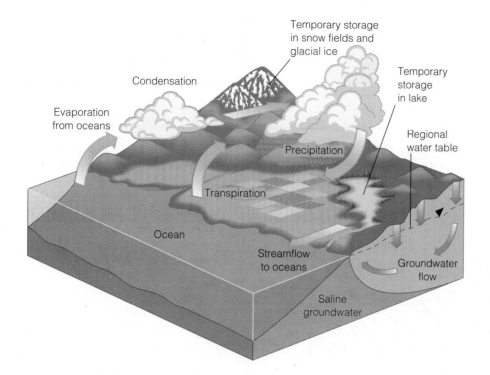

**FIGURE 2–12**
The hydrologic cycle.

tinues to rise and cool, it moves either north or south, continues to lose moisture, and eventually begins to sink as dry air in the region of 25 to 35° latitude north and south, giving rise to the subtropical high-pressure zones that produce some of the world's great deserts. Once the cool air approaches the surface, it flows south or north toward the equator. On reaching the equator the air again heats and absorbs moisture, and the cycle continues. Not all of the air sinks at the subtropical high pressure zones, however. Some of the air continues toward the poles where it eventually sinks and takes part in polar atmospheric cycles. Cold surface winds tend to blow from the poles toward the equator.

Of course, the atmospheric cycle is not quite that simple. Two effects in particular modify it. First, the Earth spins on its axis, causing the air in the convection cells to cycle at an angle rather than directly north and south. This is known as the Coriolis effect. To understand the Coriolis effect, imagine yourself standing on the geographical North Pole. The Earth is rotating toward the east. If you throw a ball, it will land to the west of where you aimed it—the Earth turns under it as it travels through the air. This effect produces the trade-winds that once carried sailing vessels across the oceans.

Second, the Earth's topography— the positions of its mountains, valleys, lakes, and oceans— greatly modify both weather and climate. The **oceans** that cover much of the surface contribute

greatly to the overall climate (■ Fig. 2–14). Moving air masses create ocean currents, which are then modified by the Coriolis effect and the continental landmasses that the currents bump into. Due to the great capacity of water to absorb and retain heat, ocean currents play an important role in distributing heat over the Earth's surface.

**FIGURE 2–13**
General circulation in the Earth's atmosphere.

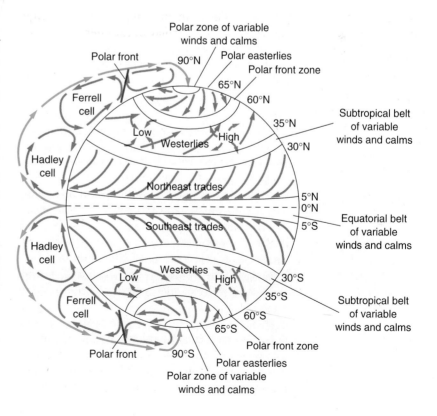

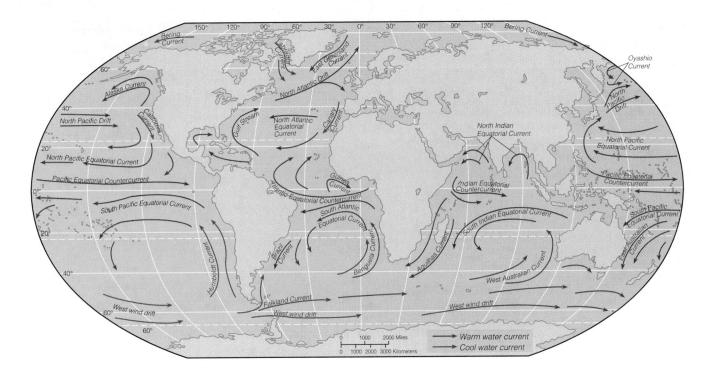

**FIGURE 2–14**
Global surface ocean currents.

On land the topography greatly influences weather patterns. For example, mountains may create rainshadows causing deserts to form on their leeward sides. When a warm moist air mass encounters a mountain, the air begins to sweep up the mountain's windward side. In so doing, the air rises, cools, and loses much of its moisture as precipitation. Once across the mountain, the now dry air flows down the other side, becoming warmer as it reaches lower elevations. Because the air has left its moisture on the other side of the mountain, a desert is created. In North America a rainshadow effect produces deserts east of the Sierra Nevada, and in South America the Andes Mountains are responsible for the extremely dry deserts found along the western coasts of Peru and Chile.

Local and global temperature and climate are also influenced by the albedo, or the proportion of the incoming solar radiation that is reflected back to space by various surfaces. Large, vegetation-free deserts and blankets of ice or snow have a large reflective capacity—a high albedo. Oceans and other large bodies of water, which have the ability to absorb heat, as well as areas covered with thick vegetation, have a low albedo.

Dust in the atmosphere can also have a high albedo and reflect significant amounts of radiation including heat back into space. As the Prologue described, the dust and ash emitted by the volcano Tambora had worldwide ramifications for the weather. The impact of a huge meteorite, could throw up blankets of dust and particulate matter that would have the same effect. Conversely, other additions to the atmosphere can lead to higher temperatures. Various greenhouse gases, most notably carbon dioxide, when added to the atmosphere (either artificially or naturally) create a blanket that allows radiation to enter, but blocks the escape of heat (see Chapter 18), thus leading to global warming.

## Rotation, Orbits, and Seasons

In addition to its short-term, day-to-day fluctuations, weather is seasonal, changing on an annual basis. These cyclical variations in the weather are due to changes in the orientation of the Earth's axis. As you know, the Earth rotates on its axis once a day as it orbits around the Sun once a year. The Earth's axis of rotation is not perpendicular to the plane of its orbit, but rather is inclined at an angle of about 23.5°. Consequently, as the Earth follows its orbit, different parts of the surface are exposed to more direct rays from the Sun (Fig. 2–15). In the Northern Hemisphere during the summer, the axis is tilted toward the Sun, causing sunlight to fall more directly on this part of the world. During the winter months, when the axis is tilted away from the Sun, the sunlight reaches the surface at an oblique angle. The seasons create fluctuating surface temperatures that stay within a moderate range. Without the seasons, large amounts of heat might be permanently trapped at the equator, and huge regions of permanently frozen wasteland would exist at moderate and high latitudes.

# ORIGIN AND PHYSICAL DEVELOPMENT OF THE EARTH

The Earth is not a stagnant, unchanging planet. Since its origin around 5 billion years ago, our planet has been progressively developing and evolving. Atmospheric composition, climate and weather, continental and ocean positions, surface topography, sea level heights, and many other factors have varied in the past.

Therefore, if we are to evaluate the modern environment in a holistic context (taking into account the functional relationships between the parts and the whole), we need to take an historical perspective. For instance, to evaluate the current concentration of greenhouse gases and the predictions of global warming, we need to consider the changing composition of the atmosphere through geologic time and the oscillations in climate that have occurred over the past few million years (see Chapter 18). Similarly, we must compare present extinction rates of species to extinction rates over the last 500 million years (see Chapter 12).

## Origin of the Solar System and Earth

The present universe is believed to be between 8 and 20 billion years old. Our little bit of the universe—our Sun and solar system—is very much younger, though. The Sun, Earth, and solar system originated about 5 billion years ago when a gas and dust cloud in our region of the galaxy began to collapse and coalesce. The material rotated more and more swiftly around its center, flattening the cloud into a disc shape and causing the accretion and condensation of particles of matter.

In the middle of the disc, the proto-Sun (the material that would become our Sun) condensed, and at various distances from the center eddies concentrated particles in clusters that formed planetesimals (small planet-like bodies). Through gravitational attraction and accretion, these bodies eventually became our familiar planets. By about 4.6 or 4.5 billion years ago, the Sun ignited, giving off tremendous heat and light. The influence of the Sun may have produced the basic arrangement of the planets we observe today, with the innermost planets being the "rocky" planets (Mercury, Venus, Earth and its Moon, and Mars) that can withstand the higher temperatures closer to the Sun, and the outer planets (Jupiter, Saturn, Uranus, Neptune, and Pluto) being frozen, gassy or icy planets.

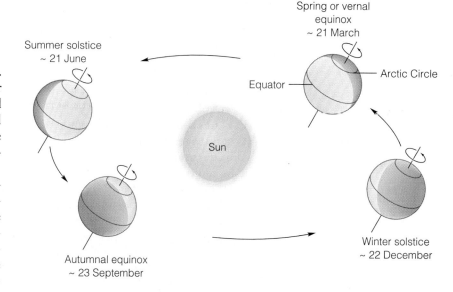

**FIGURE 2–15**
Rotation of the Earth around the Sun.

On the Earth, a period of intense heating caused the various components to melt and to separate into layers of heavier and lighter components. The dense iron-nickel components sank to the core while the lighter silicates rose and formed the mantle and crust. Many sources for the heat that led to this differentiation have been suggested, such as the impact energy of meteorites and asteroids, but in all likelihood, the main source was the radioactivity of elements trapped within the planet.

## Origin of the Oceans

By about 4 billion years ago, the Earth probably had an ocean. We can assign an approximate date because among the oldest known rocks, formed some 3.8 billion years ago, are sedimentary rocks that show evidence of water weathering and erosion. But where did the water come from? Various hypotheses have been proposed. Many scientists believe that during the early accretion of the Earth, much water (initially in the form of water vapor) and large amounts of other gases were released by volcanoes. Modern volcanoes also spew out water, although much of their output may actually be recycled seawater. A significant amount of water may also have been deposited by icy comets that collided with the primitive Earth.

Over time, the oceans have accumulated salts as weathered material from the rocks of the continents has washed into them. The oceans contain ions, or salts, of such elements as sodium, magnesium, and chlorine along with smaller amounts of calcium, silica, potassium, and various dissolved gases including oxygen, carbon dioxide, and sulfur dioxide.

## Origin of the Atmosphere

The earliest atmosphere of which we have any direct evidence, that of about 3.5 to 4 billion years ago, was very different than the atmosphere of today. It almost certainly originated from the Earth's interior as the planet underwent melting and segregation into a core, mantle, and crust. This early atmosphere probably contained large amounts of nitrogen gas, appreciable amounts of carbon dioxide, some methane and ammonia, and virtually no molecular oxygen.

So where did the present atmosphere's oxygen come from? Two basic processes are known to produce oxygen gas in some abundance in the natural world: (1) the breakdown of water into hydrogen gas and oxygen gas by ultraviolet radiation and (2) plant photosynthesis, the process of using the energy of sunlight to combine carbon dioxide and water into carbohydrates, giving off free oxygen gas as a by-product. The latter process is much more efficient at producing oxygen.

Currently, photosynthesis produces an estimated 22 billion tons (20 billion metric tons)* of oxygen per year. Many scientists believe that the high oxygen level of our current atmosphere is largely the result of photosynthetic organisms dumping this once lethal toxic waste into the environment over the last 3 billion years. As the levels of oxygen in the atmosphere increased, organisms evolved the ability to utilize oxygen in an efficient form of metabolism known as aerobic respiration; ultimately these changes allowed the evolution of very complex, multicellular life-forms.

## NATURAL HAZARDS

Humans have always had to deal with "unpredictable" **natural hazards**—earthquakes, volcanic eruptions, floods, avalanches, droughts,

---

*Unless otherwise noted, *tons* refers to short tons (2000 pounds).

fires, tornadoes, hurricanes, and so forth (● Table 2–1). For most of human history such phenomena were beyond human control: they were neither caused by humans, nor was there much humans could do to predict their occurrences or mitigate (make less severe) their consequences.

Although many acts of nature still cannot be controlled, we have learned to better predict their occurrences and mitigate their effects. Furthermore, we have come to understand that some types of phenomena have a large anthropogenic (produced or caused by humans) component. Flash floods and avalanches may be caused, or at least exacerbated, by human deforestation in hilly regions. Abnormal droughts, storms, and other unusual weather phenomena may be caused or magnified by human interference with the atmosphere, such as the emission of high levels of greenhouse gases. Earthquakes, at least on a local level, may be caused by the pumping of fluid wastes into rocks lying deep below the surface.

As the Earth's human population increases, the damage done by naturally occurring, periodic "disasters" is magnified. A coastal area may be hit by a major storm once every century, a river may swell over its "normal" banks covering the floodplain only once every few centuries, or a naturally set forest fire may periodically burn off dead underbrush and litter on the forest floor. Viewed on a temporal scale of millennia (thousands of years), such events form an integral part of the natural ecosystem cycle; from a natural, holistic perspective, they are not disasters at all. But when dense human populations inhabit a coastal area or a river's floodplain and depend on a forest for lumber products or for scenic beauty, these events are perceived as terrible disasters—and so they are from a human perspective. But they are disasters that, given a little knowledge of the natural world, should have been easily anticipated. In this section, we briefly introduce some of the basic types of natural hazards that civilization must face as we continue to live in a natural environment.

---

**TABLE 2–1** *Estimated Deaths Due to Major Natural Hazards 1960–1995*

| HAZARD TYPE | ESTIMATED TOTAL DEATHS | EXAMPLES OF MAJOR EVENTS | DEATHS |
|---|---|---|---|
| Tropical cyclones | 800,000 | East Pakistan (Bangladesh) 1970 | 500,000 |
| Earthquakes | 600,000 | Tangshan, China 1976 | 250,000 |
| Floods | 46,000 | Vietnam 1964 | 8,000 |
| Avalanches, mudslides | 38,000 | Peru 1970 | 25,000 |
| Volcanic eruptions | 35,000 | Colombia 1985 | 23,000 |

## Earthquakes and Volcanoes

Earthquakes and volcanic eruptions are geological phenomena that humans may be able to predict (though not always), but can virtually never control. With few exceptions, earthquakes and volcanoes are due to processes that take place deep within the crust and mantle. Volcanic eruptions are usually accompanied by at least minor to moderate earthquakes, but very large earthquakes can occur in the absence of volcanic activity. As we have already discussed, earthquakes and volcanic activity are associated with the boundaries of the lithospheric plates (refer to Fig. 2–4), and can be explained in terms of moving and/or subducting plates. But earthquakes (and less commonly volcanoes) can also occur in the middle of plates; indeed, no place on the surface of Earth is immune to earthquake activity.

### Earthquakes

**Earthquakes** are essentially shock waves that originate when large masses of rocks suddenly move relative to each other below the Earth's surface. For instance, along a plate boundary where two lithospheric plates are sliding past each other, the plates may "hang up," allowing strain (frictional drag) to accumulate until it is finally relieved by rock movement—causing an earthquake. Earthquakes can originate up to 450 miles (700 km) below the surface. When the sudden rock movement occurs, various types of shock, or seismic, waves are transmitted through the Earth, causing the shaking or trembling felt by humans on the surface. A large earthquake may be detectable around the world.

Earthquakes are a constant threat to human life and well-being in some areas. Perhaps the most devastating set of earthquakes occurred near Shensi, China, in 1556 killing an estimated 830,000 people. A dozen earthquakes that caused the death of 100,000 people or more, have been recorded. Estimates are that, on average, earthquakes kill at least 10,000 people a year and cause about $500 million in property damage. Japan, a nation always at risk for earthquakes, suffered devastating consequences in 1995 when a quake hit the Kobe area killing over 5000 people, injuring another 25,000, and initially leaving over 300,000 homeless ( Fig. 2–16).

The intensity, magnitude, or strength of an earthquake is commonly measured either on the Richter scale (in North America) or the Mercalli scale (in Europe). The Richter scale (see Issues in Perspective 2–1) is based on the amplitude

of the seismic waves recorded by seismographs (instruments that record the motions of the Earth's surface) coming from a particular earthquake. The Richter scale is a logarithmic scale so that every unit corresponds to a 10-fold increase in the amplitude of the seismic waves. Thus a 7.0 earthquake is characterized by seismic waves with an amplitude of 100 times that seen in a 5.0 earthquake. Theoretically, the Richter scale has no upper limit, but some of the largest recorded earthquakes (such as the Lisbon earthquake of 1755 immortalized in Voltaire's *Candide*) have been ranked at about 8.9–9.0 ( Table 2–2).

**FIGURE 2–16**
The 1995 Kobe earthquake killed more than 5000 people and disrupted the lives of hundreds of thousands more. (*Source:* Bunyo Ishikawa/ Sygma.)

# *Forget the Richter Scale?*

Most members of the American public automatically associate an earthquake's size with a number on the "Richter scale." But, in fact, the original Richter scale, devised by Charles Richter in 1935 to measure the magnitude of southern California earthquakes using a then common—but now obsolete—seismograph, is outdated and virtually never used ( Fig. 1). Indeed, Richter originally devised his scale not for scientific purposes, but as a way to express the relative sizes of earthquakes to inquiring journalists. Over the years, seismologists have continued to devise various scales to measure parameters such as the magnitude of earthquake waves passing through the Earth's crust, waves passing through the planet's interior, and long-period vibrations that measure the energy released at the earthquake's source (often known as the "moment magnitude").

Journalists in the popular press may refer to any of these scales as a "Richter scale," and for any particular earthquake, the magnitude that is measured may vary depending on the scale used. Another complication is that one unit of magnitude on a Richter–style scale originally corresponded to 10 times more "shaking" of the ground a certain distance from the earthquake as recorded on a certain type of seismograph. Yet seismographs (as well as people) stationed closer to or further from the epicenter may detect a different set of frequencies and vibrations or "shaking." And 10 times more shaking does not correspond to ten times more energy released by the earthquake; on a typical Richter–style scale, a magnitude 7.0 quake will release about 33 times as much energy as a 6.0 quake and 1000 times as much as a 5.0 quake. Thus, the use of the term "Richter scale" has led to widespread confusion. A recent trend in the

**FIGURE 1**
Charles Richter, inventor of the "Richter Scale," standing next to an old seismograph. (*Source:* UPI/Bettmann.)

popular press is simply to use the generic term "magnitude" to refer to the relative size and strength of an earthquake; such magnitudes are often based on moment magnitudes.

But if the Richter scale has outlived its usefulness, what will replace it? Professional seismologists compare different earthquakes using seismic moments, which are calculated on the basis of such factors as the length of the fault rupture, the amount of rock movement, and the stiffness of the rock, but these are considered too complex for the public. The long-established Mercalli scale measures the intensity of earthquake damage—which may be what most people are concerned about. Another suggestion is that the energy released by earthquakes might be converted into atomic bomb or TNT equivalents. Thus, a magnitude 5.0 earthquake is equivalent to the detonation of approximately 1000 tons of TNT while a magnitude 6.0 earthquake releases about the same amount of energy as was released by the atomic bomb dropped on Hiroshima. Another possibility is to describe earthquakes in terms of the ground's acceleration as it shakes, perhaps using the unit "g" (the acceleration due to gravity on the surface of Earth, which is equal to 32 ft/sec² [9.8 m/sec²]). An earthquake that results in ground shaking in excess of 0.2g (20% of the force of gravity) may cause structural damage to many buildings.

The Mercalli scale ( Table 2–3) is more qualitative, based primarily on observations of the effects caused by an earthquake close to its origin. This scale classifies earthquakes into a dozen basic categories, from instrumental (earthquakes so small that they can be detected only on seismographs) to catastrophic (earthquakes where local destruction is virtually total). The Mercalli scale is easily related to the Richter scale in an approximate way (Table 2–3).

Much research has recently gone into devising ways to predict earthquakes in both the long term and the short term. Some work has attempted to discover long-term earthquake cycles, based on the movements of the lithospheric plates and also perhaps correlated with such phenomena as meteoritic impacts, variations in the Earth's geomagnetic field, sunspot activity, and variations in the length of the day. Such work is very difficult to pursue, and no method has been able to predict long-term earthquake events with any degree of accuracy.

As for the short term, researchers have identified several precursors that often signal the probability of a major earthquake in earthquake-prone areas. The most commonly utilized precursors are unusual land deformation, seismic activity, geomagnetic and geo-electric activity, groundwater fluctuations, and natural phenomena such as animal behavior and unusual weather conditions (see Issues in Perspective 2–2 on page 49).

Although we usually do not think of earthquakes as being caused by human activity, some earthquakes are indeed anthropogenically induced (caused by humans). Earthquakes have been induced by nuclear blasts, conventional blasting, mining activities, fluid injection and extraction from rocks deep underground, and the building of dams and reservoirs. A now classic example of human-induced faulting and seismic activity occurred near Denver in the early 1960s, when nerve-gas waste was disposed of by pumping it down a well to great depths where it would be below groundwater supplies. Pumping the waste down the well at high pressures triggered a series of earthquakes. Since then it has been verified experimentally in oil fields that pumping fluids into the ground (and in some cases extracting them, such as the pumping out of oil) can induce seismic activity.

The most important cause of human-induced earthquakes seems to be the construction of large dams and reservoirs. In the case of at least six major dams around the world, including Hoover Dam on the Colorado River, earthquakes of a magnitude greater than 5 on the Richter scale (moderately strong earthquakes, capable of minor damage) have apparently been induced by the impounding of water in large reservoirs. Over 1000 earthquakes of various magnitudes have been felt since Hoover Dam was constructed in 1935; before 1935 the area was not known for earthquake activity. Worldwide dozens of dams have been associated with seismic phenomena. It is thought that water in the reservoir may penetrate the underlying bedrock and cause rock slippage that generates earthquakes. The

**TABLE 2–2** *Some of the Largest Earthquakes, by Magnitude on the Richter Scale*

| YEAR | LOCATION | MAGNITUDE |
|---|---|---|
| 1755 | Lisbon, Portugal | 9.0 |
| 1906 | Andes (Colombia) | 8.6 |
| 1906 | Valparaiso, Chile | 8.4 |
| 1906 | San Francisco, United States | 8.25 |
| 1911 | Tienshan, China | 8.4 |
| 1920 | Kansu, China | 8.5 |
| 1923 | Tokyo, Japan | 8.2 |
| 1933 | Japanese trench | 8.5 |
| 1950 | North Assam, India | 8.6 |
| 1960 | Chile | 8.3–8.9 |
| 1964 | Alaska | 8.6 |
| 1976 | Tangshan, China | 8.2 |
| 1977 | Sumba, Indonesia | 8.9 |
| 1977 | Argentina | 8.2 |
| 1979 | Indonesia | 8.1 |
| 1985 | Mexico City, Mexico | 8.1 |
| 1994 | Bolivia | 8.2 |

huge mass of water in the reservoir also exerts tremendous pressures on the underlying rocks, and this can cause downwarping and subsidence of the land's surface.

Given that humans have inadvertently caused earthquakes, some people suggest that in the future we might be able to intervene to control natural earthquake activity. Perhaps, in an active earthquake zone, we could selectively induce a series of small earthquakes by either injecting or extracting fluids from the rocks. The small, relatively harmless earthquakes might relieve the strain on the rocks and thus allow us to avoid a single large, very destructive earthquake.

## Volcanoes

**Volcanoes** are basically spots in the Earth's crust where hot, molten rock (magma) wells up to the surface (  Fig. 2–17). Active volcanoes are found almost exclusively in three geologic settings: at convergent plate margins where one lithospheric plate subducts under another, melting the rock which rises to the surface as volcanoes (for instance, in Indonesia and elsewhere along the Pacific rim); at divergent plate margins where magma wells up to the surface as two lithospheric plates pull apart from each other, forming a rift (as in the middle of the Atlantic Ocean); and over mantle hot spots, areas that lie over a hot mantle plume that breaks through the crust and spews molten rock onto the Earth's surface (as in the Hawaiian Islands).

**TABLE 2-3** *The Mercalli Scale of Earthquake Intensity*

| SCALE | INTENSITY | DESCRIPTION OF EFFECT | MAXIMUM ACCELERATION (MM SEC$^{-2}$) | CORRESPONDING RICHTER SCALE |
|---|---|---|---|---|
| I | Instrumental | Not felt except by a very few under especially favorable circumstances. | <10 | |
| II | Feeble | Felt only by a few persons at rest, especially on upper floors of buildings. Delicately suspended objects may swing. | <25 | |
| III | Slight | Felt quite noticeably indoors, especially on upper floors of buildings, but many people do not recognize it as an earthquake. Standing automobiles may rock slightly. Vibration like a passing truck. | <50 | <4.2 |
| IV | Moderate | During the day felt indoors by many, outdoors by few. At night some awakened. Dishes, windows, doors disturbed; walls make cracking sound. Sensation like heavy truck striking building. Standing automobiles rock noticeably. | <100 | |
| V | Slightly strong | Felt by nearly everyone, many awakened. Some dishes, windows, etc., broken; a few instances of cracked plaster; unstable objects overturned. Disturbances of trees, poles, and other tall objects sometimes noticed. Pendulum clocks may stop. | <250 | <4.8 |
| VI | Strong | Felt by all, many frightened and run outdoors. Some heavy furniture moved; a few instances of fallen plaster or damaged chimneys. Damage slight. | <500 | <5.4 |
| VII | Very strong | Everybody runs outdoors. Damage negligible in buildings of good design and construction; slight to moderate in well-built ordinary structures; considerable in poorly built or badly designed structures; some chimneys broken. Noticed by persons driving automobiles. | <1000 | <6.1 |
| VIII | Destructive | Damage slight in specially designed structures; considerable in ordinary substantial buildings, with partial collapse; great in poorly built structures. Panel walls thrown out of frame structures. Fall of chimneys, factory stacks, columns, monuments, walls. Heavy furniture overturned. Sand and mud ejected in small amounts. Changes in well water. Persons driving automobiles disturbed. | <2500 | |
| IX | Ruinous | Damage considerable in specially designed structures; well-designed frame structures thrown out of plumb; great in substantial buildings, with partial collapse. Buildings shifted off foundations. Ground cracked conspicuously. Underground pipes broken. | <5000 | <6.9 |
| X | Disastrous | Some well-built wooden structures destroyed; most masonry and frame structures destroyed with foundations destroyed; ground badly cracked. Rails bent. Landslides considerable from river banks and steep slopes. Shifted sand and mud. Water splashed (slopped) over river banks. | <7500 | <7.3 |
| XI | Very Disastrous | Few, if any (masonry) structures remain standing. Bridges destroyed. Broad fissures in ground. Underground pipelines completely out of service. Earth slumps and land slips in soft ground. Rails bent greatly. | <9800 | <8.1 |
| XII | Catastrophic | Damage total. Practically all works of construction are damaged greatly or destroyed. Waves seen on ground surface. Objects are thrown upwards into the air. | >9800 | >8.1 |

(*Source:* United States Geological Survey.)

# Predicting Earthquakes

The careful periodic surveying of known benchmarks on the Earth's surface can lead to the detection of movement within the crust. Benchmarks may have moved relative to each other, suggesting possible faulting. In some areas where an active fault zone has been identified, accurate surveys across the fault zone can detect very slight movements (on the order of millimeters) that may be precursors of larger earthquake activity to come. In known earthquake-prone areas, instruments called tiltmeters can be used to monitor the surface of the Earth; if the surface starts tilting rapidly, an earthquake is usually imminent.

Daily monitoring of seismic activity is useful in an earthquake–prone area. Changes in the background seismic activity, especially increases in activity (sometimes referred to as foreshocks), can herald a major earthquake. The Earth's surface is characterized locally by magnetic fields and electric currents flowing through the rocks. Anomalous geo-magnetic and geo-electric activity may be detectable months, days, or hours before an earthquake strikes. Another technique that has been used very successfully in China is to monitor groundwater levels in wells. Fluctuations in normal water levels may precede an earthquake by hours to over a week. Radon levels in groundwater may increase for years before a major earthquake; this is probably due to the movement of water through new cracks that open up in the rocks before the onset of an earthquake.

Some of the most interesting and useful predictors are also extremely low-tech and poorly explained from a scientific perspective (indeed, they almost verge on superstition): namely, the behaviors of various animals in the days and hours before an area experiences an earthquake. The Japanese have observed that catfish exhibit unusual behavior before an earthquake, becoming very active and even jumping out of the water ( Fig. 1). All kinds of domestic animals become restless and exhibit odd behaviors prior to an earthquake: dogs bark, pigs become very aggressive, horses refuse to go into their stables, and so forth. Wild animals also show unusual behavior: burrowing animals leave the ground, rats run around randomly, snakes attempt to leave the area, and worms crawl from the ground to the surface in large numbers. In the San Francisco area, the behavior of zoo and marine animals is monitored daily as part of the local earthquake prediction system.

Possibly, certain animals are sensitive to vibrations (or ultrasound) generated by small earthquakes undetectable to humans that precede a major earthquake. Perhaps some animals are extremely sensitive to the smell of methane that may leak from the ground prior to an earthquake. Another possibility is that electrostatic particles may be coming from the ground; furry and feathered animals, such as mammals and birds, are generally very sensitive to electrostatic charges.

Reports of unusual weather before major earthquakes have often been dismissed as nonsense. However, some researchers have suggested that degassing of methane and other gases from below the Earth's surface may precede a major earthquake and could account for unusual weather phenomena such as strange mists, glowing skies, and flashes of light. If electrostatic particles are released prior to an earthquake, this also might help explain unusual weather phenomena.

All in all, predicting earthquakes is still a tricky business, perhaps more art than science. But China in particular has a very good track record; the Chinese have been able to predict a number of major earthquakes in time to evacuate cities before they were hit. Although substantial financial losses may still be unavoidable, by removing people from the area, the death toll can be kept at a minimum.

**FIGURE 1**

The Japanese have used catfish behavior as a predictor of earthquakes, and according to Japanese legend earthquakes are caused by the movement of a giant catfish. This antique illustration shows people attempting to subdue the giant catfish that causes earthquakes. (*Source:* Katsuhiko Ishida.)

**FIGURE 2–17**
Volcanoes, evidence that the Earth is still geologically young and active, inspire fear and awe in humans. Illustrated here is the 1980 eruption of Mount St. Helens, Washington. (*Source:* Swanson/USGS.)

**FIGURE 2–18**
Seen here are the remains of St. Pierre, a once thriving city of 30,000 on the island of Martinique, that was destroyed by the 8 May 1902 eruption of Mount Pelée. (*Source:* USGS.)

Volcanoes can be classified according to whether they extrude predominantly basaltic or andesitic magma. Volcanoes at divergent plate boundaries and hot spots tend to produce basaltic magma which is relatively silica-poor and originates from the mantle. Andesitic magma contains a higher percentage of silica and is generally formed from the remelting, differentiation, and recrystallization of previously existing crustal or mantle material. Thus andesitic volcanoes are commonly found in subduction zones where rock is remelted.

Basaltic magmas are hotter and much less viscous than andesitic magmas, which tend to contain a much higher percentage of gases (often predominantly water vapor). Consequently, whereas lava may flow smoothly out of the crater of a basaltic volcano, andesitic volcanoes tend to be much more explosive, shooting out steam and other gases, rock fragments of various sizes, and volcanic ash.

Volcanic eruptions can affect hu-

mans on both a local and a global scale. On a local level, volcanic eruptions can destroy local towns and cities. In A.D. 79 ash falls and mudflows triggered by the eruption of Mount Vesuvius in Italy buried the towns of Pompeii and Herculaneum. The eruption of Mount Pelée on Martinique in 1902 destroyed the city of St. Pierre, killing some 30,000 people in a span of two minutes ( Fig. 2–18). As we have seen, large volcanic eruptions can have worldwide effects by spewing dust, ash, and gases (including material that can form acid rain) into the atmosphere, affecting global weather patterns. For example, the 1883 eruption of Krakatoa, a volcano in the Sunda Straits between Sumatra and Java, spewed 4 cubic miles (18 km³) of rock, ash, and other debris into the atmosphere to heights of 50 miles (80 km). The materials initially reduced the amount of incoming solar radiation reaching the Earth's surface by an estimated 13%. Even two years later, the amount of incoming solar radiation over France was still 10% below normal.

The eruption of Krakatoa also set off tsunami that caused damage throughout the Pacific basin. Tsunami (Japanese for "harbor wave") are huge waves, sometimes caused by explosive volcanic activity in or near the oceans or by large undersea earthquakes (usually registering higher than 6.5 on the Richter scale) or landslides. Fortunately, tsunami are relatively rare; however, they can be extremely destructive. The waves can range in height from less than 3 feet (1 m) to nearly 200 feet (60 m).

In 1692 an earthquake destroyed Port Royal, Jamaica, and the resulting tsunami threw harbored ships inland over two-story buildings. The Lisbon earthquake of 1755 sent a wave across the Atlantic Ocean that temporarily raised the sea by 10 to 13 feet (3–4 m) in Barbados.

Even with modern technology and knowledge, predicting future volcanic activity is extremely difficult. Although we know where to expect active volcanoes relative to lithospheric plates and can determine if a volcano is active or dormant (based on the time since its last eruption), we cannot predict exactly the timing and intensity of future eruptions. Researchers use many of the same techniques used for predicting earthquakes. Seismic activity, land deformation, geomagnetic and geo-electric parameters can be monitored. Any anomalous behavior, like a change in seismic activity or active deformation of the sides of a volcano, can herald an imminent eruption. But estimating the strength and type of eruption that will occur is difficult. The analysis of gases given off by volcanoes holds some promise for predicting volcanic activity, at least in the short term. But sampling gases being vented from an active volcano that may be near eruption can be very difficult and dangerous.

## Land Instability

A very widespread form of natural geologic hazard, usually brought on by human ignorance of the principles of geology and soil mechanics, is the collapse of soil or weathered rock material. Landslides, rockfalls, and avalanches may bury roads, buildings, and other human structures. Soils may fail to support buildings, thus causing them to collapse. Such phenomena may occur simply because humans erect structures in areas that are geologically unstable and thus unsuitable for building. Human activity, such as clear-cutting a mountainside, may induce land instability. Of course, natural phenomena such as earthquakes and volcanic eruptions may also induce landslides, rockfalls, avalanches, surface subsidence, and so forth.

## Weather Hazards

Hurricanes, typhoons, tornadoes, droughts, floods, heat waves, wind storms, dust storms, and other "irregular" weather patterns can wreak havoc on human settlements. Full discussion of this large and complex topic is beyond the scope of this book, but here we will briefly mention some major types of storm hazards. Due to possible global warming brought on by the greenhouse effect (see Chapter 18), some researchers expect a dramatic increase in irregular weather patterns, particularly the number of violent storms, in the relatively near future.

### *Tropical Cyclones*

Tropical **cyclones** are intense storms that develop over warm tropical seas (  Fig. 2–19). When they occur in North America, tropical cyclones are generally referred to as hurricanes; when they occur in Southeast Asia, they are known as typhoons. Approximately 100 to 120 tropical cyclones develop worldwide every year, and many of them travel far inland as well as posing hazards

to coastal areas. Every five years or so, a hurricane along the east coast of North America crosses the Appalachian Mountains and enters the Great Lakes region.

In terms of deaths, tropical cyclones are among the worst natural hazard that humans currently face. Between 1960 and 1995 approximately 800,000 people died as a result of tropical cyclones compared with 600,000 people killed by

**FIGURE 2–19**
Tropical cyclones, more commonly known as hurricanes and typhoons, are among the most destructive of natural hazards. Here we see Cutler Ridge, Florida, after being hit by Hurricane Andrew, August 1992. (*Source:* B. Wisser/Gamma Liaison.)

# SUGGESTED READINGS

Archer, A. A., G. W. Luttig, and I. I. Snezhko, eds. 1987. *Man's dependence on the Earth*. Paris: UNESCO.

Bryant, E. A. 1991. *Natural hazards*. Cambridge: Cambridge University Press.

Ernst, W. G. 1990. *The dynamic planet*. New York: Columbia University Press.

Friday, L., and R. Laskey, eds. 1989. *The fragile environment*. Cambridge: Cambridge University Press.

Goudie, A. 1990. *The human impact on the natural environment*, 3d ed. Cambridge, Mass.: MIT Press.

Mannion, A. M. 1991. *Global environmental change: A natural and cultural history*. New York.: John Wiley.

Margulis, L., and L. Olendzenski, eds. 1992. *Environmental evolution*. Cambridge, Mass.: MIT Press.

Monroe, J. S., and R. Wicander, 1995. *Physical geology: Exploring the Earth (second edition)*. St. Paul: West Publishing Company.

Officer, C., and J. Page. 1993. *Tales of the Earth: Paroxysms and perturbations of the blue planet*. New York: Oxford University Press.

Pipkin, B. W., 1994. *Geology and the environment*. St. Paul: West Publishing Company.

Robinson, A. 1993. *Earth shock: Hurricanes, volcanoes, earthquakes, tornadoes and other forces of nature*. London: Thames & Hudson.

Turner, B. L., II, W. C. Clark, R. W. Kates, J. F. Richards, J. T. Mathews, and W. B. Meyer, eds. 1990. *The Earth as transformed by human action*. Cambridge: Cambridge University Press.

Van Andel, T. H. 1985. *New views on an old planet: Continental drift and the history of the Earth*. Cambridge: Cambridge University Press.

**F**

A vortex
wind spe
miles an
single to
incredib
small ar

# ᴛHE BIOSPHERE

**PROLOGUE**    *Restoring the Biosphere by Applying Ecology*

𝒲e are privileged to live at a time when the diversity of life on Earth is about the richest it has ever been. Since the first microscopic life originated more than three billion years ago, the number of species on Earth has slowly climbed, as evolution has produced new kinds of adaptations. The 5 to 50 million species present today are many more than Earth held at the time of the dinosaurs, for instance. This richness makes the current "extinction crisis" all the more lamentable.

PHOTO    *Restoration ecology seeks to return natural habitats, such as the tall-grass prairies, to their original state. (Source: Ron Klataske.)*

By some estimates, as many as 100 species are becoming extinct every day. Many people recognize the importance of saving biodiversity and understand that preserves of native habitat must be set aside if we are to save species. The new fast-growing science of conservation biology seeks to discover the best ways of designing preserves. What is the best size for a preserve? The best shape? Exactly which species are most at risk of extinction? Such questions do not have simple answers, but the science of biological preservation has made enormous strides over the last few years.

Furthermore, one subfield of conservation biology seeks to go beyond preserving species before they go extinct. This subfield, called restoration ecology, seeks to restore entire ecosystems and biological communities to their former state. The tall-grass prairie, on which buffalo once fed, was reduced to a few tiny fragments around railroad tracks and other undeveloped areas in the American Midwest. Restoring this prairie has involved gathering the seeds and plants of remnant species and replanting them in carefully watched plots of land. But this is just the first step. Interactions among the native plants and animals, such as insect pollinators, must be established if a true biological community is to be re-created. Native grazing animals, birds, and many other prairie natives must ultimately be established if the tall–grass prairie is to live again. Doing this will be difficult, time-consuming, and expensive. So will be the task of restoring the Kissimmee River and Everglades of Florida and many other areas of the United States where restoration ecology is being applied. But to people who value biodiversity, the potential benefits are enormous. Instead of simply preserving remnants of biodiversity, we have the possibility of restoring whole ecosystems that we would otherwise never see again.

# INTRODUCTION

In Chapter 2, we saw that the Earth is a dynamic entity that gave rise to life over 3.5 billion years ago when the first microbes appeared. Since that time, life has co-evolved with the Earth's atmosphere, hydrosphere, and lithosphere to create an integrated "living planet." Living things help cycle the elements and sustain an oxygen atmosphere while the Earth provides a habitable environment for life. In this chapter, we examine the fundamentals of ecology, which is the science of how organisms interact with each other and with the physical environment. These ecological principles have great practical value in determining just how much humans are disturbing biological systems and how this disruption can be minimized.

# EVOLUTION OF THE BIOSPHERE

The very early appearance of life on Earth implies that natural processes readily produce life under appropriate conditions. Beginning in the early 1950s with the work of Stanley Miller and Harold Urey, scientists have shown that complex molecules possessed by all living things are readily produced under laboratory conditions that duplicate early environments on Earth. As ▄ Figure 3–1 shows, the early atmosphere is thought to have been composed of ammonia ($NH_3$), methane ($CH_4$), water vapor ($H_2O$), and other gases. When these are subjected to electricity, which simulates lightning and sunlight, chemical reactions occur that produce **amino acids**. Amino acids are complex molecules that are the "building blocks" of proteins. Proteins make up enzymes and many other components of life such as muscles, hair, and skin.

Of course, protein molecules alone are not living things. Organisms are composed of molecules organized in very complex ways. The basic organizational unit of life is the cell. Remarkably, in the late 1950s, Sidney Fox found that heated amino acids can form cell-like structures sometimes called **protocells**. These structures are not true cells but have many cell-like properties such as being semi-permeable to certain materials.

Producing amino acids and protocells in the lab is far from creating life in the lab. Even the simplest bacteria are vastly more complex than these protein and protocellular building blocks. Nevertheless, the readiness with which these first steps toward life occur, combined with the fossil record, support the idea that life readily arose through natural processes.

## Diversification of the Biosphere

### Evolution through Natural Selection

Once life originated, it began to diversify into different kinds of organisms through biological evolution. As Charles Darwin first documented in

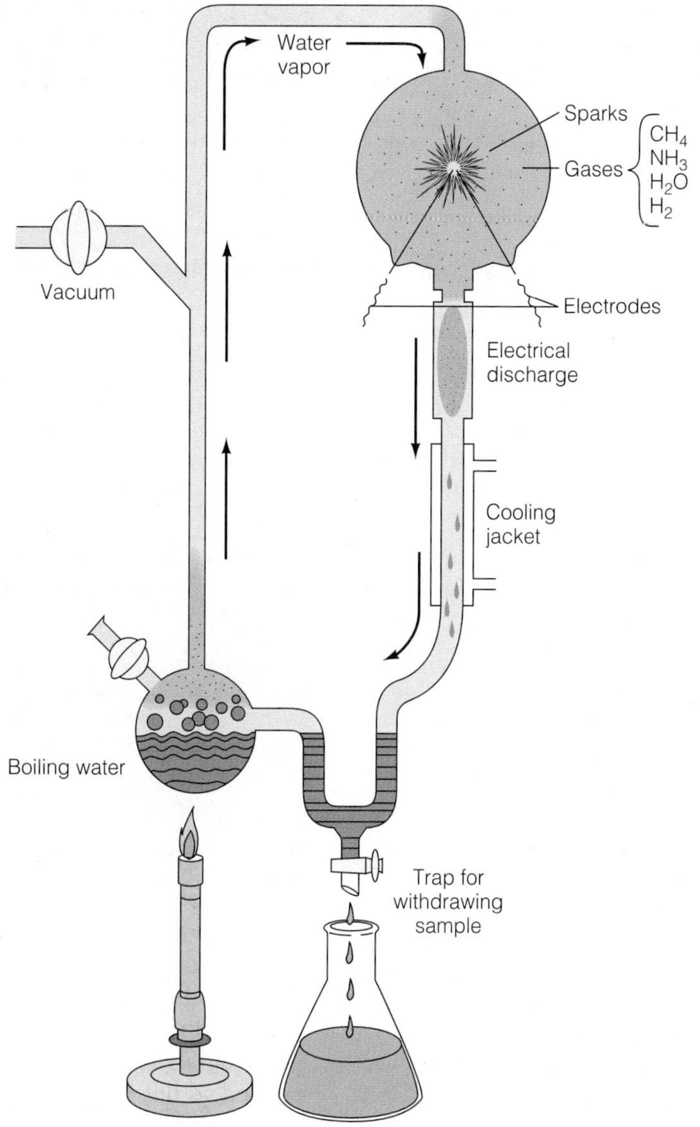

**FIGURE 3-1**
Experimental apparatus that Miller and Urey used to show that organic molecules could be produced from the chemical components of the Earth's early atmosphere.

1859, biological evolution occurs from **natural selection** of individual variation:

1. Nearly all populations exhibit variation among individuals.
2. Individuals with advantageous traits will tend to have more offspring.
3. Advantageous traits will therefore become widespread in populations.

Variation in neck length in giraffes is an example. We know from fossils that early giraffes had relatively short necks. A few individuals, however, had slightly longer necks. In some localities, these giraffes had a feeding advantage because they could browse on leaves in taller trees. Consequently, in populations living where tall trees were common, longer-necked giraffes tended to have more offspring so that longer necks became more common.

If this process occurs with many traits over a long period of time, the population will eventually become very different from other populations and will create a new species. Figure 3-2 shows how isolation of populations promotes speciation. The different populations are exposed to different environments, which favor different traits, causing the populations to diverge through time. But when do two different populations become two different species? Biologists generally define a **species** as a group of individuals that can interbreed to produce fertile offspring (this definition applies only to sexual organisms; the issue of defining nonsexual species is a matter of debate in biological circles). A new species is therefore formed when members of a diverging population can no longer successfully mate with populations of the ancestral species. Closely related species, which have often diverged relatively

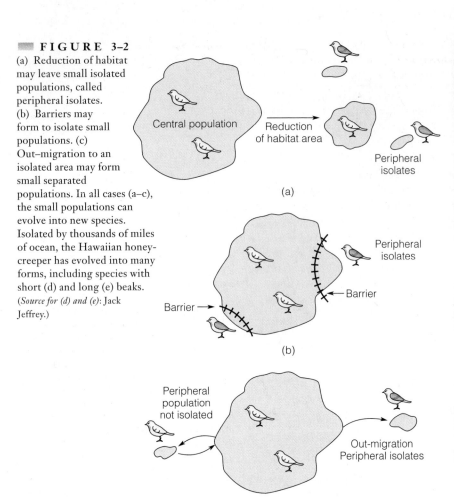

**FIGURE 3–2**
(a) Reduction of habitat may leave small isolated populations, called peripheral isolates. (b) Barriers may form to isolate small populations. (c) Out–migration to an isolated area may form small separated populations. In all cases (a–c), the small populations can evolve into new species. Isolated by thousands of miles of ocean, the Hawaiian honeycreeper has evolved into many forms, including species with short (d) and long (e) beaks. (*Source for (d) and (e)*: Jack Jeffrey.)

**(a)** Central population — Reduction of habitat area — Peripheral isolates

**(b)** Barrier — Barrier — Peripheral isolates

**(c)** Peripheral population not isolated — Out-migration Peripheral isolates

(d)

(e)

recently, are grouped together within the same genus. Similar genera are then grouped together within the same family. This method of classifying species according to hierarchically nested categories is a form of **taxonomy**. Applying this traditional system to humans, we have the following:

Kingdom Animalia

Phylum Chordata

Class Mammalia

Order Primates

Family Hominidae

Genus *Homo*

Species *H. sapiens**

Where does individual variation come from? This question is crucial because without the ini-

---

*Note that a species name must always be associated with a genic name or abbreviation (in this case *H.* for *Homo*). Thus humans are the species *Homo sapiens*; it is incorrect to call humans simply *sapiens*.

tial variation in the population, natural selection would have nothing to act upon. This question troubled Darwin himself because he was not aware of the work of Gregor Mendel who is credited with discovering the laws of inherited variation in 1865. Indeed, Mendel's work was not well publicized and was not rediscovered by scientists until the early 1900s. Mendel discovered that traits are passed on by **genes**, which are the basic units of heredity. Humans, for instance, have an estimated 50,000 to 100,000 genes that determine our traits. Variation in a population, or "gene pool," occurs because individuals possess different sets of genes that produce different traits. But how do different sets of genes arise? Reproduction is one way. Genes are shuffled when sperm and egg cells are fused causing offspring from the same parents to have different genes. A second cause of genetic variation is **mutation**, which is a spontaneous change in a gene. Genes are composed of **DNA** molecules, and mutations occur when DNA molecules are altered. Mutation is the ultimate source of all genetic variation.

## Patterns of Diversification

Evolution through natural selection has produced an increasingly diverse biosphere, with the total number of species becoming greater through time. Initially, evolution was relatively slow. The right side of ▬ Figure 3–3 summarizes the evolution of life on Earth. For about 2 billion years after the first appearance of fossils, relatively few species of simple single-celled organisms, such as various bacteria and cyanobacteria (formerly known as blue-green algae), appear in the fossil record. A major change occurred about 1.5 billion years ago when more complex cells, called **eukaryotes** evolved. These cells had a true nucleus, chromosomes, and specialized cellular organelles such as mitochondria. Apparently, such complex cells were a main cause of increasing rates of evolution. Multicellular organisms, including sponge-like and jellyfish-like creatures, appeared in the oceans by at least 1 billion years ago. These probably evolved from colonies of single-celled eukaryotes, such as protozoa, that became progressively more specialized and integrated.

About 570 million years ago, the fossil record shows a rapid diversification sometimes called the **explosion of life**, when most of the major groups of animals first appear. Note in Figure 3–3 that this "explosion" corresponds to the time when modern oxygen levels were attained in the atmosphere. This permitted the evolution of more complex animals, which have a greater metabolic need for oxygen.

Following the explosion of life, living things diversified into new environments. As shown in Figure 3–3, life colonized the land (lithosphere) and the air (atmosphere) during the Paleozoic Era, which began with the explosion of life and ended with a global mass extinction. The Mesozoic Era, sometimes called the "age of dinosaurs," was the second major era, and it also ended with a mass extinction. The third and last era is the Cenozoic Era, sometimes called the "age of mammals." Although catastrophes, especially from global climate change, have temporarily caused species numbers to decrease at very rare intervals through mass extinctions, the overall trend throughout these eras is toward increasing numbers of species as life has adapted

▬ **FIGURE 3–3**
The left side of this diagram summarizes the changes in the Earth's continents, oceans, and atmosphere, while the right side summarizes the evolution of life on Earth. (*Source:* Modified from McKinney, M. L., *Evolution of Life.* Copyright © 1993, p 190. Reprinted by permission of Prentice Hall, Upper Saddle River, NJ.)

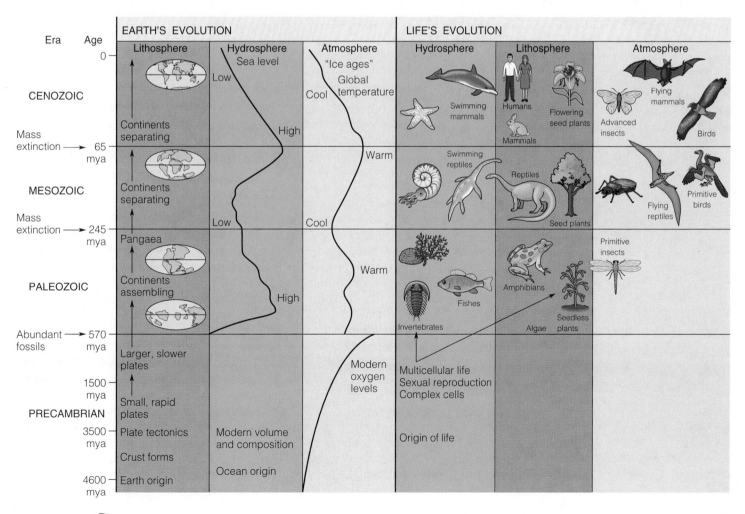

## What Is "Ecology"?

The term "eco-" is derived from the Greek word *oikos*, which means "home." Since *logia* means "study of" in Latin, *ecology* is the "study of home." The word *economics* has the same derivation: *nomos* is Greek for "managing" so *economics* means "managing the house." Ironically, these two words—ecology and economics—which derive from the same word, are often thought to represent opposing interests. Even more ironically, "studying" the home and "managing" the home seem to have resulted in very different sets of priorities about how the home (that is, our environment) should be treated.

Henry David Thoreau was apparently the first to use the word *ecology* in one of his letters in 1858, but he did not give it a specific definition (and possibly Thoreau's *ecology* was simply a misspelling for some other intended word). Instead, the German biologist Ernest Haeckel is generally credited with introducing, in 1866, the word (originally spelled "oecologie") as it is now used in biology to mean the study of organisms and their interactions with each other and their physical environment.

Although scientists still use this technical definition, ecology has come to mean many other things, especially to nonscientists. As environmental awareness has risen over the last few decades and environmental issues have come to be discussed in social rather than scientific contexts, ecology has taken on new meanings. Thus, many people who express concern about the environment call themselves "ecologists" and are interested in "ecology." This label has even been extended to political ideologies that reflect these concerns. Thus, the political scientist William Ophuls has said that "ecology is a profoundly conservative doctrine in its social implications."

The confusion arises when ecology is expanded beyond its restricted meaning as a branch of biology that studies natural environments ("ecosystems") to refer to the social and political ideas of people who are actively concerned with preserving those natural environments ("ecosystems"). For reasons of clarity, we might do better to use *environmentalist* as a general term for someone who actively wants to *preserve* the natural environment, while reserving *ecologist* for scientists who *study* it. (Of course, a person can be, and often is, both an ecologist and an environmentalist.) Ophuls should say that *environmentalism* is a conservative doctrine because the "study" of something is not a doctrine at all: a doctrine is a system of beliefs.

In addition to being expanded to mean social and political environmental action, ecology has also been generalized as an academic term. Many students, perhaps even yourself, have enrolled in ecology courses expecting to learn about water pollution, solar power, and many other aspects of environmental problems. They are often surprised to find that the course focuses on the study of natural communities, unaltered by humans. While the study of natural laws governing such communities is basic to understanding how humans affect them, many students desire a broader perspective that includes pollution and other ways that humans modify the natural world. Environmental science, such as the course you are enrolled in now, has arisen in recent years to fulfill this need. Because environmental science is such a broad area of study, it is taught in a variety of traditional science departments, including biology, geology, chemistry, and geography. College courses labeled "ecology" are often primarily for students in biology or with interests in the specific study of natural communities.

to new environments and found "new ways of doing things" through mutation and natural selection. Ironically, we now live in a biosphere that is one of the most diverse in life's long history, although this will not be true in a few decades if current rates of species extinction continue (Chapter 12).

## BIOSPHERE INTERACTIONS: POPULATIONS

The biosphere today, as in the past, is hierarchical: organisms, composed of atoms, molecules, and cells, are grouped into populations. Populations form communities, which then form ecosystems. Finally, ecosystems, when considered together, form the biosphere which subsumes all life on Earth ( Fig. 3–4). This figure illustrates the interconnectedness of life because each level is composed of the units in the level below. Furthermore, the hierarchy is not static. Each level is dynamic, with many interactions occurring among its units. For instance, the organisms that compose populations interact in many ways, as do the populations that compose communities.

**Ecology** is the study of how organisms interact with each other and their physical environment. Because interactions occur at many levels in the hierarchy of life, ecology is very complex

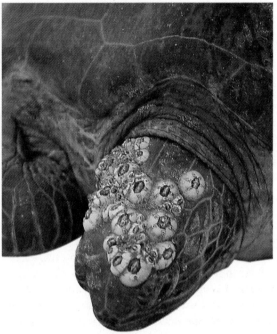

**FIGURE 3–8**
Parasites, such as this leech, often do not kill their hosts. (*Source*: Visuals Unlimited/© Glenn Oliver.)

tualism is the coexistence of algae within the tissue of the tiny animals that build coral reefs. The algae are provided with a protected living space while the coral animals are supplied with nutrients from the algae's photosynthesis. Similarly, a lichen is actually a fungus and algae growing together symbiotically. Mutualism is thus a factor regulating the abundance of certain types of algae because their numbers are influenced by the abundance of coral or fungal hosts.

**Parasitism** is similar to predation in that one species benefits while harming the other species (Fig. 3–8). The main difference is that parasites act more slowly than predators and do not always kill the prey (host). **Commensalism** occurs when one species benefits and the other is not affected. For example, Spanish moss (a lichen) hangs from trees for support but causes the trees no great harm or benefit. Barnacles attach to crab shells in a similar way, deriving food from the surrounding water (Fig. 3–9). **Amensalism** occurs when one population inhibits another while being unaffected itself. Harm to one species is simply an incidental by-product of the actions of another. For example, when elephants crash through vegetation, they often have a detrimental effect on it, while gaining relatively few benefits (of course, the elephants get where they want to go).

## The Real World: Complex Interaction of Abundance Controls

Our brief description of the various controls on abundance (physical fluctuations, competition, predation, and symbioses) has greatly oversimplified by discussing each control separately. In reality, most natural populations are governed not by a single control, but by several controls often acting simultaneously. When two populations of beetles interact in the laboratory, for example, competition leads to a high abundance of one species and a very low abundance of another. When a third species, a parasite, is introduced, the formerly abundant species becomes the rarer one because it is more susceptible to the parasite (Fig. 3–10).

Now consider that natural communities are often composed of hundreds to many thousands of species. Any single population will often have many competitors, predators, and symbionts such as commensals. Abundance changes in any of these could have a major influence on the abundance of that population. At the same time, changes in physical conditions could also influence any of the populations, with each responding differently to a physical change. This complex interaction of abundance controls in natural ecosystems means that small changes in one control, such as the abundance of a prey species, can have a cascading domino effect throughout the ecosystem, causing other changes in the abundance of other species. Abundance of all species is therefore nearly always fluctuating in response to natural fluctuations in physical conditions and in other species.

## Physically versus Biologically Controlled Systems

For over 60 years, ecologists have debated which of the abundance controls, if any, is the most important. Some have argued that physical factors play the major role. This is sometimes called

FIGURE 3–10

(a) With two competing species of beetles, the superior competitor can drive the other to a very low abundance. (b) The addition of a parasite can drive the formerly abundant species to rarity and allow the formerly rare species to increase. (*Source*: Modified from T. Park, *Ecological Monographs* 18 [1948]: 265–308. Reprinted with permission of Ecological Society of America.)

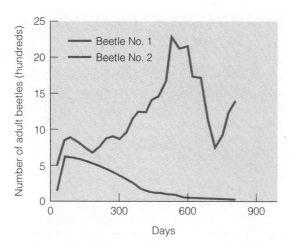

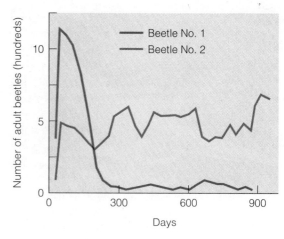

(a) Parasite absent

(b) Parasite added

**density-independent regulation** because physical processes usually operate independently of the present abundance. For example, a severe drought or storm can drastically reduce abundance of populations regardless of how many individuals exist when it strikes. Similarly, a volcanic eruption might kill all individuals on an island, whether there are dozens or millions. Other ecologists argue that biological interactions, especially competition and predation, are the major controls. This is sometimes called **density-dependent regulation** because current abundance plays a role in determining population change. For instance, the effect of a predator in reducing a prey species's abundance depends greatly on how many prey there are. As noted earlier, if a prey species's population becomes too low, the predator may switch to another prey.

Most ecologists now recognize that, in reality, population abundance is regulated by both physical and biological constraints, although one type of constraints may dominate in certain environments. We can depict environments on a continuum as in Figure 3–11. At one end are environments that are often subjected to physical disturbances or stress. An example is a beach,

where wave action from storms and hurricanes can often cause great disturbances. At the other end are environments, such as the offshore tropical waters of a coral reef, where disturbances are rarer. Rapid changes in physical parameters such as water energy and temperature are neither common nor severe, so biological interactions are the major determinant controlling the abundance of the many reef species. But even in these extremes, many factors still interact to control abundance. For instance, even though physical processes may be the dominant regulators of abundance in beach environments, competition, predation, and other biological interactions are still occurring, affecting abundance.

## Population Decline

While even stable populations rise and fall in abundance during fluctuations, given enough time, eventually most populations decline to zero and become extinct. Extinction is the elimination of all individuals in a group. In a local extinction, all individuals in a population are lost, but a new population can be reestablished from other populations of that species living else-

**FIGURE 3–11**
Population abundance is regulated by both physical and biological processes. In some environments, such as a beach, physical processes may play a much larger role than in other environments, such as a coral reef.

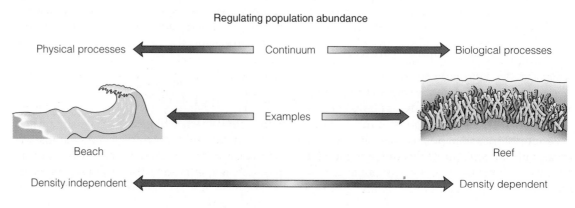

Regulating population abundance

Physical processes ← Continuum → Biological processes

Examples

Beach

Reef

Density independent ← → Density dependent

where. Species extinction occurs when all populations of the species become extinct.

The inevitability of population decline is clear when we consider that over 99% of all species that have ever existed are now extinct. The vast majority of these became extinct before humans, so decline and extinction are natural processes. Ultimately, decline and extinction are caused by environmental change: one or more of the abundance controls becomes altered leading to an abrupt or gradual decline in abundance. For instance, many extinctions in the fossil record resulted largely from physical changes such as cooling temperatures. Similarly, the fossils reveal cases where competition from new groups apparently caused decline, such as when placental mammals invaded South America and replaced most marsupials.

## Human Impact on Population Growth and Decline

Increasing human population and technology have caused progressively greater disruption in natural populations. Pollution, agriculture, and many other kinds of human alterations of the environment have destabilized populations by affecting the various abundance controls. Depending on the population, humans may cause (1) population growth by removing previous limitations or (2) population decline by imposing new limitations.

### Human Impact on Population Growth

Populations grow when there is an excess of resources relative to the number of individuals available to exploit them. Humans commonly contribute to population growth in the four ways listed in ● Table 3–2; each involves removing a control on abundance.

Increase of available resources can be planned or unplanned. Agriculture and animal domestication are obvious examples of how humans can greatly increase the populations of plants and animals that they favor. We do this by providing far more food and other resources than those organisms would find in their natural state. The effect of humans on cat numbers provides a striking example. In England alone, domestic cats occur in such numbers that more than 300,000 cats must be destroyed each year. Yet before humans began to domesticate them a few thousand years ago (to catch mice in grain storage areas), the small, wild ancestors of our pet cats were relatively rare and were probably limited to the Middle East and Europe, a relatively small area compared to their present range. Similarly, corn,

potatoes, and many other domesticated organisms had much smaller ancestral ranges.

Unplanned increases in available resources by humans also have major effects. Pollutants, for example, generally represent unplanned releases of substances into water or air. These substances are often nutrients that are in short supply. Recall from Liebig's law of the minimum that growth is limited by the resources in shortest supply. Phosphorus and nitrogen are very often the two most limiting nutrients for plants in water or on land. When fertilizers rich in these nutrients are carried into rivers and lakes, the result is often runaway plant growth. This enrichment of nutrients in waters is called eutrophication. Eutrophication is a classic example of "too much of a good thing" because the decomposition of the accumulating plants uses up increasing amounts of oxygen, causing fishes and other organisms to suffocate.

Competitive release is common when humans try to eliminate a population of one species, allowing its competitors to increase in numbers. The most economically important examples occur when farmers try to eradicate pests from crops with pesticides. Because poison tolerance varies among species, some pests will not be killed by the poisons and will actually increase in numbers

| TABLE 3–2 *Four Ways That Humans Cause Population Growth* | |
|---|---|
| | EXAMPLES |
| Increase available resources | Agriculture |
| | Nutrient pollution in lakes |
| Competitive release | Poisoning of insect pests |
| Predator release | Overhunting of large carnivores |
| Introduce to new areas | Game releases |

when their competitors are gone. This is called a "secondary pest outbreak." A dramatic example occurred in Central America where cotton crops were sprayed in 1950 to kill boll weevils. The effort was highly successful until 1955, when populations of cotton aphids and cotton bollworms soared. When a new pesticide was used to remove them, five other secondary pests emerged. Such experiences have led to new methods of pest control (Chapters 13 and 15).

Predator release is common where humans hunt, trap, or otherwise reduce populations of predators, allowing the prey species's population to increase. For example, large mammalian predators such as wolves and panthers have long been the target of ranchers and farmers because they

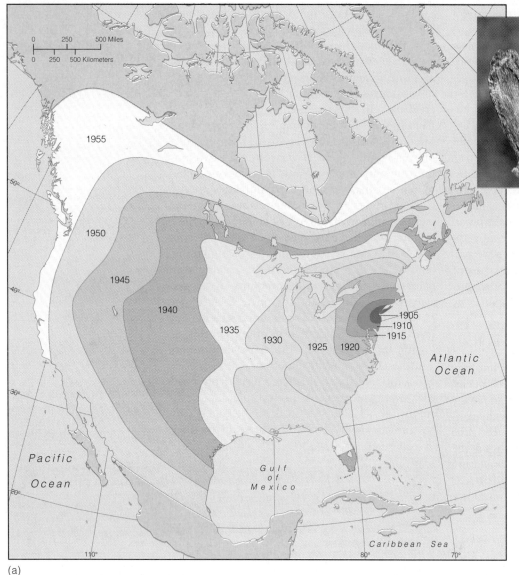

(a)

(b)

24 families of fishes have been successfully introduced into North America. The extent of this introduction is even more impressive considering that the vast majority of populations die out when initially introduced. A recent analysis of ballast water in a tanker revealed that it contained the live larvae of 367 species of marine organisms carried from Japan to the Oregon coast. Such ballast waters are routinely discharged. Once an organism is introduced and established, expansion can be quite rapid. The European starling covered North America in just a few decades after it was introduced in New York for a Shakespearean play in the early 1900s ( ▬ Fig. 3–12).

▬ **FIGURE 3–12**
(a) This map shows the rapid migration of the European starling across North America after its introduction in New York. (b) The European starling is now one of the most common birds in North America. (*Sources*: (a) C. B. Cox and P. Moore, *Biogeography* [Cambridge, Mass.: Blackwell, 1993], p. 62. Reprinted by permission of Blackwell Science, Inc.; (b) Harold Hoffman/Photo Researchers.)

prey on domesticated animals. The result has been a rapid increase in the predators' natural prey. Deer have shown an especially spectacular rise. Indeed, most experts estimate that more deer are now living in the United States than were here before Europeans arrived. Unfortunately, the excess populations often lead to overgrazing and death by starvation. For this reason, game hunting by humans is a justifiable activity, at least based on ecological criteria. By prudently culling deer and other prey, humans are essentially carrying out the role of predators that no longer exist.

Introduction of nonnative (also called "exotic") species into new areas may be the single greatest alteration of nature carried out by humans so far. Few people realize the enormous scale on which humans have, either accidentally or purposely, transferred organisms from one area to another. For example, more than 1500 insect species and

*Human Impact on Population Decline*

Humans are causing the decline and extinction of species at thousands of times the natural rate in nearly all parts of the biosphere. We will examine the causes of extinction in more detail in Chapter 12, but note here that humans alter the environment in four basic ways that cause population decline ( ● Table 3–3). All are directly related to the abundance controls. Habitat disruption occurs when humans disturb the physical environment in which a population lives. This disturbance can range from minor, such as mild chemical changes from air pollution, to major, such as total destruction of a forest by bulldozers or fire.

As Table 3–3 shows, humans change the biological environment in three ways that cause population decline. As we have seen, many new species have been introduced in various parts of the world. Introduced species are competitors, predators, or symbionts (including diseases and parasites) in the native biological system. Island species are especially susceptible to introduced species. An example of competitive decline in island species is the introduction of rabbits to Australia; the voracious appetite and rapid reproduction of rabbits led to decreased abundance of many native marsupials.

Human overkill is the shooting, trapping, or poisoning of certain populations, usually for sport or economic reasons. It is very difficult for humans to cause the extinction of "pest" species, such as roaches or mice, in this way because they are so abundant and reproduce so rapidly. However, overkill has been very effective in eliminating populations of large animals because they are much fewer and reproduce much more slowly. Leopards, elephants, rhinos, pandas, and many other large animals comprise a disproportionate number of threatened and endangered species in the world (Chapter 12). Secondary extinctions occur when a population is lost due to the extinction of another population on which it depends, such as a food species.

It is not necessary for these environmental changes to reduce a population to zero in order to cause extinction. Even if many individuals survive, the population may never recover if it becomes too small. Small populations are beset by many breeding problems, such as inbreeding and lack of mates, and are also more likely to become extinct from environmental fluctuations

such as hurricanes, droughts, and so on. Ecologists often refer to "minimum viable population" (MVP): if population abundance drops below the MVP, the population will probably never recover (Chapter 12).

## Population Range

In addition to varying through time, abundance may vary geographically. Populations tend to have a maximum abundance near the center of their geographic range, which is the total area occupied by the population ( Fig. 3–13). This central

**TABLE 3–3** *Four Ways That Humans Cause Population Decline and Extinction*

The actions are listed in approximate order of importance in causing extinctions. In other words, habitat disruption causes the most extinctions today; secondary extinctions cause the least.

| | EXAMPLES |
|---|---|
| Change physical environment: | |
| 1. Habitat disruption | Draining a swamp, toxic pollution |
| Change biological environment: | |
| 2. Introduce new species | New predator |
| 3. Overkill | Big-game hunting |
| 4. Secondary extinctions | Loss of food species |

**FIGURE 3–13**
Organisms tolerate a range of conditions but thrive in an optimum range.

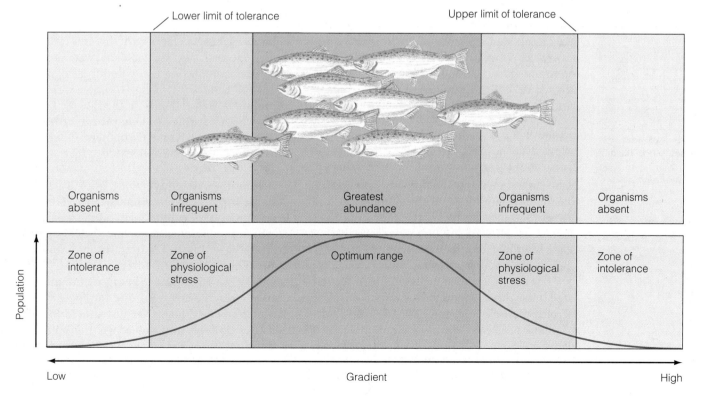

very patchy environment, individuals are commonly clumped together with gaps in between.

The size of the geographic range of populations also varies among species. **Endemic species** are localized and may have just one population that inhabits only a small area. This pattern is especially common in tropical organisms and in organisms that are highly specialized to live on resources with limited distributions or that have narrow environmental tolerances (▬ Fig. 3–14).

*Human Impact on Population Ranges*

Humans have both decreased and expanded the geographic ranges of populations. On the one hand, range decrease has commonly accompanied declining populations and extinction. Habitat destruction such as cutting down trees can also reduce a population's range. If the habitat disappears, the population's geographic range can be reduced to zero. This is a major reason why tropical extinctions are particularly destructive; with the high number of endemic populations, it does not take much habitat destruction to reduce the geographic range to zero. On the other hand, we saw how humans have often expanded geographic range by domesticating and introducing wild species into new areas (see Fig. 3–12).

## ℬIOSPHERE INTERACTIONS: COMMUNITIES AND ECOSYSTEMS

A **community** consists of all populations that inhabit a certain area. The size of this area can range from very small, such as a puddle of water, to large regions encompassing many hundreds of square miles (or thousands of km²). The extent of a community thus depends on the size of the area one wishes to denote. An **ecosystem** is the community plus its physical environment. Therefore, ecosystems can also be delineated at many spatial scales.

Because ecosystems include both organisms and their physical environment, the study of ecosystems often tends to focus on the movement of physical components, such as the flow of energy and the cycling of matter, through the "system." This approach is often called the "functional" view. In contrast, because communities consist only of organisms, one can focus on describing how organisms are distributed in communities through time and space: this approach is called the "structural" view. We turn first to the community, or structural, view.

maximum occurs where the physical and biological factors that control abundance are the most favorable. As one moves away from this central optimum into the zone of physiological stress, abundance generally begins to decline. This decline is usually gradual because both physical and biological limiting factors tend to follow a gradient. Physical conditions such as temperature and salinity usually change gradually geographically, as do biological limits such as the abundance of competitors and predators. Eventually, the zone of physiological stress grades into the zone of intolerance, where the population is absent. The zone of intolerance occurs because some limiting factor has become so great that the species can no longer survive.

Abundance is almost never uniformly distributed throughout a population's geographic range because the environment is rarely uniform enough to follow perfect gradients. Instead, many irregularities occur; ecologists call this the patchiness of the environment. In populations that inhabit a

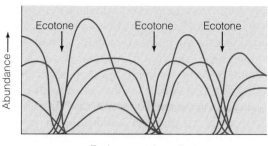

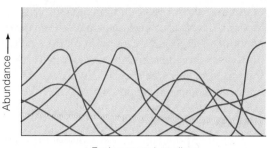

(a) Closed communities

(b) Open communities

**FIGURE 3–15**
Each curve represents the abundance of a single species. (a) In closed communities, the species boundaries tend to coincide. (b) In open communities, the species boundaries are more randomly distributed. (*Source*: R. E. Ricklefs, *Ecology* [New York: W. H. Freeman, 1990], p. 659. Copyright © 1990 by W. H. Freeman and Company. Used with permission.)

## Community Structure

Populations are not randomly distributed in communities. Indeed, discovering the various spatial patterns by which species are distributed has been one of the major accomplishments of ecology over the last century. Two of the most important patterns are the open structure of communities and the relative rarity of most species in communities.

### Open Structure of Communities

A key question about community structure is whether the populations that comprise a community have about the same geographic range and abundance peaks. Proponents of *closed community* structure argued that populations in most communities had similar range boundaries and abundance peaks. A closed community was thus a discrete unit with sharp boundaries called **ecotones** ( Fig. 3–15a). In contrast, proponents of open communities argued that most communities had populations with highly varied abundance peaks and range boundaries. Open communities were said to have populations distributed more-or-less randomly relative to one another (Fig. 3–15b).

Decades of data collection have finally resolved this debate, showing that most communities are indeed open. For example, populations of the many plants comprising a typical forest community have highly varied ranges that almost appear randomly distributed. In the case of forests, tolerance to moisture is a major determinant: some species do best in wetter areas while others thrive in a wide range of moisture. As a result, population ranges very often overlap to various degrees depending on how similar the populations' tolerances to moisture are. Areas where drastic changes occur in the physical environment are the major exception to the generally open structure of communities. In such areas, boundaries between communities can be sharp because popu-

lation tolerances are abruptly exceeded. A beach where land and sea come together, producing an ecotone, is an example. Because changes in the physical environment are usually more gradual, population abundance between communities also changes gradually.

The fact that communities are not closed makes their study more complicated because it is difficult to characterize, describe, and even name a community when it changes gradually in nearly every geographic direction. Ecologists often use advanced statistical methods, such as gradient analysis, to quantitatively describe the spatial changes in species composition. At any point along the gradient, the community is usually assigned a name on the basis of the most common species. One might refer to an oak-hickory forest community or a barnacle–blue mussel tidal zone community.

Another major implication of open communities is that communities are not tightly integrated assemblages of organisms that can be destroyed in an all-or-nothing fashion. Some ecologists once argued that communities were closed, highly-integrated units forming a "superorganism." They maintained that if we destroyed just one or a few populations, the whole superorganism would die, just as an organism dies if a key organ is removed. The fact that species come and go in communities, however, means that communities are generally not as integrated as the superorganismic concept said. This point is significant because many nonscientists still hold the superorganismic concept of biological communities.

### Most Species Are Rare in Communities

A second basic population pattern is the relatively low abundance of most populations in communities. As we have seen, populations tend to have their peak abundance near the center of their range, where optimum conditions prevail. In the example of the forest community above, optimum moisture level seems to be a primary determinant of abundance. At any given point on the gradient, however, a large percentage of the individuals belong to just a few tree species. Even at their maximum abundance, most populations are much less abundant than a few dominant populations such as beech, maple, oak, and pine.

This high population abundance of only a few species is found in nearly all natural communities and in many kinds of organisms. From deep-ocean to mountain communities, populations of just a few species almost always dominate in abundance, with many species being represented by only a few individuals. The result is a logarithmic pattern because when we plot the number of individuals per species, the number of species with few individuals rises rapidly.

What causes this abundance dominance by a few species? This question is currently being debated among ecologists, but most agree that the general cause is related to resource partitioning. In any environment, a limited amount of resources is available. Because of their evolutionary history, individuals of only a few species are best able to exploit a large part of the available resources. These species were the first to evolve the ability to obtain and eat a common food in the community. Other species must partition the remaining resources and are therefore less abundant. A species that is very rare in one community, however, may be very abundant in a nearby community if conditions are different enough that the species's particular adaptations are more effective in exploiting the resources there.

## Kinds of Communities

Many thousands of communities exist on the Earth. Rather than describe each in detail, we will examine the basic categories into which communities can be grouped.

The most basic distinction is between terrestrial (land) and aquatic (water) dwelling communities. The terrestrial group is often considered to include six major types of biomes ( Fig. 3–16); the aquatic group includes two:

1. *Terrestrial*. Tundra, grassland, desert, taiga, temperate forest, tropical forest (including tropical rainforests).
2. *Aquatic*. Marine, freshwater.

A **biome** is a large-scale category that includes many communities of a similar nature.

Both terrestrial and aquatic biomes (and thus the communities within them) are largely determined by climate, especially temperature. Climate is so important because it affects many aspects of the physical environment: rainfall, air and water temperature, soil conditions, and so on. Many secondary factors such as local nutrient availability, are also important, however. In all cases, biomes illustrate the key point that species will often adapt to physical conditions in similar ways, no matter what their evolutionary heritage. For instance, a desert biome in the western United States looks similar to a desert biome in North Africa even though the plants have different ancestries.

### Terrestrial Biomes

● Table 3–4 describes six basic land biome types. The tundra and desert biomes represent adaptations to the extreme conditions of very low temperature and low water, respectively. Not surprisingly, communities in these biomes tend to have the least number of species because organisms have difficulty adapting to the extreme physical conditions. In contrast, the tropical rainforests tend to be richest in species, in part because the tropics have the most moderate conditions.

Figure 3–17, page 79, shows the distribution of the major land biomes, by altitude and latitude. This figure demonstrates the importance of temperature, which decreases with both increasing altitude and increasing latitude; similar changes result in both cases. The more detailed global view in Figure 3–18, page 80, shows some of the true complexities of the latitudinal pattern. For example, tropical forests are not always neatly confined to equatorial areas, and there are various types of tropical forests, such as tropical scrub and tropical rainforests.

### Aquatic Biomes

In general, conditions in water are much less harsh than those on land. Water experiences many fewer temperature fluctuations and provides more buoyancy as support against gravity. All of these differences occur because water, as a liquid medium, is much denser than the gaseous air. Most important perhaps, living in water eliminates the danger of drying out, whereas water is often scarce on land. Not surprisingly, then, life originated in the oceans and took many millions of years to adapt to land. Yet even though water covers about 71% of the Earth's surface, most of it contains relatively little life; most of the open ocean is a vast aquatic desert with few nutrients.

(a)

(b)

(f)

(c)

(d)

(e)

**FIGURE 3–16**

Six major terrestrial biomes (clockwise from top left): (a) Canadian tundra; (b) natural grassland in South Dakota; (c) the Mojave desert; (d) taiga forest in Canada; (e) temperate forest in the Great Smoky Mountains; (f) tropical rainforest in Australia. (*Sources*: (a) Joe McDonald/ Visuals Unlimited; (b) Ron Spomer/Visuals Unlimited; (c) Simon Fraser/Science Photo Library/Photo Researchers; (d) Dean DeChambeau; (e) Dick Poe/Visuals Unlimited; (f) D. Cavagnaro/Visuals Unlimited.)

**TABLE 3–4**  *Six Major Land Biomes*

The biomes are listed in approximate order going from the equator to the poles.

1. *Tropical rainforest.* The most complex and diverse biome, containing over 50% of the world's species while occupying only 7% of the land area. This high diversity is largely due to the relatively constant temperatures at all times: daily and seasonal changes (fluctuations) are usually less than a total of 9°F (5° C). Rainfall is very heavy, over 80 inches (200 cm) annually. Major plants include deciduous trees that form a multilayered canopy, including understory trees. Herbs and shrubs that tolerate intense shade form the ground flora. Insects are extremely abundant; perhaps 96% of insect species are found here.

2. *Grasslands.* Rainfall is scarce, about 10–30 inches (25–75 cm) per year, causing grasses to be the most prominent plants. Fires are common. Major animals include grazers, such as the bison in North America. Economically, this is the most important biome, providing grazing land for sheep, cattle, and other food animals, as well as the richest cropland in the world. The rich soils are formed by the relative lack of rain and held in place by grass roots.

3. *Deserts.* Rainfall is very scarce, less than 10 inches (25 cm) per year. Temperatures can be very hot or very cold. Desert plants are widely spaced to allow maximum moisture per plant. Plant adaptations to arid conditions include (1) storage of water as in cacti, (2) shedding leaves in dry periods by deciduous shrubs, and (3) rapid growth and reproduction during rare rainy periods. Animal adaptations are similar to plants, with some storing large amounts of water (such as camels) and others exhibiting rapid growth and reproduction after rains (such as desert toads).

4. *Temperate forests.* Rainfall is abundant, 30–60 inches (75–150 cm per year), with distinct seasonal change. Deciduous trees dominate, such as oak and hickory (western United States) and beech and maple (north-central United States). Ground cover of shrubs and herbs. These forests lack the spectacular diversity of tropical forests, but are still more diverse than coniferous forests. Animals include deer, foxes, squirrels, raccoons, and many other familiar forms.

5. *Taiga.* Also called coniferous forests, these occur in a broad belt in northern North America and Asia. Diversity is relatively low. Plants are dominated by conifers (evergreens), which are tolerant of dry, cold conditions. Prominent types of evergreens include spruce, firs, and pines whose needles conserve water and withstand freezing better than leaves. Animals include moose, snowshoe hare, wolves, and grouse. Due to acidic, thin soils, cleared taiga makes poor cropland.

6. *Tundra.* An extensive treeless plain whose topsoil is frozen all year except for about 6 weeks in summer. Below this is permafrost soil, which is frozen all year long and poses a hazard for building. During the brief summer thaw, life grows and reproduces rapidly. Lichens (algae and fungi symbionts), grasses, and small shrubs are dominant plants. Prominent animals include caribou (reindeer), arctic hare, arctic fox, and snowy owl. Many migratory birds arrive for the rich summer growing season, characterized by billions of insects, bright flowers, and marshy conditions.

Aquatic communities do not divide into distinctive biomes like those found on land because the liquid state of water makes nonclimatic conditions more important in determining what can live in a particular environment. Water is a powerful solvent and also readily carries many substances in suspension; these substances, which range from toxins to nutrients, influence life locally. Furthermore, water readily transports heat so warm currents, such as the Gulf Stream, can warm large areas even near the poles. This prevents a simple latitudinal gradient from forming. Therefore, ecologists often designate only two aquatic biomes: the marine biome and the freshwater biome.

Marine waters differ from fresh waters in containing more dissolved minerals (salts) of various kinds. On average, marine waters have about 3.5% salt, mainly sodium chloride, and many other materials as well. The marine biome is the largest biome by far (over 70% of the Earth's surface), but can be subdivided relatively easily into (1) **benthic** (bottom-dwelling), and (2) **pelagic** (water column) zones (Fig. 3–19, page 81). Benthic communities are further subdivided by depth: littoral (shore), continental shelf, and abyssal (deep-sea, including the hydrothermal vent communities mentioned in Chapter 2). Benthic organisms include burrowers (such as worms), crawlers (such as snails), and stationary filter-feeders (such as barnacles). Pelagic organisms include (1) planktonic organisms (floaters) and (2) nektonic organisms (swimmers). The **photic zone** is the upper part of the biome where light penetrates; usually, this zone extends to about 150 feet (46 m) below the water surface. The photic zone is the main zone of photosynthesis and therefore is crucial to life in the

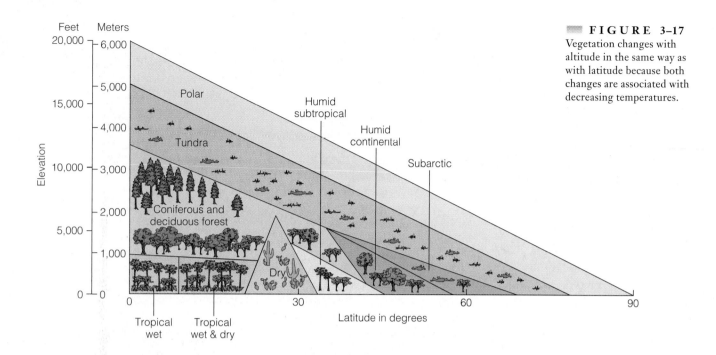

**FIGURE 3-17**
Vegetation changes with altitude in the same way as with latitude because both changes are associated with decreasing temperatures.

biome. The photosynthesizing plants, which form the base of the marine food pyramid, are mainly tiny planktonic organisms, such as diatoms. Much of the ocean is too deep for light to penetrate and drive the photosynthetic food base, though, so life is largely absent. Another reason why much of the ocean is a "biological desert" is that many nutrients in the ocean flow in from land and consequently are found only close to shore.

The freshwater biome can be subdivided into two zones: running water, such as rivers and streams, and standing water, such as lakes and ponds. Rivers and streams are not sharply delineated from lakes and ponds. In general, rivers and lakes are larger and more permanent than streams and ponds. The faster motion of running waters tends to keep them more highly oxygenated and more difficult to pollute. The slower motion of water in lakes and ponds leads to *stratification* of the water: the uppermost layer of water has plenty of oxygen while the oxygen decreases with depth. The uppermost layer is also much warmer during the summer and cooler during the winter than the lower layers. Most of the mixing between the uppermost and deeper layers occurs during seasonal changes known as spring and fall overturn. Like the marine biome, the freshwater biome has benthic (bottom-dwelling) and pelagic (swimming and planktonic) organisms and communities. Most of these have relatives in the marine realm (clams, snails, fishes, and plankton, for example), where the groups originated hundreds of millions of years ago.

## Community Diversity

Diversity refers to how many kinds of organisms occur in a community. Diversity is therefore often expressed in terms of species richness, or the number of species in a community. Many factors influence diversity, and the importance of any single factor varies with the particular community. Nevertheless, most of these factors can be summarized by two diversity trends. The **latitudinal diversity gradient** describes how species richness in most groups steadily decreases going away from the equator. Consequently, richer communities are found in tropical areas. For instance, 2.5 acres (1 hectare) of tropical forest typically contain from 40–100 tree species. In contrast, a typical temperate zone forest has about 10–30 tree species while a taiga forest in northern Canada has only 1–5 species. Furthermore, the number of insect species living on those trees increases with the kinds of trees (resources) available to exploit, so tropical forests also have vastly more kinds of insects and other animal species per acre. As a result of this richness, habitat destruction in tropical countries generally leads to many more extinctions per acre than destruction elsewhere (Chapter 12).

Ecologists generally agree that this gradient is largely due to three interrelated factors: (1) environmental stability, (2) community age, and (3) length of growing season. Greater environmental stability in equatorial areas means that communities are exposed to less environmental change on a daily, seasonal, and even hundred-

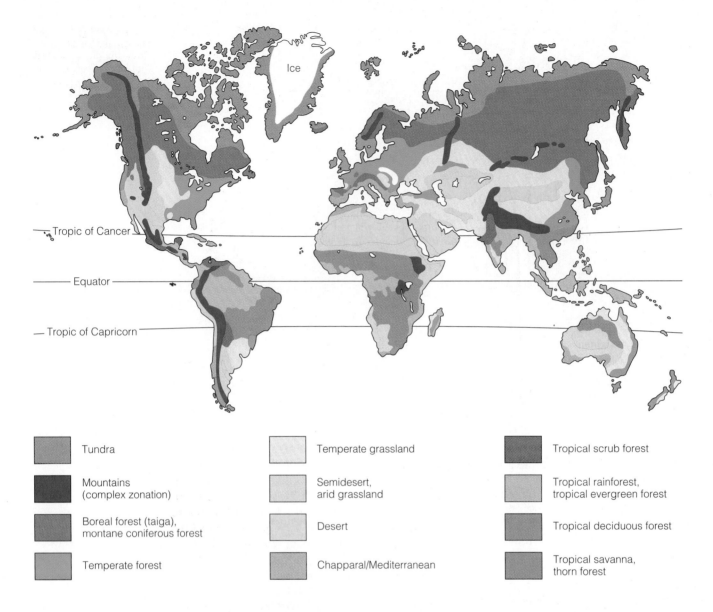

Ice

Tropic of Cancer

Equator

Tropic of Capricorn

| | Tundra | | Temperate grassland | | Tropical scrub forest |
| | Mountains (complex zonation) | | Semidesert, arid grassland | | Tropical rainforest, tropical evergreen forest |
| | Boreal forest (taiga), montane coniferous forest | | Desert | | Tropical deciduous forest |
| | Temperate forest | | Chapparal/Mediterranean | | Tropical savanna, thorn forest |

**FIGURE 3–18**
Major terrestrial biomes of the world.

year basis. This stability allows more kinds of species to thrive because high disturbance or stress generally reduces diversity. Equatorial communities are older because they have been less disturbed by advancing ice sheets and other climatic changes over the long span of geologic time. Hence evolution has had more time to create new species. The longer growing season in equatorial areas leads to more photosynthesis and plant growth, which forms the food base for all life. As we will see, higher plant productivity supports a greater diversity of organisms that depend on the plants.

The second important diversity trend is the **depth diversity gradient** found in aquatic communities. This gradient shows how species richness increases with water depth, down to about 6560 feet (2000 m) deep, and then begins to decline. This gradient is due to (1) environmental stability and (2) nutrients. Environmental stabil-

ity increases as one moves away from the higher water energies of the beach and shoreline. As we have seen, stability allows more species to thrive. Similarly, as one moves offshore, the amount of nutrients from land runoff begins to diminish. Thus, even though deep water is very stable, it contains insufficient nutrients to permit the high productivity seen in shallower waters. Marine life depends especially on land runoff to supply limiting nutrients such as phosphorus.

To summarize, four major factors may increase diversity in any community: increasing environmental stability, age, growing season, and nutrients. Stability provides an accommodating environment for diversity to proliferate, age provides the time, and the last two factors provide the energy and nutrients to supply many types of organisms. In general, the more of these factors that a community has, the more species-rich it will be.

Labels in figure: Freshwater biome; Marine biome; Lakes; Rivers; ① Littoral (shore); ② Continental shelf; Photic zone; Pelagic (water column); Benthic (sea bottom); ③ Abyssal (deep sea)

## Community Change through Time

Biological communities change through time. This is not surprising since the physical environment that ultimately supports life is always changing. Whether we perceive change as "fast" or "slow" depends almost entirely on the time scale we are using. Two time scales are particularly useful for examining change in communities: ecological time and geological time. Ecological time focuses on community events that occur on the order of tens to hundreds of years. These events are most relevant to our own human time scale. Geological time focuses on community events that are longer, on the order of thousands of years or more, such as evolution.

### Community Succession

Community succession is the sequential replacement of species in a community by immigration of new species and the local extinction of old ones. Community succession is initiated by a disturbance that creates unoccupied habitats for colonizing species. These colonizers usually have a hardy nature and are adapted for widespread dispersal and rapid growth, characteristics that enable them to become the first species to appear and thrive (see Issues in Perspective 3–2). This initial community of colonizing species is called the **pioneer community**. Eventually, other species migrate into the community. These new species are usually poorer dispersers and slower growing than the colonizers, but they are more efficient specialists and better competitors and therefore begin to replace the colonizers. This process continues, as still newer species migrate in, until the **climax community** is reached. The climax community, continues to change, although at a much slower pace.

Succession has been most fully documented in forest communities ( Fig. 3–20, page 83). Pioneering plant species include lichens, mosses, and herbs, which give way to shrubs, small trees, and finally large trees in the climax community. Various animals, such as the bird and mammal species shown, also appear in sequence. The animal sequence is determined largely by the appearance of the plants they rely on.

Succession is characterized by a number of trends ( Table 3–5, page 84). One of the most basic is the decrease in productivity. Pioneering plants tend to be smaller in size and exhibit rapid growth that maximizes productivity. In later stages, as more specialized, slower-growing species begin to migrate in, productivity declines. As these later species immigrate, diversity increases because the more specialized species more finely subdivide the resources. In addition, the later species generally have larger size and longer life cycles. Together, these trends result in

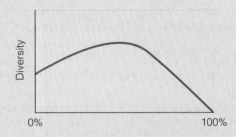

# Can Destruction Be Good?
# The Intermediate Disturbance Hypothesis

Most of us intuitively think of environmental disturbances as undesirable, negative events. Pollution, forest fires, the introduction of exotic species, and many other events that destroy organisms are regarded as invariably bad. Yet many ecologists are concluding that, in the long run, such disturbances can be beneficial for the diversity of biological communities.

How can destruction promote diversity? Consider an environment where there is little or no change. After a long time, the community often becomes dominated by a relatively small number of species. Some may be better competitors, such as toxin-secreting plants; others may be better at evading predators, such as speedy animals. For these and other reasons, some species will eventually disappear from the community.

In contrast, if the environment is disturbed, the dominant species may be removed from the disturbed area. Perhaps a fire destroys a few acres of forest. Such a

disturbance "cleans the slate" and opens up the area for species that might otherwise have been excluded by the more competitive and dominant species. Pioneer species, which are adapted for colonizing disturbed areas, are likely to be the first inhabitants after the disturbance ( Fig. 1a). Eventually, these pioneers may be excluded by the dominants if no further disturbances occur and community succession takes its course. But if another disturbance occurs nearby, the pioneers can move on.

But just as too little disturbance is bad for diversity, so is too much disturbance. If the fire or other destruction occurs over too wide an area, it could wipe out many species, including both dominants and pioneers. Thus, ecological disturbances, like most things in life, are perhaps most beneficial in moderation ( Fig. 1b). This concept has been encapsulated in the intermediate disturbance hypothesis of ecology: maximum diversity in an area is promoted when relatively small, localized

**FIGURE 2**

Moderate disturbances may promote greater diversity than either no disturbance or total disturbance.

disturbances occur in parts of the area. These disturbances allow dominant species to persist in undisturbed parts and colonizing species to live in the newly disturbed parts. The net diversity of the whole area is therefore greater than if the environment were completely unchanging or completely disturbed ( Fig. 2).

**FIGURE 1**

(a) Forest fires, such as this one in Yellowstone, will often kill many species. (b) But such disturbances create new opportunities for other, "disturbance-adapted," species. (*Source*: (a) © *Seattle Times*/Gamma Liaison; (b) © Nathan Farb/Gamma Liaison.)

(a)

(b)

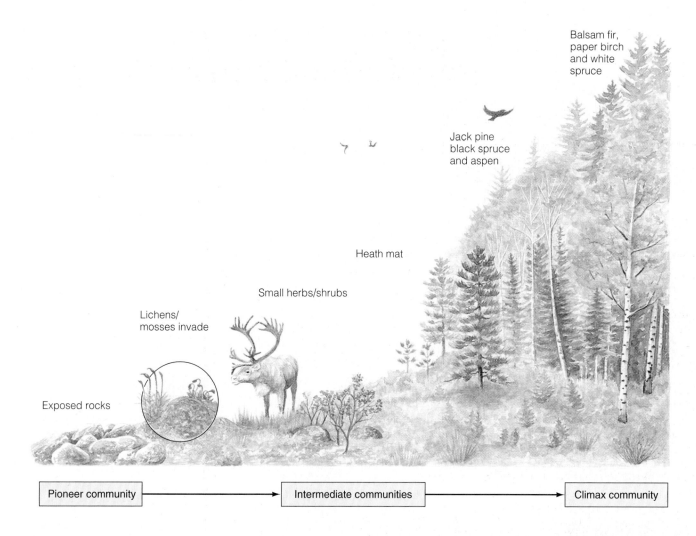

Balsam fir,
paper birch
and white
spruce

Jack pine
black spruce
and aspen

Heath mat

Small herbs/shrubs

Lichens/
mosses invade

Exposed rocks

| Pioneer community | → | Intermediate communities | → | Climax community |

more biomass in later stages because living tissue accumulates. **Biomass** is the total weight of living tissue in a community. Finally, later stages tend to have populations controlled mainly by biological or density-dependent controls such as competition and predation. In contrast, early stages mainly show physical or density-independent controls, such as physical disturbance. Some communities, such as a beach, are generally in a constant state of physical disturbance so early-successional populations become permanent dwellers.

Succession occurs because each community stage, from pioneer to climax, prepares the way for the stage that follows. Soil conditions, nutrient availability, temperature, and many other environmental traits are altered by each preceding community. For example, the pioneering stage of a forest stabilizes the soil of a bare patch of land, begins to accumulate nutrients in the soil, attracts pollinating insects, retains water, and provides ground shade, among many other processes that make the environment more livable for later stages. The process of "preparation"

is ironic in the sense that species in each community often bring about their own demise. Yet these early species are adapted by evolution to be colonists and can nearly always migrate to other, newly disturbed areas that permit them to persist. Thus, nearly all natural landscapes (including sea-bottom areas) consist of a mosaic of undisturbed patches intermixed with patches that are disturbed to varying degrees. Ecologists think that this "patchiness" of the natural environment is crucial for maintaining diversity because it allows species from different stages of succession to exist simultaneously.

### Community Evolution

Since communities are composed of populations of species, communities must also evolve. A comparison of a typical community from the Paleozoic Era, about 500 million years ago, with a typical community from the Cenozoic Era, living today, would reveal not only that the species composition of the communities differs, but that the present-day community contains more species.

**FIGURE 3–20**
Ecological succession occurs when biological communities become established in a sequence, from pioneer through climax communities.

**TABLE 3-5** *Trends in Ecological Succession*

| | STAGE IN ECOSYSTEM DEVELOPMENT | |
|---|---|---|
| ATTRIBUTE | Early | Late |
| Biomass | Small | Large |
| Productivity | High | Low |
| Food chains | Short | Long, complex |
| Species diversity | Low | High (?) |
| Niche specialization | Broad | Narrow |
| Feeding relations | General | Specialized |
| Size of individuals | Smaller | Larger (?) |
| Life cycles | Short, simple | Long, complex |
| Population control mechanisms | Physical | Biological |
| Fluctuations | More pronounced | Less pronounced |
| Mineral cycles | Open | More or less closed |
| Stability | Low | High |
| Potential yield to humans | High | Low |

(*Source*: Adapted from R. Smith, *Elements of Ecology and Field Biology* [New York: Harper & Row, 1977]. Table 8–9: Trends in Ecological Succession from *Elements of Ecology and Field Biology* by Robert Leo Smith. Copyright © 1978 by Robert Leo Smith. Reprinted by permission of HarperCollins Publishers, Inc.)

The main reason why the global diversity of life has increased through time (Chapter 12) is that organisms have evolved "new ways of doing things." For instance, there were fewer burrowers on the Paleozoic sea floor because evolution had not yet produced organisms, such as clams with enhanced digging muscles, capable of burrowing to great depths in the sediment. As species become more specialized and find new ways to exploit resources in the physical environment, evolution produces communities with more species per unit area, a development called species packing.

## Human Disturbance of Communities

Community structure is determined by species distributions, so whenever species distributions change, the structure is altered. We have seen that humans change natural species distributions in many ways from introducing new predators into pristine ecosystems to outright annihilation of large areas of habitat. However, the basic effect of nearly all human activity is community simplification: the reduction of overall species diversity (number of species).

In many cases, humans simplify communities on purpose. The farmer's agricultural and the suburbanite's horticultural communities of plants, insects, and other animals are common examples. In such cases, we seek to grow only certain species, creating a much lower diversity than normally is found in that area. The extreme case is called **monoculture**, meaning that only one particular species is grown. An example is a wheat field. Monocultures and other forms of extreme community simplification are very susceptible to diseases and other forms of destruction, such as the Irish Potato Famine. It is interesting to note that most of the plant species we cultivate for food and pleasure are species from pioneering communities. For example, corn, wheat, and many other plants are grasses that were originally adapted to colonizing disturbed areas. Humans favor them as food because they are fast-growing, rapidly reproducing organisms.

In other cases, humans inadvertently simplify communities. Construction, road building, pollution, and many other aspects of "development" act as disturbances that simplify communities. It is important to note that such stressed communities are simplified not only by having fewer species, but also by having some species that are superabundant. Although most species cannot tolerate the stressful conditions, some find the new conditions beneficial. For instance, some organisms thrive in highly polluted waters and even use the pollutants as food. Even in these inadvertent disturbances, we often favor early-successional species. Whether we are building roads, farms, cities, or lawns, one of our first actions is to bulldoze or otherwise remove the climax community. Because colonizing disturbed environments is what early-successional species are adapted to do, they have tended to thrive as we have expanded. Indeed, the term *weed* is virtually synonymous with early-successional species, which also include "weedy" animals, such as some mice and many insects. Issues in Perspective 3–2 discusses the possibility that disturbances may sometimes be beneficial.

## Ecosystems and Community Function

Although communities vary in structure, certain basic processes, or functions, unite them all. The most basic processes are (1) energy flow and (2) matter cycling. All organisms must eat (take in energy and matter) to stay alive, causing energy and matter to move through the community. All energy and matter ultimately come from, and return to, the physical environment. We must therefore observe the ecosystem (community plus physical environment) to understand the complete process.

As Chapter 4 will discuss in detail, energy flows and matter cycles through all four of the environmental spheres. The movement of energy and matter through ecosystems represents move-

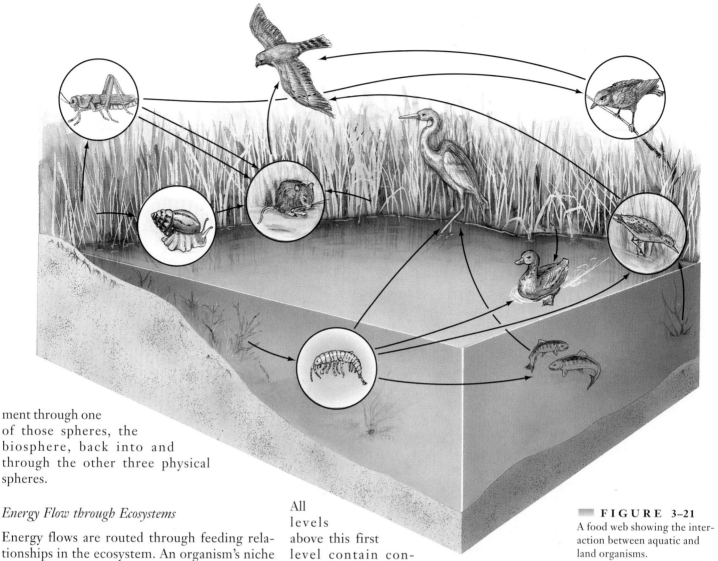

ment through one
of those spheres, the
biosphere, back into and
through the other three physical
spheres.

## Energy Flow through Ecosystems

Energy flows are routed through feeding relationships in the ecosystem. An organism's niche ("occupation") in the ecosystem is closely associated with feeding. Energy flow through any ecosystem can be represented by the food web and the biomass pyramid. The **food web** describes the complex interrelationships by which organisms consume other organisms. The food web in Figure 3–21 illustrates how even aquatic and land organisms prey on each other.

Although food webs are adequate for graphically depicting the feeding relationships in any given ecosystem, the **biomass pyramid** provides a more basic understanding of energy flow (Fig. 3–22). Biomass is the weight of living matter. The first trophic (feeding) level consists of the producers in the ecosystem, which produce the food used by all other organisms. Usually, the producers are plants, producing the food by photosynthesis; in a few deep-sea ecosystems, organisms produce food by chemosynthesis based on heat energy and compounds from underwater hydrothermal vents instead of the Sun's energy.

All levels above this first level contain consumers. First-order, or primary, consumers are herbivores that directly consume the producers, deriving energy from the chemical energy stored in the producers' bodies. As a marine example, first-order consumers include the crustaceans and other organisms that eat the phytoplankton. In a forest ecosystem, first-order consumers include deer and other plant eaters. Above the first-order consumers are the second-order (or secondary) consumers, which feed on the first-order consumers. In a marine ecosystem, second-order consumers may consist of fishes, lobsters, and other species. In a forest ecosystem, second-order consumers include wolves, panthers, and other meat eaters (carnivores) that eat the deer and other first-order consumers (Fig. 3–23). Third-, fourth-, and even higher-order consumers can occur in some ecosystems. Decomposers are a special type of consumer. Decomposers, such as many bacteria, consume the tissue of dead organisms from all lev-

**FIGURE 3–21**
A food web showing the interaction between aquatic and land organisms.

Second-order consumers

First-order consumers

Producers

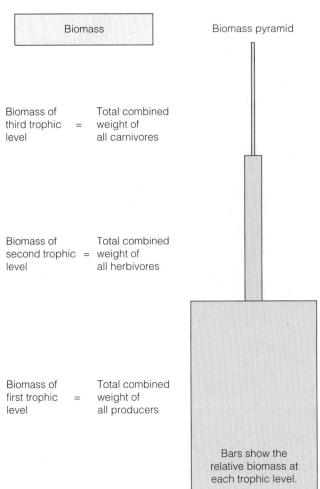

Biomass

| Biomass of third trophic level | = | Total combined weight of all carnivores |

| Biomass of second trophic level | = | Total combined weight of all herbivores |

| Biomass of first trophic level | = | Total combined weight of all producers |

Biomass pyramid

Bars show the relative biomass at each trophic level.

■ **FIGURE 3–22 (above)**
A biomass pyramid. In most land food webs, biomass decreases from one feeding (trophic) level to the next highest.

■ **FIGURE 3–23 (at right)**
The gray wolf is a predator high on the biomass pyramid. (*Source*: Art Wolfe/Tony Stone Images.)

els of the food pyramid. Although they are inconspicuous, decomposers are extremely important in energy flow; in virtually all ecosystems, they consume the largest part of the energy flow.

Why does the biomass pyramid form? Biomass declines with each higher trophic level because progressively less food is available. Much of the food an animal consumes is not passed on to the animal that eats it. Instead, much of the food is (1) lost as undigested waste, or (2) "burned up" by the animal's metabolism to produce heat (■ Fig. 3–24). For example, a deer excretes about 25% of its ingested calories as undigested waste. Of the 75% that is digested, most is lost as metabolic waste products (such as urine) and, especially, body heat generated from movement and other kinds of maintenance. Thus, of all the calories eaten by the deer, less than 20% are converted into the deer's body tissue, which can be eaten by wolves or other animals that feed on the deer. Other organisms are more energy-efficient. Insects and other cold-blooded organisms can convert ingested calories into tissue much more ef-

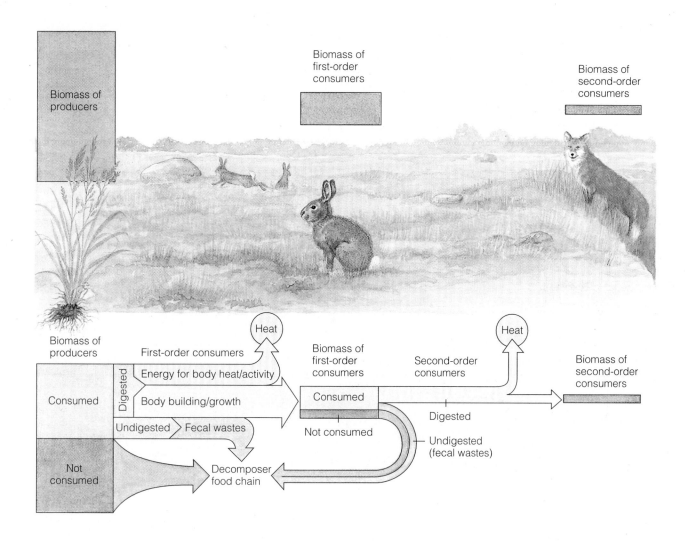

ficiently than mammals because they have slower metabolisms. Even so, these organisms convert less than 50% of ingested calories into tissue. The result is a "leakage" of energy between each feeding level. This inefficiency is why feeding relationships form a pyramid. In general, about 80-95% of the energy is lost in the transfer between each level, depending on the organisms involved. Because so little energy is left, very few ecosystems have food pyramids with more than five levels. This is also why large carnivores are rare: they are the organisms at the top.

## Ecosystem Productivity

The amount of food generated by producers at the base of the food pyramid varies greatly among ecosystems. Productivity is the rate at which biomass is produced in a community. **Net primary productivity (NPP)** is the rate at which producer, usually plant, biomass is created. Among the most productive terrestrial ecosystems are tropi-

cal forests and swamps (● Table 3–6), which produce plant biomass (NPP) at many times the rate of deserts. Temperate communities such as grasslands and temperate forests have intermediate productivities. The main reason for this pattern is that productivity on land increases where the growing season is longer. As ▬ Figure 3–25 shows, productivity tends to increase toward the equator where winters are milder and shorter. Deserts are the exception to this trend because lack of water limits growth, even though the growing season is long.

In terms of productivity per unit area, among the most productive aquatic ecosystems are estuaries and reefs, which may be up to 10 times more productive than certain other freshwater or marine ecosystems (Table 3–6). By this measure, the open ocean is the least productive by far. This point is crucial because the open ocean constitutes about 90% of the ocean. Therefore, 90% of the ocean, which is over half of the Earth's surface, is essentially a "marine desert"

▬ **FIGURE 3–24**
Flow of biomass and energy through a food pyramid. Note that much of the biomass is consumed by decomposers.

**TABLE 3–6** *Ecosystems and Productivity*

| ECOSYSTEM TYPE | AREA (10^6 km²)[b] | NET PRIMARY PRODUCTIVITY, PER UNIT AREA (g/m² or t/km²)[a] Normal Range | Mean | WORLD NET PRIMARY PRODUCTION (10^9 t)[c] |
|---|---|---|---|---|
| Tropical rainforest | 17.0 | 1000–3500 | 2200 | 37.4 |
| Tropical seasonal forest | 7.5 | 1000–2500 | 1600 | 12.0 |
| Temperate evergreen forest | 5.0 | 600–2500 | 1300 | 6.5 |
| Temperate deciduous forest | 7.0 | 600–2500 | 1200 | 8.4 |
| Boreal northern forest | 12.0 | 400–2000 | 800 | 9.6 |
| Woodland and shrubland | 8.5 | 250–1200 | 700 | 6.0 |
| Savanna | 15.0 | 200–2000 | 900 | 13.5 |
| Temperate grassland | 9.0 | 200–1500 | 600 | 5.4 |
| Tundra and alpine | 8.0 | 10–400 | 140 | 1.1 |
| Desert and semidesert shrub | 18.0 | 10–250 | 90 | 1.6 |
| Extreme desert, rock, sand, and ice | 24.0 | 0–10 | 3 | 0.07 |
| Cultivated land | 14.0 | 100–3500 | 650 | 9.1 |
| Swamp and marsh | 2.0 | 800–3500 | 2000 | 4.0 |
| Lake and stream | 2.0 | 100–1500 | 250 | 0.5 |
| Total continental | 149 | | 773 | 115 |
| Open ocean | 332.0 | 2–400 | 125 | 41.5 |
| Upwelling zones | 0.4 | 400–1000 | 500 | 0.2 |
| Continental shelf | 26.6 | 200–600 | 360 | 9.6 |
| Reefs | 0.6 | 500–4000 | 2500 | 1.6 |
| Estuaries | 1.4 | 200–3500 | 1500 | 2.1 |
| Total marine | 361 | | 152 | 55.0 |
| Full total | 510 | | 333 | 170 |

[a] t/km² = g/m² = metric tons/km² = approximately 2.85 tons per square mile.
[b] 10^6 km² = approximately 386,000 square miles.
[c] 10^9 t = 1 billion metric tons = approximately 1.102 billion tons.

(*Source*: M. Begon, J. Harper, and C. Townsend, *Ecology*, 2d ed. [Cambridge, Mass.: Blackwell, 1990] Reprinted by permission of Blackwell Science, Inc.)

in terms of productivity per unit area. Due to the size of the open ocean, however, it does make a significant contribution to the world's net primary productivity (Table 3–6). Reefs and estuaries are highly productive ecosystems despite their small areas. Unlike terrestrial ecosystems, the productivity of these nearshore areas is not strongly determined by the length of the growing season. Instead, nutrient availability tends to be the main limiting factor in marine ecosystems. The open ocean is relatively "starved" for some nutrients, especially phosphorus, because the source of the nutrients is runoff from land. Zones of upwelling can be highly productive, however, because the upwelling currents often carry many nutrients that have settled and been swept up from the ocean bottom. The upwelling zones west of Peru, which support a great fishing industry, are an example.

Net secondary productivity (NSP) is the rate at which consumer and decomposer biomass is produced. In other words, NSP includes all biomass except plants. A general rule of ecology is that primary and secondary net productivity are correlated: communities that have high primary productivity almost always have high secondary productivity. If the base of the food pyramid is producing much biomass, the organisms that consume and decompose plants will usually produce more biomass, too.

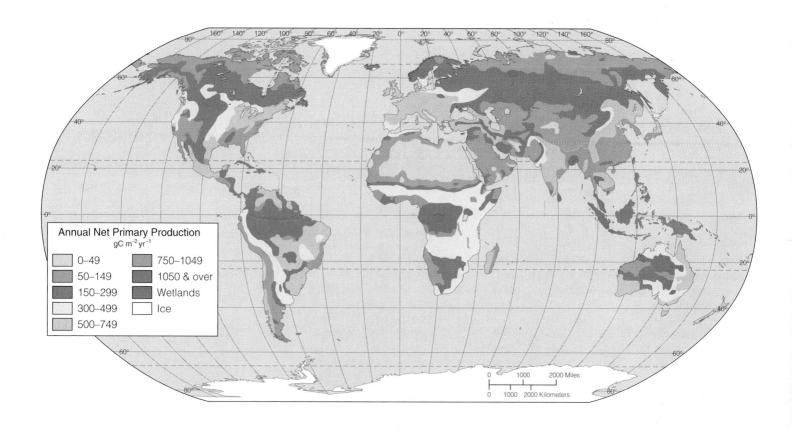

Annual Net Primary Production
gC m⁻² yr⁻¹

- 0–49
- 50–149
- 150–299
- 300–499
- 500–749
- 750–1049
- 1050 & over
- Wetlands
- Ice

## Human Disturbance of Energy Flow and Productivity

The extent to which humans have altered ecosystem energy flow is demonstrated by a startling statistic: nearly 40% of the potential terrestrial NPP and about 2% of the oceanic ecosystem NPP is directly used, diverted, or lost (such as when forests are paved over to construct shopping malls) due to the activities of humans. This means that nearly half of the energy potentially converted by land plants is largely not available to species in natural ecosystems. Instead of trickling upward into the natural food pyramids, the energy flow is either "re-channeled" for human needs, such as directly feeding ourselves, feeding our pets, running our factories, or simply lost due to human activities (such as when we destroy tropical rainforests). This energy loss to nature is particularly striking considering that up to 90% of all species on Earth live on land. If we add the NPP of the aquatic food pyramid to that of the land pyramid, humans redirect an estimated 25% of global NPP.

Another way humans disturb productivity is by causing extinctions. Issues in Perspective 3–3 discusses evidence that humans not only "usurp" natural productivity, but also reduce what ecosystems can produce.

## Matter Cycling through Ecosystems

The second basic ecosystem function, matter cycling, occurs because, unlike energy, matter is not always converted into less useful forms when used. Dozens of elements are cycled through ecosystems in biogeochemical cycles, which carry the elements through living tissue and the physical environment such as water, air, and rocks. An example is the biogeochemical cycle of carbon, which has a major influence on global climate (Chapter 4).

Most of the elements that cycle through ecosystems are trace elements, used in small amounts by organisms. Living things use carbon, hydrogen, oxygen, nitrogen, sulfur, and phosphorus in large amounts, however. Because organisms both metabolize and store these elements, ecosystems exert great control over how fast elements cycle. Some elements cycle in a matter of days while others may be buried for millions of years. For example, carbon may spend millions of years underground stored in fossil fuels such as coal and oil or as limestone (Chapter 4).

Ecosystems are generally very efficient in cycling matter, in that most matter is cycled over and over within the ecosystem itself (■ Fig. 3–26). For instance, the carbon atoms in a plant will be incorporated into a deer. These, in turn, will be incorporated into the tissue of a

■ **FIGURE 3–25**
Annual net primary productivity (NPP) on the Earth's land surface. In photosynthesis plants extract carbon from the atmosphere and utilize the carbon to form biomass. Therefore, one way to measure NPP is in terms of the amount of carbon converted into biomass per unit area per year. In this figure NPP is measured using the units grams of carbon per square meter per year (g C m⁻² yr⁻¹). [1 gram C per m² per year is approximately 0.029 ounce C per yd² per year.] Note that productivity is high in tropical forests and very low in arid regions. (*Source:* J. M. Melillo, *et al.*, *Nature* 363 [1993]: p. 237. Reprinted with permission from *Nature.* Copyright © 1993 Macmillan Magazines Limited.)

# Does Extinction Reduce Ecosystem Productivity? How "Experimental Ecology" Answers Key Questions

If an ecosystem loses plant species, is its primary productivity reduced? After all, the ground could be completely covered with just one species. Some ecologists, however, have argued that the more plant species in an ecosystem, the more biomass it can produce because they provide buffers against seasonal and other environmental changes. If one species suffers from cold, for instance, another can take over the photosynthetic processes.

After years of debate, evidence is accumulating that plant diversity does indeed tend to increase primary productivity. John H. Lawton and his colleagues at the Imperial College in England have per-

formed a series of experiments that measured productivity of ecosystems under environmentally controlled laboratory conditions. As Figure 1 shows, their general finding was that plant productivity remained relatively high during the initial loss of species in very species-rich communities. But as the number of species continued to decline, productivity began to decrease until species-poor communities, with 1–5 plant species, showed significantly lower productivity. Much further work is needed to verify this finding, but it shows how experimental methods can answer crucial environmental questions that otherwise become embroiled in fruitless debates.

Another series of experiments conducted by David C. Tilman of the University of Minnesota produced another key finding: Increased diversity also increases ecosystem resistance to disturbance. Figure 2 shows that in Minnesota grasslands, species-poor communities produce much less relative biomass during drought years than species-rich communities. Apparently, having more species helps buffer the ecosystem against disturbances because some species can tolerate the disturbance better than others. By having more species, an ecosystem is more likely to have at least some species that can tolerate a disturbance and continue to produce biomass.

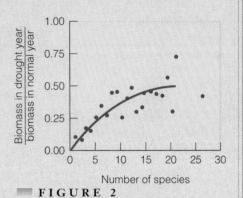

### FIGURE 2

Communities with more species produce relatively more biomass in drought years than communities with fewer species. (*Source*: Redrawn from J. Lockwood and S. Pimm, "Do Species Matter?" *Current Biology* 4 [1994]: p. 456. Reprinted with permission from Current Science.)

The studies by Lawton and Tilman illustrate how ecological experiments can answer crucial questions about how extinction is impacting the environment. Species loss not only diminishes our world aesthetically and economically, it apparently impairs (1) ecosystem functioning such as biomass production and (2) ecosystem resistance to disturbance. A species-poor ecosystem has lower productivity during normal years, and this reduced productivity is even more drastically lowered during times of stress.

### FIGURE 1

Declines in the number of species ultimately lead to declines in productivity.

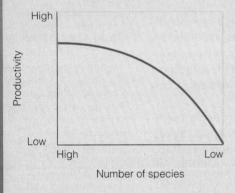

wolf that eats the deer. When the wolf dies, decomposers will incorporate the same carbon atoms. All of these changes take place within the ecosystem. Nevertheless, a small amount of matter will be lost from the ecosystem over time. Leaching from rainfall will carry off carbon in the form of decaying organic matter, leaves, and so on. In undisturbed ecosystems, this output loss is roughly balanced by an equal input gain of the

same matter. For instance, carbon enters the ecosystem via weathering of rocks and is carried into the ecosystem by rainwater. In undisturbed natural ecosystems, both the input and the output are small relative to the amount of matter "locked up" and recycled within the biomass of the ecosystem itself (Fig. 3–26).

Both the rate and efficiency of matter cycling vary between ecosystems. The cycling of matter

Matter input
(rock weathering, rain)

Matter

Ecosystem

Matter output
(runoff, leaching)

Excess input,
disturbance
(such as eutrophication)

Excess output
(such as slash and burn
agriculture)

(a)

(b)

**FIGURE 3–26**
(a) A healthy ecosystem cycles
most of its matter over and
over through the food web.
Excess input and excess output
are symptoms of an unhealthy
ecosystem. An example of
excess input, where too much
matter enters into the system,
is fertilizer or nutrient excess.
An example of excess output is
the rapid loss of matter caused
by slash and burn agriculture.
(b) Slash-and-burn farming of
the rainforest releases nutrients normally stored in plant
biomass. (*Source*: (b) Jacques Jan-
goux/Tony Stone Images.)

is generally faster in tropical ecosystems, such as tropical rainforests and coral reefs, because biochemical reaction rates tend to increase with temperature. Matter cycling is also especially efficient in tropical ecosystems, where high rainfall will leach elements from the soil unless plants incorporate them quickly and efficiently into their tissue. Similarly, coral reefs thrive mainly in nutrient-poor tropical waters, so the elements in the nutrients must be utilized quickly and recycled very efficiently into the tissues of the marine life.

### Human Disturbance of Matter Cycling

Matter cycling in the ecosystem is disturbed when humans alter the balance between the input and output of matter by creating (1) excess output, or (2) excess input (Fig. 3–26). Excess output occurs when humans suddenly release the large quantity of matter retained in the biomass of the ecosystem. For instance, in **slash and burn agriculture,** trees are cut down and burned. The burning releases the nutrients into the soil for agriculture. Unfortunately, the nutrients are quickly leached out of the soil where rainfall is heavy, as in the tropics where slash and burn techniques are common. This massive output of matter from the ecosystem is not fully replaced by input for many hundreds or perhaps thousands of years. During this time, the area can sustain only a relatively barren ecosystem with a fraction of its former diversity. In the meantime, farmers must move on and burn another area of tropical forest to produce arable land. This practice is contributing to massive tropical deforestation worldwide. Another example of excess output is the massive burning of fossil fuels. Billions of tons of carbon are released into the atmosphere annually from the burning of the tropical forests and other ecosystems. These emissions are contributing to the likelihood of global climate change (Chapter 18).

Disturbance by excess input commonly occurs when runoff from agricultural activity carries large amounts of fertilizer, organic waste, and other nutrients into natural ecosystems. This also destroys diversity because the excess nutrients cause eutrophication, leading to unrestrained growth of some organisms, such as algae in a lake. When the algae die, the decay of their now-abundant bodies by bacteria uses up so much oxygen that fish and many other organisms die.

## SUMMARY

The very early appearance of life on Earth implies that natural processes readily produce life under appropriate conditions. The components of the early atmosphere are thought to have been ammonia, methane, water vapor, and other gases. When these are subjected to electricity, which simulates lightning and sunlight, chemical reactions occur that produce amino acids, complex molecules that are the building blocks of proteins. Proteins make up enzymes and many other components of life. The basic organizational unit of life is the cell.

Once life originated, it began to diversify into different kinds of organisms through biological evolution. Biological evolution occurs from natural selection of individual variation. Isolation of populations promotes speciation. Among sexual organisms, a species is a group of individuals that can interbreed to produce fertile offspring. Traits are passed on by genes, which are the basic units of heredity. Variation in a population, or "gene pool," occurs because individuals possess different sets of genes that produce different traits, as well as by mutation, which is spontaneous change in a gene.

The biosphere is hierarchical: organisms, composed of atoms, molecules, and cells, are grouped into populations. Populations form communities, which then form ecosystems. Ecosystems, when considered together, form the biosphere, which subsumes all life on Earth. Ecology is the study of how organisms interact with each other and their physical environment. A population is a group of individuals of the same species living in the same area. All populations undergo three distinct phases during their existence: (1) growth, (2) stability, and (3) decline. The potential for increase in a given population is called the intrinsic rate of increase. The intrinsic rate of increase = birth rate – death rate. Four basic abundance controls can limit population growth: (1) physical limitations, (2) competitors, (3) predators, and (4) symbiosis. Eventually, all populations become extinct. The ultimate cause of decline and extinction is environmental change.

Human alterations of the environment have led to destabilization of populations by affecting the various abundance controls. The result has often been either (1) population growth as previous limitations are removed or (2) population decline as new limitations are imposed.

Diversity refers to how many kinds of organisms occur in a community. The latitudinal diversity gradient describes how species richness in most groups steadily decreases going away from the equator. Thus, richer communities are found in tropical areas. The second important diversity trend is the depth diversity gradient found in aquatic communities: species richness increases with water depth down to a point about 6560 feet (2000 m) deep and then begins to decline. This gradient is caused by (1) environmental stability and (2) nutrients.

Although communities vary in structure, they all experience certain processes. The most basic of these processes are (1) energy flow and (2) matter cycling. All organisms must eat (take in energy and matter) to stay alive, causing energy and matter to move through the community. All energy and matter ultimately come from, and return to, the physical environment.

The food web describes the complex interrelationships by which organisms consume other organisms. The biomass pyramid provides a more basic understanding of energy flow. Biomass can be thought of as the weight of living matter. The first trophic level consists of the producers in the ecosystem, which produce the food used by all other organisms. All the levels above the first level contain consumers. First-order, or primary, consumers are herbivores that directly consume the producers, deriving energy from the chemical energy stored in the producers' bodies. Above the first-order consumers are the second-order consumers, which feed on the first-order consumers. Third-, fourth-, and even higher-order consumers can occur in some ecosystems. Decomposers consume the tissue of dead organisms from all levels of the pyramid. Decomposers are extremely important in energy flow, consuming the largest part of the energy flow in virtually all ecosystems. Humans now divert or redirect, for their own use, about 40% of the net primary productivity of all land plants on Earth.

Matter cycling occurs because, unlike energy, matter is not converted into less useful forms when used. Dozens of elements are cycled through ecosystems in biogeochemical cycles, which carry the elements through living tissue and the physical environment such as water, air, and rocks. Most of the elements that cycle through ecosystems are trace elements, used in small amounts by organisms. Living things do use carbon, hydrogen, oxygen, nitrogen, sulfur, and phosphorus in large amounts, however. Matter cycling is disturbed when humans alter the balance between input and output of matter through ecosystems by creating (1) excess output, or (2) excess input.

# KEY TERMS

age structure
amensalism
amino acids
benthic
biomass
biomass pyramid
biome
carrying capacity
climax community
commensalism
community
competition
competitive exclusion
DNA (deoxyribonucleic acid)
density-dependent regulation
density-independent regulation

depth diversity gradient
ecological release
ecology
ecosystem
ecotones
endemic species
eukaryotes
explosion of life
food web
genes
habitat
intrinsic rate of increase
latitudinal diversity gradient
law of the minimum
life history
monoculture
mutation

mutualism
natural selection
net primary productivity (NPP)
niche
parasitism
pelagic
photic zone
pioneer community
population
predation
protocells
slash and burn agriculture
species
symbiosis
taxonomy

# STUDY QUESTIONS

1. What is the basic organizational unit of life?
2. What is a protocell? What cell-like properties do protocells have?
3. What is a species?
4. What was Mendel's discovery? Explain.
5. What is the ultimate cause of all genetic variation?
6. What is the suggested reason for the "explosion of life"? Why would this promote life?
7. What are the three phases during a population's existence?
8. What is biomass? Monoculture?
9. What is the intrinsic rate of increase? What is its symbol?
10. Define age structure. Explain the meaning of the three diagrams in Figure 3–6.
11. What is the latitudinal diversity gradient?
12. What is the abundance control in the physical environment? What are the three abundance controls in the biological environment?
13. Explain the law of the minimum.
14. If a population doubles each day and begins with two individuals, what will the population be in five days?
15. What is the intrinsic rate of increase in a population with a birth rate of 100 per day and a death rate of 98 per day?

# ESSAY QUESTIONS

1. Describe the process of evolution by natural selection. How has the physical environment affected the history of life?
2. Compare and contrast density-independent regulation and density-dependent regulation.
3. How do humans affect the biosphere? Include the following in your discussion: population growth, population decline, population ranges, communities, the energy flow and productivity, and matter cycling.
4. Discuss the difference between closed and open structure communities. Why are most communities open structure? What is an exception to this?
5. List and briefly describe six major land biomes and two major aquatic biomes.

# SUGGESTED READINGS

Begon, M., J. Harper, and C. Townsend. 1990. *Ecology*, 2d ed. Cambridge, Mass.: Blackwell.

Cox, G. W. 1993. *Conservation ecology*. Dubuque, Iowa: W. C. Brown.

Freedman, B. 1989. *Environmental ecology*. New York: Academic Press.

Odum, E. P. 1993. *Ecology and our endangered life support system*, 2d ed. Sunderland, Mass.: Sinauer.

Primack, R. B. 1993. *Essentials of conservation biology*. Sunderland, Mass.: Sinauer.

Ricklefs, R. E. 1990, *Ecology*, 3d ed. New York: W. H. Freeman.

Smith, R. L. 1990. *Elements of ecology and field biology*, 4th ed. New York: Harper & Row.

# ENVIRONMENT: AN INTEGRATED SYSTEM OF FOUR SPHERES

## OUTLINE

## PROLOGUE    *Stardust and Caesar's Last Gasp*

*A* song about the famous Woodstock concert of the late 1960s said, "we are stardust, we are golden." Artistic metaphors aside, this is at least half true: all of us—and indeed all living things—are stardust. Many of the atoms in our bodies were forged by nuclear reactions in ancient stars over five billion years ago. The original Big Bang produced a universe containing only the two simplest elements, hydrogen and helium. Carbon, phosphorus, and all the heavier elements that comprise not only life but the Earth itself were formed from nuclear reactions produced by stars. Our "spaceship Earth" condensed, along with the rest of our solar system, from the remains of an exploded star.

The stardust that composes us and our global environment is always moving, always cycling. Because Earth is a relatively isolated island in space, the same matter is cycled over and over in ourselves and in our environment. Many of the atoms that composed your body as

PHOTO    *The Earth is an ancient entity. The air, land, sea and life have evolved together.* (*Source:* Frederic Edwin Church, *Cotopaxi* (1862). Oil on canvas, 48 in. x 7 ft. 1 in. Copyright © The Detroit Institute of Arts, Founders Society Purchase with funds from Mr. and Mrs. Richard A. Manoogian, Robert H. Tannahill Foundation Fund, Gibbs-Williams Fund, Dexter M. Ferry, Jr. Fund, Merrill Fund, and Beatrice W. Rogers Fund.)

a child are long gone, having been lost as new cells replaced dead cells. Atoms move through the environment in a similar fashion. A single oxygen atom that starts in molten magma may become an oxide molecule in a rock. A chemical reaction may release this atom into the atmosphere to form the oxygen we breathe. A famous chemical calculation illustrates the amazing extent of this "atomic recycling." Less than one-tenth of a cubic inch (one cubic centimeter) of air contains more than a billion billion molecules. Virtually every time you breathe, you may inhale some of the same air molecules contained in Julius Caesar's last gasp because the trillions of molecules he exhaled have had many hundreds of years to diffuse and mix into the global atmosphere.

We are recycled ancient stardust living out a tiny life span on an island of stardust that is five billion years old. When our lives are over, our atoms will once again join the dynamic, complex chemical web of our environment, and our descendants will inhale the atoms that we breathed.

# INTRODUCTION

Everything in the universe is either matter or energy. The four spheres (atmosphere, hydrosphere, lithosphere, and biosphere) are composed of matter in the gaseous, liquid, or solid states. Energy is what makes matter move. One of the most basic laws of physics is the **law of conservation of matter and energy**, which says that matter and energy cannot be created or destroyed. However, matter and energy can be *transformed* into different kinds of matter and energy. For example, gases condense to become liquid; oxygen reacts with iron to form "rust" (iron oxide). The amount of matter on Earth is finite, but it is constantly being recycled, changing from one form to another. Any matter in our environment, from resources to wastes, simply represents a temporary storage of matter in one place and in one form. Ultimately, physical processes (such as evaporation) or chemical processes (such as oxidation) will cause the matter to be transported or change its chemical environment in the Earth's dynamic system of cycles.

## Biogeochemical Cycles: An Introduction

When observing the cycles of matter such as water, rocks, nutrients, and other substances within and among the spheres, scientists often find it useful to focus on the cycles of chemical elements that compose those substances. This approach can be used to simplify our models of environmental cycles because just a few basic elements participate in many of the most important cycles on Earth. These cycles of chemical elements through the atmosphere, lithosphere, hydrosphere, and biosphere are called **biogeochemical cycles**.

Among the most important biogeochemical cycles are the six cycles that transport the six elements most important to life: carbon, hydrogen, oxygen, nitrogen, phosphorus, and sulfur. Of the approximately 90 elements that occur naturally on Earth, these six comprise the vast majority of atoms in the tissue of all living things. As ● Table 4–1 shows, oxygen alone accounts for more than 62% of the weight of the human body and more than 77% of the weight of the alfalfa plant. Carbon and oxygen together account for more than 80% of the weight of a human.

● Table 4–2 shows the relative abundances of the most common elements in the Earth's crust. Oxygen is the most abundant, just as it is most common in the human body. But the second most common human element, carbon, is hundreds of times rarer in the crust. Instead, silicon, which is virtually absent from the human body, is extremely abundant in the crust. You can see other major discrepancies by comparing Tables 4–1 and 4–2. These discrepancies illustrate how life is chemically distinct from its environment. Without biogeochemical cycles to transport and store temporary concentrations of matter for food and other uses, life could not survive.

| | **TABLE 4–1** *Atomic Composition by Weight of Three Representative Organisms* | | |
|---|---|---|---|
| ELEMENT | HUMAN | ALFALFA | BACTERIUM |
| Oxygen | 62.81% | 77.90% | 73.68% |
| Carbon | 19.37 | 11.34 | 12.14 |
| Hydrogen | 9.31 | 8.72 | 9.94 |
| Nitrogen | 5.14 | 0.83 | 3.04 |
| Phosphorus | 0.63 | 0.71 | 0.60 |
| Sulfur | 0.64 | 0.10 | 0.32 |
| Total | 97.90 | 99.60 | 99.72 |

**TABLE 4–2** *The Relative Abundance by Weight of Some Chemical Elements in the Earth's Crust*

| ELEMENT (CHEMICAL SYMBOL) | RELATIVE ABUNDANCE |
|---|---|
| Oxygen (O) | 46.6% |
| Silicon (Si) | 27.7 |
| Aluminum (Al) | 8.1 |
| Iron (Fe) | 5.0 |
| Calcium (Ca) | 3.6 |
| Sodium (Na) | 2.8 |
| Potassium (K) | 2.6 |
| Magnesium (Mg) | 2.1 |
| Phosphorus (P) | 0.07 |
| Carbon (C) | 0.03 |
| Nitrogen (N) | Trace |

Each of the many biogeochemical cycles has different pathways of transport and temporary storage reservoirs. The **carbon cycle** in ▬ Figure 4–1 is a typical biogeochemical cycle. Like many cycles, the carbon cycle, appears at first glance to be quite complex with many pathways (arrows), but closer inspection shows that these pathways are based on just two processes: withdrawal from and addition to the atmosphere.

1. *Withdrawal* of carbon is largely driven by **photosynthesis** whereby plants take carbon out of the atmosphere where it resides as carbon dioxide. The $CO_2$ is combined with water ($H_2O$) to form biochemical molecules such as sugars ($CH_2O$),

and oxygen. Photosynthesis is conveniently written as:

$$CO_2 + H_2O + energy \longrightarrow CH_2O + O_2$$

This reaction is called photosynthesis because it requires energy from the Sun (*photo* = light; *synthesis* = combine).

Figure 4–1 also shows two "loops" of photosynthesis. Loop 1 illustrates the pathway of "living" carbon in the ongoing photosynthesis of modern plants. Loop 2 shows how "fossil" carbon forms. Fossil carbon is carbon that has been temporarily withdrawn from use by living organisms by becoming buried and stored. Carbon is temporarily stored in the lithosphere, when plants, such as tiny plankton in marine and fresh waters, die and sink to the bottom. After millions of years of burial, these dead plants, and the carbon in them, can become fossil fuels such as petroleum. Similarly, clams and other ocean shellfishes withdraw carbon for use in constructing their shells. When the shellfishes die, their shells contribute to the vast amounts of limestone (▬ Fig. 4–2). Indeed, the large majority of the Earth's carbon now resides in the ocean. As ▬ Figure 4–3 shows, the ocean stores much more carbon than is found in the other three sinks—the atmosphere, lithosphere (geologi-

▬ **FIGURE 4–1**
The carbon cycle. Loop 1 is "living" carbon that is still actively circulating among living organisms and their environment. Loop 2 is "fossil" carbon; it consists of carbon that is bound in molecules such as coal deposits that are deeply buried until released by burning or some other process. Combustion (and respiration) and photosynthesis ultimately cause carbon to move through both cycles.

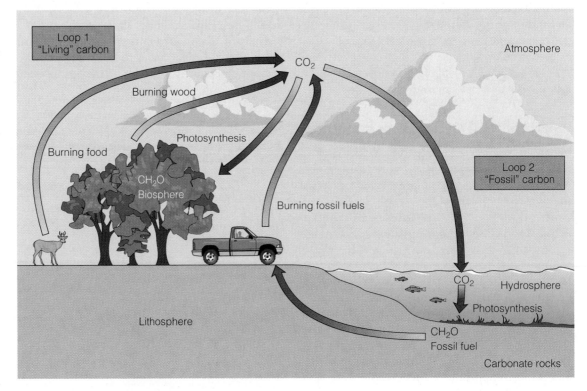

*E*NVIRONMENTAL PRINCIPLES     SECTION 1

**FIGURE 4–2**
Limestone, such as the white cliffs of Dover, is formed from shells of clams and other marine life. (*Source:* Laguna Photo/ Gamma Liaison.)

cal), and living organisms on land (terrestrial biosphere).

2. *Addition* of carbon to the atmosphere often occurs from combustion. As Figure 4–1 shows, combustion or "burning" is essentially the reverse of photosynthesis; oxygen ($O_2$) is combined with plant matter ($CH_2O$) to release $CO_2$ and $H_2O$:

$$CH_2O + O_2 \longrightarrow CO_2 + H_2O + energy$$

Setting fire to either living matter (loop 1) or fossil fuel (loop 2) will therefore release carbon dioxide. Similarly, when we digest food, we are carrying out combustion: our bodies take the oxygen we inhale and use it to break down the biochemical molecules we eat, such as plant foods. We then use the energy given off to move around, grow, and maintain our bodies. The carbon dioxide produced is exhaled into the atmosphere (loop 1). This process of biological combustion is called **respiration**.

## Biogeochemical Cycles: Major Features

The biogeochemical cycles as a group can be analyzed in terms of a number of important features. These features include the cycles' pathways, their rates of cycling, and the degree to which they are being disturbed by human activities.

*A Variety of Pathways*

Each biogeochemical cycle has *many different pathways*: many chemical and physical processes help to cycle each atom. For instance, the carbon cycle transports carbon through all four spheres. From the atmosphere, the carbon dioxide ($CO_2$ molecule) dissolves in water in the hydrosphere, where plankton use the carbon to build body tissue ($CH_2O$ molecule), thereby moving the carbon into the biosphere. When the plankton are buried and converted to fossil fuel, the carbon is converted to complex hydrocarbon molecules such as oil and becomes part of the lithosphere. When the oil is burned, the carbon is released back into the atmosphere where it may recycle through a different set of pathways. For instance, the $CO_2$ gas may be absorbed by a tropical tree the next time instead of by plankton.

Of course, each element has a different set of potential biogeochemical pathways. For example, unlike carbon, phosphorus generally does not cycle through the atmosphere because it does not easily form a gas. During its cycle, phosphorus often combines with different atoms than carbon does and therefore forms different molecules and undergoes different chemical reactions.

*Variable Rates of Cycling*

Biogeochemical cycles vary in their *rate of cycling*. Figure 4–4 shows the average amount of time

FIGURE 4-3

Major reservoirs of the carbon cycle, in billion tons of carbon. The oceans are the largest reservoir by far. (*Source:* W. M. Post, *et al.*, *"The Global Carbon Cycle,"* American Scientist 78 [1990]: 315. Reprinted by permission of *American Scientist.*)

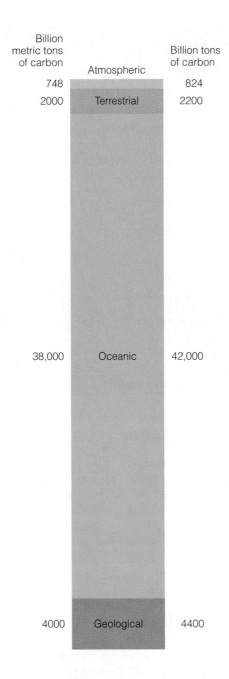

| Billion metric tons of carbon | | Billion tons of carbon |
|---|---|---|
| | Atmospheric | |
| 748 | | 824 |
| 2000 | Terrestrial | 2200 |
| 38,000 | Oceanic | 42,000 |
| 4000 | Geological | 4400 |

water, oxygen, and carbon dioxide molecules take to make a complete cycle through the four spheres. Clearly, cycling rates can vary drastically over many orders of magnitude. Carbon takes only hundreds of years to cycle whereas water takes about two million years. These times are only approximate because specific molecules may cycle much more rapidly or slowly depending on the pathway they follow. A small number of carbon atoms (fewer than 1 in 10,000) in the active, living loop, for instance, may be stored as oil deposits for over 200 million years and cycle through the much slower fossil loop.

Why do substances cycle at such different rates? Two major determinants are (1) the *chemical reactivity* of the substance and (2) whether it has a *gas phase* (occurs in the atmosphere) somewhere in the cycle. The high chemical reactivity of carbon causes it to participate in many chemical pathways and is a main reason why it cycles so quickly. In addition, carbon is abundant as the gas carbon dioxide. Because gas molecules move much more quickly than more tightly bonded molecules in liquids or solids, the existence of a gas phase allows the substance to be transported more rapidly.

Although oxygen and water cycle more slowly than carbon dioxide, they actually cycle at relatively fast rates compared to many other substances. Like carbon dioxide, oxygen and water are chemically reactive and have a major gas phase. For instance, the average water molecule has a **residence time** of 10 days in the atmosphere, where it may move thousands of miles (thousands of kilometers) before traveling back to Earth as a liquid.

Thus, to find a substance that has an extremely slow cycling time, we should look for one that has no gas phase and is also relatively unreactive in natural systems. Phosphorus is a good example because it not only has a very slow cycling rate but is one of the six most important elements of life and is therefore of much interest and very well studied. Because of its chemical and physical properties, phosphorus does not form a gas and does not readily combine with other substances. Its main mode of transport is water, which moves much slower than air, and even in water phosphorus is relatively insoluble. As ▇ Figure 4–5 shows, large amounts of phosphorus become "locked up" in storage for long periods of time as sediments in the deep ocean and the Earth's crust. Only relatively slow and rare events, such as upwelling ocean currents from the deep sea or weathering of phosphorus rich rocks, recycle the phosphorus.

Instead of the few hundreds to few millions of years typical of cycles with a gas phase, phosphorus requires many tens of millions of years to complete its biogeochemical cycle. This slow cycling rate drastically reduces the availability of this critical nutrient with profound effects for the biosphere. Phosphorus is usually the nutrient in shortest supply in most ecosystems and is therefore labeled the **limiting nutrient**. As we saw in Chapter 3, sudden availability of limiting nutrients in natural systems causes rapid growth.

## The Effects of Human Activity

Biogeochemical cycles are crucial to all life, but are being *greatly disturbed by human activity*. As human population and technology rapidly increase, huge quantities of materials are extracted through mining and other means and redistributed through all the spheres. The net result has been the disturbance of nearly all biogeochemical cycles. The most common type of disturbance is acceleration of the cycles: materials are being rapidly mined and otherwise extracted from storage reservoirs (sources) and, after use, are rapidly deposited back into the environment (sinks). This increased rate of cycling from source to sink leads to the two basic environmental problems: depletion and pollution (Chapter 1). Indeed, a basic definition of pollution is a temporary concentration of a chemical above levels that normally occur in its biogeochemical cycle.

No one really knows just how drastic or dangerous this acceleration of natural cycles will ultimately prove to be. No one doubts that major consequences will occur, however, and because biogeochemical cycles are global in nature, many of these consequences will occur on a global scale. Carbon provides a prominent example of how humans are actively disturbing a major cycle, with potentially drastic consequences. The burning of

fossil fuels, such as coal, petroleum, and natural gas, has released increasing amounts of carbon dioxide into the atmosphere. Figure 4–6a shows how global release of carbon has increased exponentially from about 1.1 billion tons (1 bil-

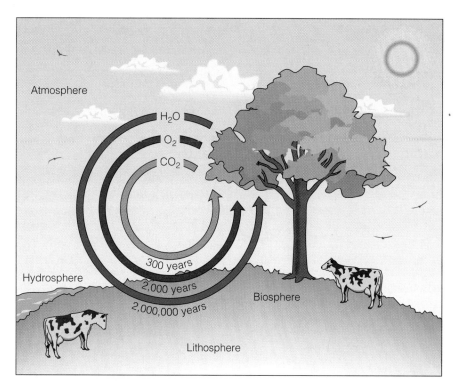

**FIGURE 4–4**

Recycling rates of water, oxygen, and carbon dioxide through the four spheres. (*Source:* L. Laporte, *Encounter with the Earth* [San Francisco: Canfield, 1975], p. 22. Modified by permission of Leo F. Laporte.)

**FIGURE 4–5**

(a) The global phosphorus cycle. The amount that flows on Earth is much smaller than the amount stored in rocks and sediment. (b) Phosphate is mined in Florida, and other areas, where ocean waters deposited phosphorus-rich sediments. (*Source:* (a) Adapted from D. Botkin and E. Keller, *Environmental Science: Earth as a Living Planet* [New York: Wiley, 1995], p. 63. Copyright © 1995 by John Wiley & Sons, Inc. Reprinted by permission of John Wiley & Sons, Inc.; (b) David Woods/The Stock Market.)

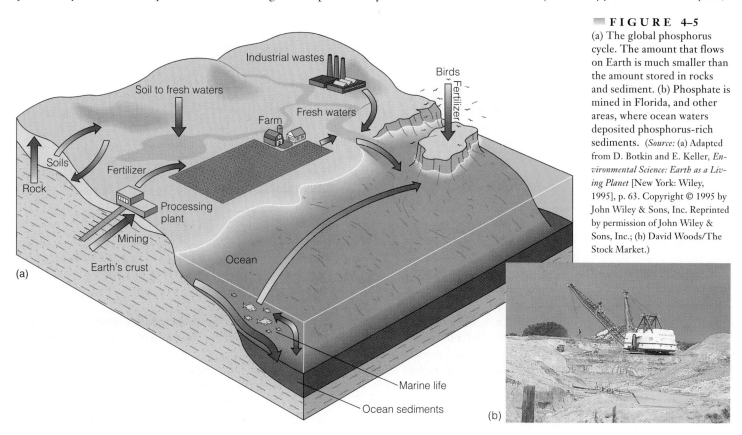

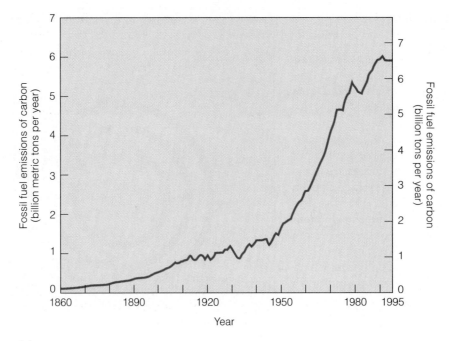

(a)

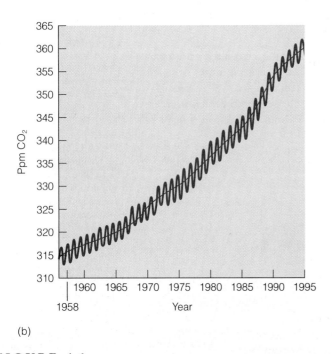

(b)

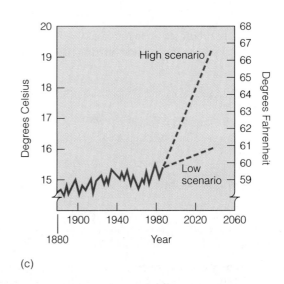

(c)

**FIGURE 4–6**

(a) Carbon from fossil fuel burning is increasing exponentially. (b) The rise of atmospheric carbon dioxide (ppm=parts per million) is correlated with (c) the rise of global temperature. Low and high scenarios represent possible future temperature, depending on predictive models and the assumptions they use. (*Source:* (a) W. M. Post *et al.*, "The Global Carbon Cycle," *American Scientist* 78 [1990]: 313. *Reprinted with permission of American Scientist.*)

lion metric tons)* per year in 1940 to an estimated 6.6 billion tons (6 billion metric tons) per year in the 1990s. It is estimated that about half of this 6.6 billion tons per year is absorbed by plant life and the oceans, but the remainder is accumulating in the atmosphere in the form of carbon dioxide (Fig. 4–6b).

This accumulation of atmospheric carbon dioxide has many potential global consequences. For example, many studies have shown that the rate of plant growth will generally increase from increasing photosynthesis. The most publicized

---

*Unless otherwise noted, *tons* refers to short tons (2000 pounds).

𝓔NVIRONMENTAL PRINCIPLES    SECTION 1

consequence is global warming. Carbon dioxide is a "greenhouse gas," meaning that it increases the ability of the atmosphere to trap heat. How much carbon dioxide can be added to the atmosphere before significant global warming will occur is much debated.

Figures 4–6c and 4–6b show that average global temperature has tended to increase along with carbon dioxide concentration, but conclusively proving that this is a simple cause-and-effect relationship is difficult. Nevertheless, many models project that major global warming will occur in coming decades under various scenarios. For instance, as developing countries industrialize, the global release of carbon will increase to an estimated 13.2 billion tons (12 billion metric tons) per year by the early twenty-first century if no attempt is made to switch to alternative (non-fossil) fuels, such as solar energy. Indeed, if all the fossil fuels (such as petroleum and coal) on Earth were burned, the atmospheric carbon dioxide concentration would increase by an estimated 10 times, or 1000%, its current level. So far, atmospheric carbon dioxide has risen only 30–40% above its level in the early nineteenth century. We will see in Chapter 18 why global warming is a matter of much concern: it can have profound effects on agriculture, sea level, and many other aspects of life.

Although the consequences of disturbing the carbon cycle are especially dramatic, all of the many dozens of biogeochemical cycles are increasingly being disturbed by humans. Some examples include excess phosphorus, which causes runaway plant growth in natural waters; nitrogen emissions, which contribute to smog; and sulfur emissions, which cause acid rain. These and other disturbances are discussed in detail in later chapters.

## Energy Flows

The **first law of thermodynamics** says that energy cannot be created or destroyed, but can be transformed. The **second law of thermodynamics** says that when energy is transformed from one kind to another, it is degraded, meaning that the energy becomes less capable of doing work. For example, only about 30% of the chemical energy in gasoline is converted to the energy of motion in a car. Similarly, photosynthesis uses solar energy to create food from carbon and other atoms. Food represents chemical energy, which is stored in the bonds between atoms, so photosynthesis is a transformation from solar to chemical energy. As ▬ Figure 4–7

shows, this transformation is far from 100% efficient. Most of the incoming energy is "lost" as heat. Heat is considered to be low-quality energy and is capable of doing less work than high-quality energy.

**Entropy** refers to the amount of low-quality energy in a system. If entropy is very high, matter will tend to disorganize to simpler states. The second law of thermodynamics is sometimes called the *law of entropy* because all energy transformations will increase the entropy of a system unless new high-quality energy, such as sunlight, enters the system to replenish it. Later in the chapter we discuss how the Earth and all living things rely on such replenishment to resist entropy and maintain high levels of organization.

Some energy transformations are more efficient than others. By carefully refining our technology, humans have managed to achieve much greater efficiencies. For example, the best solar (photovoltaic) cells convert as much as 30% of sunlight to electricity. Other examples of energy conversion are the use of nuclear energy to generate electrical energy and the conversion of gasoline (chemical energy) into mechanical energy ("energy of motion"). In each of these and all other energy transformations, however, engineers long ago accepted that no matter how advanced our technology, some loss of usable energy will always occur, if only a few percent.

Because of this loss, energy cannot be recycled like matter. Ultimately, all the energy in a system will become relatively useless (transformed to heat) unless new energy flows into the system. Thus, we say that matter cycles, but energy must flow from one source to another. On Earth, the vast majority of new energy flows from the Sun. This energy originates with nuclear reactions at the Sun's core and travels as light energy across

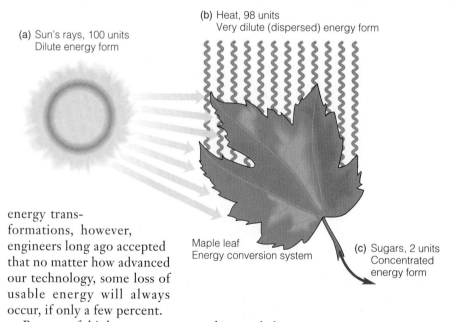

**■ FIGURE 4–7**
The two laws of thermodynamics. The first law is illustrated by the conversion of Sun energy (a) to food (chemical) energy (c). The second law dictates that heat loss (b) during conversion causes the amount of usable food (chemical) energy to be less than the Sun energy. In this case, it is much less. (*Source:* E. P. Odum, *Ecology and Our Endangered Life Support Systems* [Sunderland, Mass.: Sinauer 1989], p. 70. Reprinted by permission of Sinauer Associates, Inc.)

**(a)** Sun's rays, 100 units
Dilute energy form

**(b)** Heat, 98 units
Very dilute (dispersed) energy form

Maple leaf
Energy conversion system

**(c)** Sugars, 2 units
Concentrated energy form

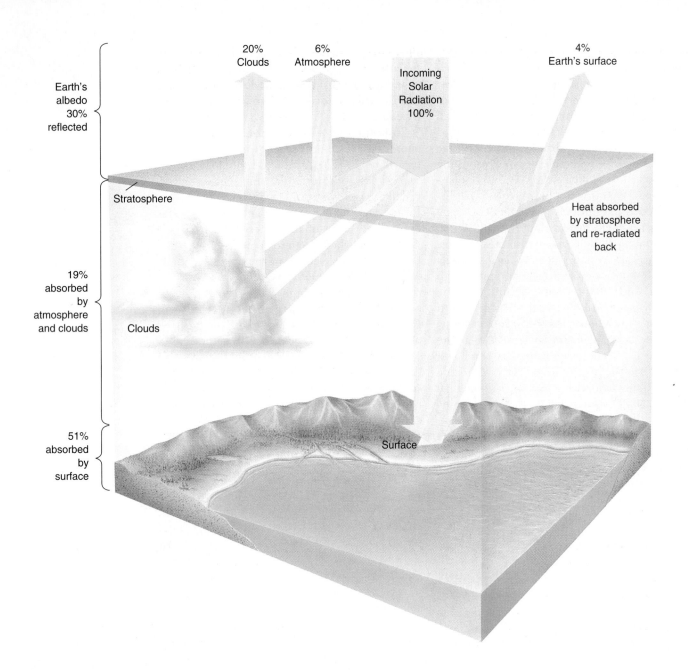

**20%**
Clouds

**6%**
Atmosphere

Incoming
Solar
Radiation
**100%**

**4%**
Earth's surface

Earth's
albedo
**30%**
reflected

Stratosphere

Heat absorbed
by stratosphere
and re-radiated
back

**19%**
absorbed
by
atmosphere
and clouds

Clouds

**51%**
absorbed
by
surface

Surface

███ **F I G U R E  4–8**
Thirty percent of the solar
radiation striking the Earth is
immediately reflected back
into space; 51% is absorbed
and radiated into space as
heat. The remaining energy
creates wind and drives the
water cycle, photosynthesis,
and other processes.

93 million miles (150 million km) to strike the
Earth. Upon striking the Earth, the energy is
transformed in many ways, depending on where
it strikes. Collectively, the various flow pathways
of all energy on Earth are called the Earth's **energy budget** ( ███ Figure 4–8). Thirty percent of
the incoming light is directly reflected back into
space, especially by white clouds. Another 51% is
absorbed and reradiated back into space as heat.
The remaining energy powers the hydrologic
cycle by evaporation, generates wind, powers
photosynthesis, and in general drives many of the
cycles within and between the spheres that we discussed earlier. Photosynthesis, for all its importance in sustaining most life on Earth, including
humans, uses a tiny fraction, just 0.06% of solar

radiation. And given the inefficiency of photosynthesis, much of this is wasted.

Actually, not all of the Earth's energy comes
from the Sun. A small fraction comes from two
other sources. One is the Moon's gravitational
pull, which causes tides in the ocean. This tidal
energy is thousands of times less than the amount
of energy provided by the Sun. The second
source of energy is the Earth's own internal geothermal energy, which is generated by radioactive minerals deep within the Earth. The heat dif-
fuses outward to the Earth's surface and melts
rocks to drive the tectonic cycle of the lithosphere
and the emission of volcanic gases into the atmosphere. It also produces the heat that creates
deep-sea vents in the ocean floor, where hot

magma provides nutrients and energy to rich marine communities.

### Human Use of Energy Flows

Humans are using ever-greater amounts of the energy flows on Earth. Modern civilization is built upon fossil fuels, which are fossilized plant materials that store solar energy from millions of years ago as chemical energy. Because they take so long to form, fossil fuels are called **nonrenewable resources**. If rates of use continue to rise, most estimates indicate that the world supply of oil will be used up within the next 100 years and world coal supplies within 300–400 years. Besides depletion, another problem with fossil fuels is the release of pollutants. Almost *all major air pollution*, including acid rain, smog, carbon monoxide, and greenhouse gases, is caused by burning fossil fuels. Although many of these pollutants can be controlled by smokestack devices, fuel cleansing, and other technical solutions, there is no economical way of removing the carbon because so much is produced. Burning just a gallon (3.785 liters) of gasoline produces over 20 pounds (9 kg) of carbon dioxide, and coal produces even more. Fossil fuels also cause many other pollution problems, such as seepage from storage tanks into groundwater and ocean spills.

Instead of using "fossilized" solar energy, it would be less damaging to use the solar energy flow as it strikes the Earth today. Because the Sun will last about five billion more years, solar energy will not soon be depleted, and the potential supply is vast. In just one month, the Earth intercepts more energy from the Sun than is contained in all the fossil fuels on the planet. Solar energy, along with tidal energy, is a form of **renewable energy**.

## $O$ VERVIEW: THE ENVIRONMENT AS A SYSTEM

As we have seen, the environment consists of four spheres, and matter cycles and energy flows through these spheres. A system approach will provide a convenient overview of this information.

### What Is a System?

A **system** is technically defined as a "set of components functioning together as a whole." A system view allows us to isolate a part of the world and focus on those aspects that interact more closely than others. For example, a cell in the system we call a human body generally interacts much more closely with other cells in the body than with the outside world. By focusing only on those cells that function in digestion, we confine our view further, to the digestive system. The key point here is that most systems are *hierarchical:* they are composed of smaller sets of systems made of smaller interacting parts.

## Three Key Traits of the Environmental System

We can analyze the global environment in terms of three system traits: openness, integration, and complexity.

**Openness** refers to whether a system is isolated from other systems. An **open system** is not isolated in that it exchanges matter or energy with other systems. A **closed system** is isolated and exchanges nothing.

The law of entropy means that energy cannot be recycled. Therefore, any system that does not have a renewing supply of energy from outside will eventually cease to exist. Not surprisingly then, the Earth is an open system in terms of energy. Figure 4–9 shows how energy flows from the Sun and is often radiated back into space. In contrast, the Earth is a closed system in terms of matter. If we discount the relatively tiny amount of matter added from meteorites and other space debris, the Earth contains all the matter it will ever have. Driven by energy from the Sun, this matter cycles over and over among the four spheres, often moving back and forth among the gas, liquid, and solid states, and participating in the metabolism of living things. Issues in Perspective 4–1 describes an attempt to create a closed system that would imitate the Earth.

**Integration** refers to the strength of the interactions among the parts of the system. For instance, the human body is a highly integrated system whose cells are interdependent and in close

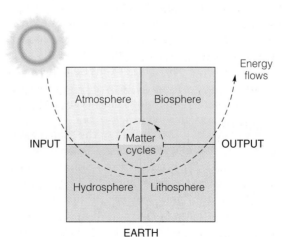

■ **FIGURE 4–9**
The Earth is open to energy, which flows into and out of it. Essentially, however, the Earth is closed to matter, which cycles over and over through the four spheres.

# Biosphere 2: A Microcosm of Earth

In September 1991, the experimental Biosphere 2 project was colonized for the first time by a team of four women and four men. Located outside Tucson, Arizona, in the Sonoran Desert, this self-contained closed ecosystem was the first facility of its kind designed to simulate Biosphere 1—our Earth. Its goal, simply put, was to create a "working substitute" of our world ( Fig. 1).

The double-laminated, glass-and-steel complex, described as "like an octopus with lumps," reaches 85 feet (26 m) at its highest point and encompasses five biomes including rainforest, desert, marsh, and ocean. Its colonists or "biospherians" were to reside in Biosphere 2 for a period of two years. During that time, they were to perform the duties necessary to maintain their environment as well as conduct research into the complex interactions found there. The plan called for large-scale recycling, with the biomes removing carbon dioxide and pollutants from the "atmosphere" in addition to releasing oxygen into the "atmosphere." All waste water was to be recycled as well. Within the 3.15-acre (1.27-hectare) complex, the biospherians planned to grow a wide variety of food crops. Designed to be totally self-sustaining, Biosphere 2 proved to be more complex than anticipated.

One of the first problems to arise was an overabundance of carbon dioxide with a subsequent decrease in oxygen levels in Biosphere 2's atmosphere. Later determined to be due to the oxidizing bacteria in the compost-rich soil, the problem forced one of the biospherians to use an oxygen mask almost nightly, and a carbon dioxide scrubber had to be installed. This addition was controversial because Biosphere 2 was supposed to be a closed system. The team also had to cope with a decline in productivity of their agricultural crops that caused all eight biospherians to lose weight. On average, the male biospherians lost in excess of 25 pounds (11 kg) in six months. The decline in productivity was attributed largely to more cloud cover than had been expected and pest-related crop damage. In addition, the biospherians had to spend more time than anticipated maintaining the health of the biomes. Difficulties ranged from an overgrowth of algae on the ocean reef to "rogue species" consuming ocean species or choking terrestrial plant species. Additionally, the plant pollinators began dying off; forcing, the biospherians to assume the role of pollinator as well. All in all, they had little time left for scientific research.

The shortage of scientific research coming out of Biosphere 2 aroused considerable controversy within the scientific community. The main area of contention was whether the project should be viewed holistically so as not to "test for effects individually," as was currently the method; or whether "a detailed, laid-out plan" of hard science should be used. Those who favored the "holistic" approach said Biosphere 2 should be allowed to "evolve" on its own while observations were made of its progress. Those wanting a more systematic research plan felt that the project's full potential as a living laboratory was being wasted. Finally, Edward P. Bass (underwriter of this $150 million project) and his co-planners opted for a more rigid scientific approach; they replaced the Bio-

communication. The loss of certain cells, such as those composing the heart or brain, can result in death of all the other cells in the system (the whole organism) because the cells are so interdependent. At the other extreme are systems with very weak integration, such as the cells in a colony of single-celled organisms (like the green algae, *Volvox*). Removal of many cells will have little effect on the remaining cells because they are less dependent on each other.

The degree of integration of the global environmental system is under debate. At one extreme are scientists who argue that the global system is a *superorganism*: the lithosphere, hydrosphere, atmosphere, and biosphere are intimately interconnected by many complex pathways. According to this **Gaia hypothesis**, the Earth is similar to an organism, and its component parts are so integrated that they are like cells in a living body. Many scientists, however, believe that the global environment is less integrated than the Gaia hypothesis argues. This does not mean that the environment is "unconnected" or even as weakly connected as a colony of cells. We have already seen that many kinds of matter cycles and energy flows interconnect the spheres and cycle within the spheres as well. As  Figure 4–10 shows, the true level of integration in the global system is probably somewhat less than a "superorganism" but considerably more than a loose collection of independent parts, such as a sponge (a sponge can be considered a colony of semi-independent

sphere 2 management team in August 1994 and initiated a new non-profit joint venture with Columbia University's Lamont-Doherty Earth Observatory. The operation would be headed by such renowned scientists as Wallace Broecker, a critic of the prior management team as well as a Lamont-Doherty geochemist.

Despite their problems, the biospherians could point to some major accomplishments. During the initial two-year period, Biosphere 2 lost only 9% of its atmosphere per year, 100% of the waste and water was recycled, and the biospherians produced 80% of their food supply. Upon review, such biomes as the marsh, coral reef, and ocean were found to be healthy.

In early March 1994, a second team of biospherians entered the Biosphere 2 facility. Based on their predecessors' results,

the new team made a few changes. This time, oxygen is being continually added to the system. Special plant species, which have a higher capacity to absorb carbon dioxide, have been added, as have shade-tolerant food crop species and pest-control species (toads and geckos) to make the agricultural plots more productive.

Problems and controversy aside, the Biosphere 2 project illustrates the intricate complexity of a closed system. It has implications for our own unique Biosphere 1—the Earth.

cells). Because the system is so vast and the interconnections so complex, the exact position of the Earth system on the "integration gradient" of Figure 4–10 will probably be the topic of much debate for many years.

**Complexity** is often defined as how many kinds of parts a system has. This definition conforms to our intuition: a tiny insect seems more complex to us than a large rock because it has many more "parts." The insect has more complex molecules, and these are used to construct cells and organs. This example also illustrates that complexity is often hierarchical, with smaller components being used to construct larger ones.

As you would expect, the environment is enormously complex. The four spheres, with their

matter cycles and energy flows, have trillions of different components operating at many spatial and temporal scales. Organisms, soils, rainwater, air, and many other components interact in complicated ways. Even the individual spheres are complex. Even with advanced computers, no one has been able to predict the weather, or even climate, very far in the future because the atmosphere is so complex. Indeed, the many interactions make unpredictability a basic characteristic of complex systems. This inability to predict how the environment will respond to changing conditions is perhaps the major reason for so much controversy and inaction over environmental problems. Issues in Perspective 4–2 examines some methods for studying complexity.

The four spheres are not a loose collection of living and nonliving things, as a cell colony can be (on the right). But neither are the four spheres a tightly integrated "superorganism." Instead the four spheres and the Earth system are somewhere between these two extremes (perhaps analogous to a jellyfish), with a moderate degree of interdependence (toward the left).

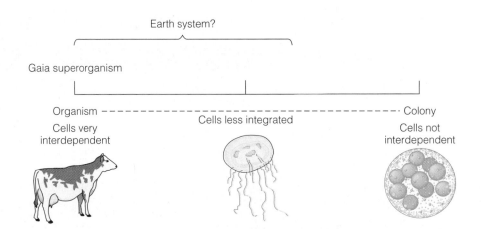

Earth system?

Gaia superorganism

Organism — — — — — — — — — — — — — — — — — — — — — — — — — — — — — — — — Colony
Cells very                                    Cells less integrated                                    Cells not
interdependent                                                                                          interdependent

### Major Obstacles: Delayed and Unpredictable Impacts

Unfortunately, social responses to environmental problems are greatly hindered by two of the key traits of the environmental system: its moderate integration and high complexity. Any system that is integrated, such as the environment, can transmit disturbances from one part of the system to another (■ Fig. 4–11). Integration results from connectedness so that resource depletion or pollution of one part of the environment can have cascading, or domino, effects into other parts. For example, removal of one species in an ecosystem will often affect the abundance of many other species, such as those that prey on or compete with it. Burning sulfur-rich coal affects the atmosphere as air pollution, but it also affects the hydrosphere when it falls as acid rain to acidify lakes. The biosphere is also affected because aquatic organisms in the lake can die from the more acidic lake water. The burning coal can even affect the lithosphere when the acid rain dissolves limestone and other alkaline rocks to form caves and sinkholes. This example shows how just one activity, burning coal, can affect all four spheres of the environment. Such wide-ranging cascading effects are anything but rare as we will see in later

■ **FIGURE 4–11**
The Mississippi River illustrates many delayed, unpredictable impacts by humans. Building of dams, for instance, has greatly reduced sediment flow into the Gulf of Mexico leading to beach erosion in many areas. (*Source: Science VU/Visuals Unlimited.*)

# Systems and Chaos Theories: Ways to Study Complexity

Studying complex systems can be difficult because they have many parts that often interact in different ways. Over the last few decades, researchers have developed several methods of studying complexity. Systems theory and chaos theory, for example, try to produce general "laws" of complexity. Such laws would not only make complex systems more understandable, but they would allow us to predict more accurately how these systems will behave. Think how important such predictions could be in a complex system like the stock market or the weather!

Unfortunately, none of these theories has been entirely successful in providing a complete understanding of complexity or producing accurate predictions of how any complex system will behave. For example, despite thousands of studies and computer models, no one knows what exactly will happen to the stock market or the biosphere on a certain day in the future. Nevertheless, these theories have provided a better idea of how complex systems will generally behave under a given set of conditions. Thus, we have a general understanding of how a lake ecosystem will respond to excess nutrients even though we cannot specify every event.

Systems theory (or general systems theory) was one of the first widely used attempts to find "laws" of complex systems. It grew rapidly in the late 1940s during the boom in automation and information technology, so it has traditionally focused on how systems are regulated and become unregulated. Systems theory treats a complex system as a "black box" with inputs and outputs (as in Chapter 1). Such a system is kept at equilibrium by negative feedback processes, defined as processes that counteract perturbations. An example is a thermostat that turns a furnace on to produce heat when a house is cold and turns on air conditioning when it is hot. In contrast, positive feedback processes amplify perturbations. For example, a cooling global climate can cause more snow to remain on the ground, which leads to more global cooling because the snow reflects sunlight back into space. This causes yet more snow, and so on (a snowball effect).

Systems theory has been widely used as a convenient scheme to classify processes, such as positive feedback. However, it has often been criticized as too general or vague because by treating a system as a "black box," the theory omits many of the details of how the system operates. Therefore, more recent efforts to study complex systems have focused on more mathematical, rigorous descriptions of them. One theory that has received much attention is chaos theory. A chaotic system is one whose workings are extremely sensitive to even the slightest change: just the slightest perturbation can become greatly amplified through positive feedback. The classic example is the weather, as first described by E. Lorenz who helped discover chaos theory in the early 1960s. Lorenz created a set of equations that precisely described atmospheric conditions and showed how even tiny changes in one of the parameters could cause a massive alteration of the weather in a few days. This is often called the "butterfly effect" by analogy with the idea that a butterfly flapping its wings in South America could eventually affect the weather in North America ( Fig. 1). By creating tiny changes in atmospheric turbulence, which in turn create cascading effects on larger air flows, the butterfly could have a major impact. (Of course, the chances that it actually will produce such a major impact are extremely low.)

Chaos theory's most important finding so far is that even simple systems, such as several atoms, often have chaotic properties. Consequently, predicting their precise behavior very far into the future is nearly impossible. How can we make predictions when a minute unseen change, as in the butterfly effect, can have cascading effects? Many theorists think it will always be impossible to accurately predict precise future behaviors in complex systems, which have even more potential for chaos than simple systems. Nevertheless, by applying chaos theory, patterns of regularity can be discerned and studied.

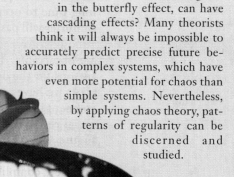

**FIGURE 1**

Can a butterfly in the rainforest affect the weather in North America? (*Source:* Kjell B. Sandved/Visuals Unlimited.)

# DEMOGRAPHY

PHOTO   *A street scene in Dhaka, the capital of densely populated Bangladesh.* (*Source:* AP/Wide World Photos.)

$\mathcal{T}$he current world population of more than 5.8 billion is cause for concern among many environmentalists. Population is one of the major factors in the I = PT (impact equals population times technology) equation that we discussed in Chapter 1. For most of history, the world's population grew only very slowly or not at all, but in the last two hundred years, it has exploded. In the late 1960s, the world population was growing at a record rate of about 2% a year, and some pessimists feared the worst—massive famine, disease, wars, civil unrest, and widespread global ecosystem collapse. Fortunately, these dire predictions have not come to pass. Due to various factors, the world population growth rate declined to about 1.75% in the 1980s and currently stands at about 1.6–1.7%. Nevertheless, even if the **growth rate** continues to decline, there will still be an estimated 8 to 10 billion people on our planet by the middle of the twenty-first century ( Fig. 5–1). Will the world be able to feed, clothe, and house all these people? And can it be done in a sustainable manner? These are major issues of our time.

The United Nations has held major intergovernmental conferences on world population every 10 years since 1974. The first conference suggested that the solution might be the rapid industrialization of the developing nations where most of the rapid population increases were occurring. The participants reasoned that since fertility rates in Europe dropped to or below replacement level after the Industrial Revolution, the same should occur as developing nations industrialize and modernize. Researchers have since questioned whether industrialization really causes a population to stabilize. Correlation does not necessarily mean causation. Furthermore, could the world sustain the potential ecological destruction that might be involved in fully industrializing all of the developing world?

The 1984 United Nations population conference emphasized increasing access to modern family planning technologies and information, including contraceptives. To a large extent, such methods have paid off with results. Worldwide contraceptive use increased from 30% in 1970 to 55% in 1990, and the average family size dropped from 4.9 to 3.5 children. Yet it is unclear how much progress can be made via increased access to family planning information and modern contraceptives.

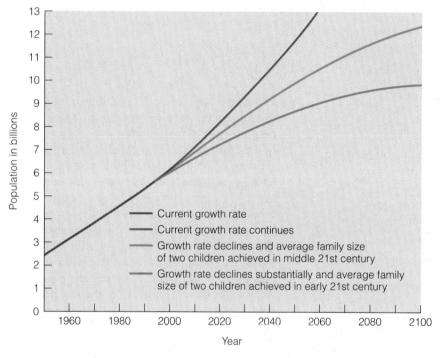

**FIGURE 5–1**
World population projections into the twenty-first century. (*Source:* Based on U.N. data and projections found in World Resources Institute, *World Resources 1992–1993* and *World Resources 1994–1995* [New York: Oxford University Press, 1992, 1994].)

Furthermore, these are emotionally, politically, and religiously charged issues. Many people associate modern family planning, rightly or wrongly, with advocacy of abortion, a practice seen by some as morally repugnant. At the 1984 conference, the U.S. government, under the Reagan administration, objected to any kind of family planning that might include the possibility of abortion and cut off funding of international groups that provided abortion counseling (funding was restored in 1993 by the Clinton administration). The Vatican opposes any forms of contraception or abortion, as do many fundamentalist Islamic groups.

Indeed, such objections made headlines during the 1994 world population conference in Cairo. The Roman Catholic church objected to much of the original language in draft documents associated with the conference, and Islamic religious leaders and scholars called for a boycott of the conference. In fact some Muslim countries, such as Saudi Arabia, Lebanon, and Sudan, withdrew their delegations.

Still, productive ideas came out of the population conference, as the interrelationships among population, poverty, inequality among individuals and nations, environmental decay, and sustainable development were discussed. No longer can population, or overpopulation, be viewed simply as a cause of environmental destruction; rather it must be viewed as a major symptom of underlying social, economic, and environmental issues. Poverty, high fertility, and environmental degradation go hand in hand, each reinforcing the other. Studies in developing countries have demonstrated that as natural resources are depleted, people perceive a need for more children to help gather increasingly scarce fuel wood, obtain clean water, or perform other necessary tasks; consequently, birth rates rise. But as a result, there are fewer resources to go around, and the people are trapped in a downward spiral. Educating women, decreasing poverty, conserving resources, and reversing environmental degradation all have the effect of depressing population growth rates. A major focus of the 1994 population conference was women's education and status. In recent years, researchers have confirmed that as women's literacy rate and social status increase in many developing regions, the fertility rate decreases.

The United Nations has stated that the low status of women is the "root cause" of population growth and poverty in many developing countries. As women's access to education increases, so does their value in the workplace and their social status. Rather than having more children, many women use their newfound education and status to improve the quality of life for the children they have. And educating the women of the world is relatively inexpensive. Estimates are that raising the education level of all women in developing nations to at least equality with men would cost only $6.5 billion per year, less than is spent on lawn care annually in the United States, and much less than is spent on video games each year in the industrialized nations.

# INTRODUCTION

Currently, approximately 5.8 billion people are inhabiting the face of our planet. Over 10,000 people are added each hour, over a quarter million persons a day. The global population is increasing by approximately 90 to 100 million persons a year. **Demography** is the study of the size, growth, density, distribution, and other characteristics of human populations.

Earth is now a very crowded planet. Only about 4.9–9.9 billion acres (2–4 billion hectares) of the Earth's approximately 37 billion acres (15 billion hectares) of land surface are potentially suitable for human cultivation, the rest being too cold, too wet, or too dry for human purposes. In actuality, only about 3.7 billion acres (1.5 billion hectares) are cultivated. Given our current population, this means only about 0.64 acre (not even a third of a hectare) of cropland is available per person. Furthermore, the amount of land per person is declining yearly as the human population increases, cultivatable lands are eroded and destroyed, forests are cleared, and grazing land is overworked.

Human overpopulation is one of the central issues in environmental science. As noted in Chapter 1, high population levels increase both major types of environmental problems: (1) resource use and (2) pollution and waste. For example, our species alone utilizes, either directly or by diverting it from other uses, an estimated 40% of the world's terrestrial green plant production. The other 60% is divided among the remaining 5 million to 50 million terrestrial species with which we share the globe.

In this chapter we will review the early development of human society, trace the initially slow and subsequently **exponential growth** of the human population, and begin to explore the ways in which human population pressure has progressively modified the environment. We will also briefly discuss what is being done to address the current "population crisis."

# WORLD POPULATION CHANGES OVER TIME

As discussed in Chapter 3, natural animal populations often exhibit an "S-shaped" growth curve—slow growth ("**lag phase**"), then rapid growth ("exponential phase"), then slowing down as limits are reached, and finally leveling out. The same curve can be applied to human populations. On a global scale, the human population is still in the rapid growth phase.

## Starting Slow: The "Lag Phase"

About one million years ago, the total human population was only some 125,000. From this small size, the population slowly increased until by about 8000 B.C., it numbered about 5 to 10 million ( Fig. 5–2). This slow increase was due to (1) the invention and development of tools

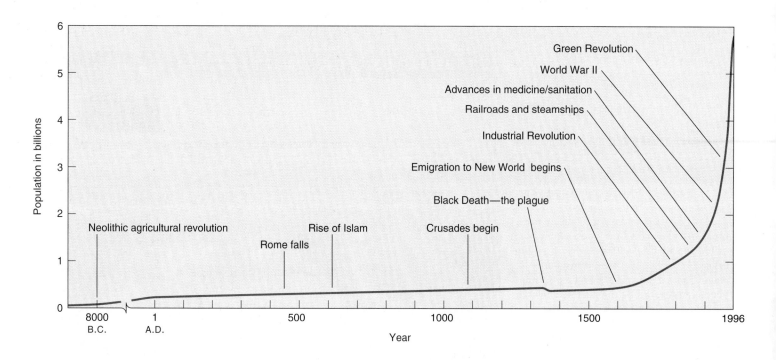

**FIGURE 5–2**
World population changes over time.

which enabled food and other necessities to be procured more efficiently and thus allowed more people to be supported in the same area, and (2) migration to new areas, as from the Old World to the Americas. Although we tend to focus on chipped stone tools because they are most readily preserved in the archaeological record, many organic tools (woven nets, baskets, clothing, tents and other shelters) also were invented. Also "discovered" and used during this period was fire—to heat, cook food, and scare away potentially harmful predatory animals.

Before 10,000 years ago, humans had spread through most of the world, reaching all of the mainland landmasses except Antarctica and the islands of the Caribbean, Polynesia, Madagascar, and New Zealand, all of which were colonized subsequently. This simple spread of people to new areas allowed the world population to increase.

The extent to which early humans impacted and permanently modified their environments remains a hotly debated topic. Some researchers believe that through overhunting and competition for environmental resources, the Upper Paleolithic hunters of Europe, Africa, Asia, and the Americas were responsible for global patterns of extinction among large mammals, such as the woolly mammoth and the woolly rhinoceros, during the later Pleistocene (around 100,000 to 10,000 years ago).

In relatively small, isolated ecosystems, such as those found on islands, it is now well documented that gatherer and hunter cultures can cause a number of species to go extinct. Within a few hundred years of the settlement of Madagascar by gatherers and hunters, a pygmy hippopotamus and a large flightless bird had gone extinct. The orginal colonists of New Zealand, also a gathering and hunting people, drove several dozen birds to extinction within 600 years of entering the island.

Another way that early humans may have modfied their environments was by setting fires. Setting forests on fire could both have made hunting easier by clearing the brush and also increased the populations of hunted herbivorous mammals, which would have thrived on the new growth of plants that would sprout up in cleared areas. Over the course of time, periodic fires would greatly modify the vegetational types in the area.

Thus, human modification of the environment is nothing new; many habitats that we think of as "natural" may in fact be the product of human intervention over tens of thousands of years. What is new in the late twentieth century is the extent, degree, and rate at which humans are modifying their environment—much quicker than we or the rest of nature can adapt to the new conditions.

## The Agricultural (Neolithic) Revolution: Beginning Exponential Growth

The advent of domestication and agriculture about 10,000 years ago led to a sharp rise in the human birth rate for reasons discussed below. Though often referred to as the **agricultural (Neolithic) revolution**, this was actually a gradual process that extended over eight or more millen-

# The Plague

In the mid-fourteenth century Europe, as well as much of Asia and Africa, was devastated by an outbreak of plague, which contemporaries called the Black Death ( Fig. 1). The disease actually took three forms: bubonic plague, pneumonic plague, and septicemic plague (all caused by the bacterium variously known as *Pasteurella pestis* or *Yersinia pestis*). It is estimated that at least 25 million, and perhaps as many as 75 million, of Europe's population of 100 million died between 1347 and 1351. As the plague raged, the social structure of Europe was destroyed. Contemporary accounts report that government and law enforcement, religious ceremonies, and medical practice disappeared in areas where the plague was worst. In an ecological sense, the plague can be viewed as a classic case of a density-dependent mechanism that served to limit the population. Six and a half centuries later, it should serve as a warning to us as we continue to overcrowd our world.

Modern research suggests that the fourteenth-century plague may have originated among the wild rodents that live in the Kirghiz Steppes of Asia, one of several apparently permanent reservoirs of plague (others are in China, India, the southern

**FIGURE 1**

Victims of the Black Death appear in this fourteenth-century French fresco. A physician lances a plague-caused bubo (a swollen and inflamed lymph node) on a woman's neck; on the left is another victim with an enlarged bubo under his arm. (*Source:* The Granger Collection, New York.)

former Soviet Union, and the western United States). Under normal conditions, the plague does not spread beyond these reservoirs, but occasionally it does—with devastating effects. In the early fourteenth century, a major outbreak ravaged China,

nia and occurred independently at different rates in different parts of the world. Full domestication of many plants and animals seems to have been established in the Old World by 8000–5000 B.C. Once agriculture and domestication were entrenched, the delicate near balance between births and deaths, which had apparently held for hundreds of millennia, was broken, and the world's human population began to increase dramatically (see Fig. 5–2). By A.D. 1 the world population had increased to between 150 million and 300 million, and cities such as Rome had populations as high as one million. By contrast, the world population

had taken a million or more years to reach a total of, at most, 10 million people.

The dramatic increase in human population has been attributed to several factors: (1) Settlement on farms may have allowed women to bear and raise more children for, without the nomadic lifestyle, they no longer had to carry young offspring for great distances. Previously, women may have chosen to raise fewer children, perhaps using natural contraceptives and practicing primitive forms of abortion or infanticide to get rid of unwanted offspring. (2) Children are more useful in agricultural communities than in hunter and

India, and other eastern and Middle Eastern populations, killing millions. The plague spread west, and rumors of the terror spread even more quickly.

In the mid-fourteenth century, the city of Genoa in Italy controlled the Crimean port of Caffa on the Black Sea, which was attacked by Mongolian Tartars (Tatars) who had traveled west across Asia from the Kirghiz Steppes. While laying siege to Caffa, the Tartars began to die of a strange disease, characterized by fever, delirium, pneumonia, and in some cases enlarged, pus-filled, lymph nodes (buboes) that opened to the skin and drained spontaneously. The Tartars decided to withdraw, but before leaving, they catapulted the bodies of their dead comrades into the city—an early and particularly gruesome instance of biological warfare. The inhabitants of Caffa subsequently contracted the plague, and when infected Genoese returned to Italy in 1347, they carried the disease to Europe.

Medieval Europeans had no idea what caused the plague or how to control it. It is now known to be caused by a bacterium that can be carried by rodents, such as rats and squirrels, and is transmitted from rodents to humans by a flea. For tens of thousands, or even millions, of years, populations of *Yersinia pestis* have been living in the guts of fleas that feed on rats and infect them with the plague. Once the rat dies, the fleas seek another host, carrying with them the plague bacilli. Eventually, the plague-carrying flea also dies, but often not before it has infected other mammalian hosts and thus indirectly other fleas that feed on the same host. In the case of Caffa, rats probably fed on the bodies of the dead Tartars and became infected, fleas fed on the rats, and the fleas subsequently bit and infected humans.

Even today bubonic plague is not well understood—and isolated cases and small outbreaks continue to occur among humans. Why does it remain contained among rodent colonies for centuries, then suddenly and unexpectedly spread at an alarming rate among the human population? And why does the outbreak subside? Do only individuals who have some type of natural resistance to the plague remain? Are reservoirs of plague perhaps always in waiting, ready to spread when conditions are right? Unfortunately, we may not know what those "right" conditions are.

We should remember that, even with our advanced medical knowledge and technology, we could conceivably find ourselves again facing an unknown or poorly understood, but rampant and devastating, disease. Some would even suggest that the current AIDS (Acquired Immune Deficiency Syndrome) crisis is a roughly analogous situation. In fact, a 1994 report compiled by the U.S. Census Bureau's Center for International Research predicted that AIDS could have a significant impact on death rates and population sizes in many countries, including Uganda, Zambia, Zaire, Brazil, Haiti, and Thailand. For instance, according to the center's projections, if AIDS did not exist, Uganda, Thailand, and Brazil would be predicted to have populations of 49.8 million, 76.6 million, and 210.5 million, respectively, in 2020, but incorporating AIDS mortality their respective populations are expected to reach only 34.1 million, 62.9 million, and 197.5 million in 2020. Moreover, AIDS could devastate the economies of some poorer nations. Increased resources will need to be directed toward caring for people with AIDS, and as AIDS continues to spread, the productivity of the workforce will decrease.

---

gatherer cultures and therefore more highly valued. This would have increased the incentive to have more children. (3) Agriculture and domestication may have made softer foods available, which allowed mothers to wean their children earlier. Thus women could bear additional children over the course of their lifetimes. (4) Agriculture and domestication, by their very nature, allowed and promoted higher densities of people. Indeed, with farming one family or group of persons could raise more food than they personally needed. This surplus led directly to the rise of cities and civilization because it allowed people to develop and concentrate on manufacturing, trading, and other specializations. In a classic example of positive feedback, this in turn led to rapid advances in technology, art, and other innovations.

After late ancient times, the world's population slowly but steadily increased, except for a slight decline in the fourteenth century due to the plague (see Fig. 5–2 and Issues in Perspective 5–1), until the mid-seventeenth century when it totaled approximately 500 million. Since about 1650, the human population has grown at an ever increasing rate, reaching 800 million around 1750, 1.2 billion in 1850, slightly over 2.5 billion

# Thomas Malthus, the Original Population Pessimist

The English political economist Thomas Robert Malthus (1766–1834) is generally credited with being the first modern pessimistic thinker concerning population growth rates and the overpopulation problem. Indeed, the term **neo-Malthusian** is often used to refer to those who believe that the modern rapid increase in human population is extremely detrimental. Neo-Malthusians generally believe that we will run out of resources and seriously damage or destroy our environment unless we can control our breeding.

In his *An Essay on the Principle of Population, as It Affects the Future Improvement of Society* (1798, revised and enlarged in 1803), Malthus suggested that while the size of a population increases geometrically or exponentially, the means that support the population tend only to increase arithmetically; thus, increasing populations invariably outstrip their resource bases ( Fig. 1). As this occurs, the poor get poorer and more desperate, leading to misery and vice. If humans do not intervene of their own accord, such as through "moral restraint" (restraint in breeding),

**FIGURE 1**
A "Malthusian view" of an overcrowded London of the future is shown in this 1851 George Cruikshank etching. (*Source:* The Granger Collection, New York.)

then the population increase will ultimately be checked by natural means, such as widespread famine, disease, and possible warfare. Although Malthus did not necessarily advocate direct birth control, he did suggest that early marriages should be avoided and self-restraint should be cultivated. Most neo-Malthusians are strong proponents of accessible birth control and family planning services.

Since his *Essay* first appeared, Malthus's ideas have been widely discussed—both admired and heavily criticized—and have greatly influenced subsequent generations. The effects of his writings have been profound in economic, political, social, and biological circles. It was from reading a version of Malthus's *Essay* that Charles Darwin hit upon the idea of natural selection and "survival of the fittest" as the major mechanism underlying biological evolution.

---

layer, have been taking place on a global level. Some observers have interpreted these changes as indicating that we have finally reached, and perhaps begun to exceed, Earth's carrying capacity for humans.

## Growth Rate and Doubling Time of the World's Human Population

Many demographers are concerned that the human population growth rate has generally been increasing; the doubling time for the human population has been getting smaller and smaller. Between 10,000 years ago and A.D. 1650, the **annual growth rate** was less than 0.1% a year for a doubling time of over 1000 years. Between 1650 and 1850, however, the human population doubled again, reaching one billion in the mid-

dle of the nineteenth century. This was a doubling time of only 200 years, or an average annual growth rate of about 0.35%. In the next 80 years or so, the population doubled again, giving an average annual growth rate approaching 0.9%. In the late 1960s and into the 1970s, the annual growth rate hovered around 2.0%, and thus the doubling time was about 35 years. An annual growth rate of 2.0% may seem small, but it is enormous—especially in comparison with the annual growth rate during the vast majority of human history and prehistory. The human species has been adding more and more individuals at a faster and faster pace (study Figure 5–2 closely).

During the 1970s and 1980s, the annual rate of growth of the world's population began to decrease slightly, from about 2.0% per year to approximately 1.7% in 1987. For 1988, however, the annual growth rate rebounded to nearly 1.8%. For the period 1985 to 1990 (the latest for which accurate statistics exist), the average annual growth rate was 1.74%. Currently, it may actually be as low as 1.6%.

Today the world population stands at 5.8 billion, and opinions differ as to where it will stand in the future. In 1988 the United Nations predicted a global human population of 6.25 billion in the year 2000. If the growth rate continues at about 1.7%, there will be over 28 billion humans on Earth by the end of the twenty-first century. On the other hand, current projections, based on a declining growth rate, suggest that the world population will be approximately 8.5 billion in 2025. If we could stabilize at two children per family by 2015, then the world population might stabilize at about 9.3 billion in 2095. If it takes until 2060 to arrive at an average of two children per family, then the world population will perhaps stabilize at about 14.2 billion in the year 2120. Considering the current status of global family planning, and extrapolating what advances can be reasonably expected over the next century, many demographers have recently suggested that the global human population may top out at 11 or 12 billion sometime around the year 2100.

## DISTRIBUTION OF THE EARTH'S HUMAN POPULATION

The present human population is distributed somewhat unevenly over the Earth ( ▬ Fig. 5–3) —even more so in terms of access to and use of resources. A select few tend to be moderately to very well off, while the many lead mediocre, marginal, or substandard existences. Likewise, such basic statistics as infant mortality, **crude birth** and **death rates**, longevity, and so on vary widely from country to country.

Of the 5.8 billion people on the planet in 1996, 59.7% live in Asia (exclusive of the former Soviet Union), 13% in Africa, 9% in Europe, 7.3% in North and Central America, 5.5% in South America, 5% in the former Soviet Union, and 0.5% in Oceania (including Australia and New Zealand). More important perhaps is that in 1996 approximately 1.2 billion people live in **more developed countries** or **MDCs** (basically the countries of North America, Europe, Japan, Australia, New Zealand, and the former Soviet Union), whereas the remaining 4.6 billion people live in **less developed countries** or **LDCs**. As ▬ Figures 5–4 and 5–5, page 123, show, past and predicted future changes in population size are unevenly distributed among the continents and between the MDCs and LDCs. Whereas the population growth curve for Europe is essentially flat, it is sharply rising for Asia and Africa.

The population of the MDCs as a whole is increasing only very slightly; indeed, Austria, Belgium, and Italy have achieved zero population growth, and the populations of Germany and Hungary are declining. As a whole, the industrialized countries of the world have about a 0.4% growth rate. In contrast, the population of the LDCs is surging; as a whole, the developing world has a 2.0% growth rate. If the UN projections are correct, the world population will reach some 8.5 billion by 2025; of the 3.2 billion increase between 1990 and 2025, over 3 billion will be added to the LDCs ( ● Table 5–1). Furthermore,

**TABLE 5–1** *Population Size and Projections for Major World Regions, 1950–2025*

| Region | POPULATION (MILLIONS) | | | | | PERCENT SHARE OF WORLD POPULATION | | | | |
|---|---|---|---|---|---|---|---|---|---|---|
| | 1950 | 1970 | 1990 | 2000 | 2025 | 1950 | 1970 | 1990 | 2000 | 2025 |
| **World total** | **2516** | **3698** | **5292** | **6261** | **8504** | **100.0** | **100.0** | **100.0** | **100.0** | **100.0** |
| Industrialized countries | 832 | 1049 | 1207 | 1264 | 1354 | 33.1 | 28.4 | 22.8 | 20.2 | 15.9 |
| Developing countries | 1684 | 2649 | 4086 | 4997 | 7150 | 66.9 | 71.6 | 77.2 | 79.8 | 84.1 |
| Africa | 222 | 362 | 642 | 867 | 1597 | 8.8 | 9.8 | 12.1 | 13.8 | 18.8 |
| North America | 166 | 226 | 276 | 295 | 332 | 6.6 | 6.1 | 5.2 | 4.7 | 3.9 |
| Latin America | 166 | 286 | 448 | 538 | 757 | 6.6 | 7.7 | 8.5 | 8.6 | 8.9 |
| Asia | 1377 | 2102 | 3113 | 3713 | 4912 | 54.7 | 56.8 | 58.8 | 59.3 | 57.8 |
| Europe | 393 | 460 | 498 | 510 | 515 | 15.6 | 12.4 | 9.4 | 8.1 | 6.1 |
| Oceania | 13 | 19 | 26 | 30 | 38 | 0.5 | 0.5 | 0.5 | 0.5 | 0.4 |
| Former Soviet Union | 180 | 243 | 289 | 308 | 352 | 7.2 | 6.6 | 5.5 | 4.9 | 4.1 |

(*Source:* World Resources Institute, *World Resources 1992–93* [New York: Oxford University Press, 1992], p. 76. Copyright © 1992 by The World Resources Institute. Reprinted by permission of Oxford University Press, Inc.)

**FIGURE 5-3**

Map of world population densities. Note that one square kilometer equals approximately 0.386 square mile, thus a population density of 10 persons per square kilometer equals approximately 26 persons per square mile.

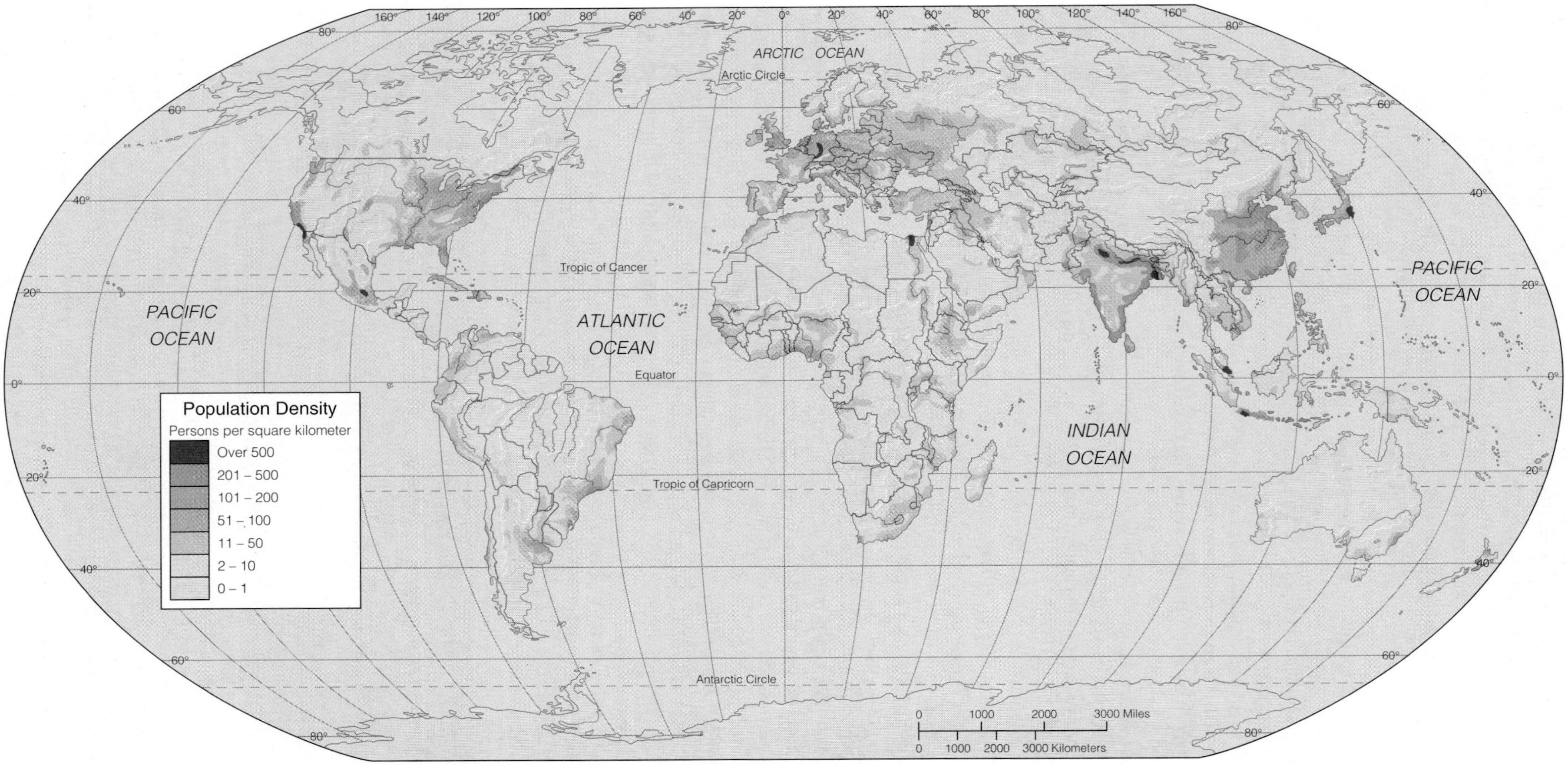

**Population Density**

Persons per square kilometer

Over 500
201 – 500
101 – 200
51 – 100
11 – 50
2 – 10
0 – 1

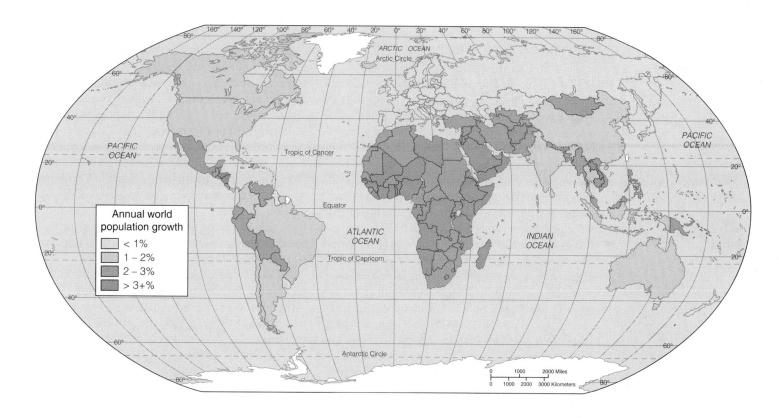

much of the estimated growth in the developed world will occur in the United States.

In 1996, 77% of the world's population lives in LDCs; in 2025, 84% will live in LDCs. These numbers are not incompatible with the estimate that currently only 16% of the world's people live an affluent American-like lifestyle, while 50% do not have adequate food or other necessities, and 34% live in extreme poverty. Such disparities may increase in the future.

**FIGURE 5-4**
Average annual population growth rates around the world in the 1990s. (*Source:* Based on data from World Resources Institute, *World Resources 1994–95* [New York: Oxford University Press, 1994], Table 16.1, pp. 268–269.)

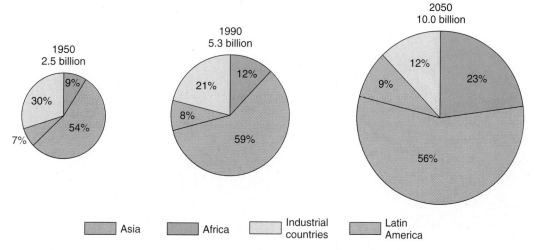

**FIGURE 5-5**
The shifting balance of the world's population by region, 1950–2050. Note that virtually no growth in the population of the present industrial countries is predicted between 1990 and 2050, yet the size of the world's population will continue to increase. Therefore, people of those industrial countries will account for a much smaller percentage of the world's population in 2050. In contrast, the populations of Asia and Africa will increase sharply, with the highest growth rates occurring in Africa. In 2050 the number of Asians could be greater than the number of all people on Earth in 1990. (*Source:* Reprinted with permission from Wade Roush, "Population: The View from Cairo." *Science* 265 [August 26, 1994]: 1166. Copyright 1994 American Association for the Advancement of Science.)

# AGE STRUCTURES

When comparing populations between different countries and regions, one must consider the **age structures** or the population **age profiles**. The age structure of a particular population is essentially a frozen profile of the population at any one instant ( Fig. 5–6); the age structure of a population will often change over time.

There are two common patterns in age structures. A typical Western industrialized country, which is an example of an MDC, has a relatively flat or uniform age structure profile (Fig. 5–6a); that is, in each age category from about age 0 to 30 or older, there are approximately the same number of people (of course, as people get much older than 50, their numbers drop off dramatically as they die of old age). In comparison, a typical LDC (Fig. 5–6b) has an age profile that is strongly skewed toward the younger categories, indicating that there are many more younger people than older people. The United Nations currently projects that in the year 2025, 18% of the populations of the MDCs will be under age 15, and 19% will be over 64, so the ratio of young to old will be about 1 to 1. In 2025, the LDCs will have 26% under age 15, and only 8% over 64, setting the ratio of young to old at 3.25 to 1.

In absolute numbers, a population that is skewed toward the young will continue to grow even as the birth rate falls. In fact, the **fertility rate** of a population can drop to, or below, the replacement fertility rate (approximately 2.1 children per woman; see Issues in Perspective 5–2), yet the population will continue to increase in size for some time. As the population ages, more women will reach their reproductive years (generously regarded as 15 to 49 years in many UN statistics) and bear offspring. Thus, even as each woman, on the average, may have fewer children, many more women will be having children. In contrast, a flat age structure profile combined with replacement fertility will result in stable population numbers. As individuals age and move from one age category to the next, and ultimately to death, they will be replaced by equal numbers of individuals being born.

It is useful to take two-dimensional age structure profiles and plot them into three-dimensional graphs, the third dimension representing time ( Fig. 5–7). Such a diagram summarizes the major trends in a population over the period of time it covers. A three-dimensional age structure chart also helps us to visualize earlier population events and see how they may affect later events. Note that a diagonal on such a chart (see Fig. 5–7) represents a single cohort (or group born within the same time period); as the members of a given cohort age, they move to higher age groups. In other words, individuals who fall in the 0–5-year age interval at one particular time will be the individuals who will compose the 6–10-year age interval 5 years later, the 11–15-year age interval 10 years later, and so on. Figure 5–7 presents selected three-dimensional

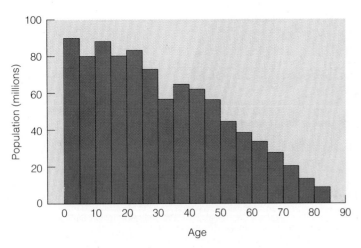

(a) More developed regions

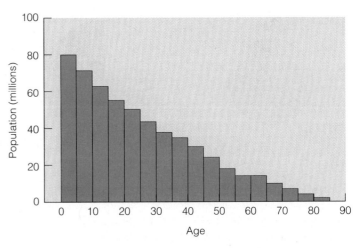

(b) Less developed region

### ■ FIGURE 5–6

Examples of age structure profiles in two dimensions: (a) a typical more developed region; (b) a typical less developed region, such as Latin America. An age structure profile for a particular population records the relative numbers of people in different age categories, in these cases by five-year intervals (0–5 years, 6–10 years, 11–15 years, 16–20 years, and so on). (*Source:* World Resources Institute, *World Resources 1990–91* [New York: Oxford University Press, 1990], p. 50. Copyright © 1990 by The World Resources Institute. Reprinted by permission of Oxford University Press, Inc.)

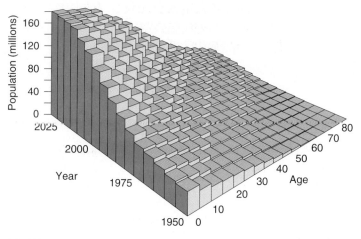

(a) Africa

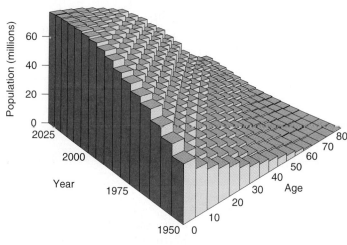

(b) Latin America

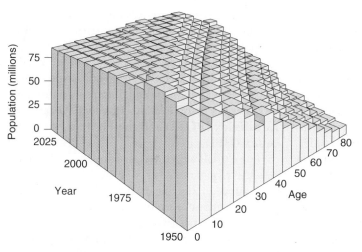

(c) More developed regions

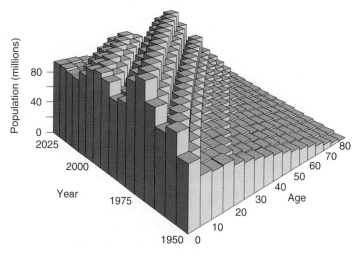

(d) China

age structure profile diagrams for various parts of the world, and  Figure 5–8 shows the age structure profiles for the world as a whole in 1995 and the year 2050 (estimated projection).

# THE CONSEQUENCES OF OVERPOPULATION

Rapid population growth and overpopulation have many far-reaching effects ecologically, economically, and societally. The increasing population is putting a greater and greater burden on the Earth's natural resource base and environment. As Paul Ehrlich (1988, p. 305) points out:

> One can think of our species as having inherited from Earth a one-time bonanza of nonrenewable resources. These include fossil fuels, high-grade ores, deep agricultural soils, abundant groundwater, and

the plethora of plants, animals, and microorganisms. These accumulate on time-scales ranging from millennia (soils) to hundreds of millions of years (ores) but are being consumed and dispersed on time-scales of centuries (fuels, ores) or even decades (water, soils, species).

Most people readily acknowledge that fossil fuels, such as oil and coal, are nonrenewable. However, many fail to realize that, from the human perspective, soils and much fresh water that is pumped from underground aquifers are also nonrenewable resources (see Chapters 11 and 13). Topsoils are being eroded at a tremendous rate, and in many regions the water table is being drawn down to alarmingly low levels. Another example is phosphorus, an extremely important element that is mined from nonrenewable rock deposits primarily in order to make modern fertilizers. A 1971 study concluded that known supplies of phosphorus would be exhausted by

**FIGURE 5–7**
Three-dimensional age structure diagrams for various regions, 1950–2050. (a) Africa; (b) Latin America; (c) more developed regions; (d) China. (*Source:* World Resources Institute, *World Resources 1990–91* [New York: Oxford University Press, 1990], pp. 52, 53, 54. Copyright © 1990 by The World Resources Institute. Reprinted by permission of Oxford University Press, Inc.)

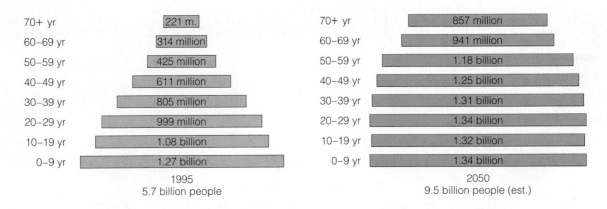

| 70+ yr | 221 m. |
| 60–69 yr | 314 million |
| 50–59 yr | 425 million |
| 40–49 yr | 611 million |
| 30–39 yr | 805 million |
| 20–29 yr | 999 million |
| 10–19 yr | 1.08 billion |
| 0–9 yr | 1.27 billion |

1995
5.7 billion people

| 70+ yr | 857 million |
| 60–69 yr | 941 million |
| 50–59 yr | 1.18 billion |
| 40–49 yr | 1.25 billion |
| 30–39 yr | 1.31 billion |
| 20–29 yr | 1.34 billion |
| 10–19 yr | 1.32 billion |
| 0–9 yr | 1.34 billion |

2050
9.5 billion people (est.)

**FIGURE 5–8**
Age structure profiles of the world as a whole in 1995 and 2050 (estimated projection). (*Source: U.S. News and World Report,* September 12, 1994, p. 58. Copyright, Sept. 12, 1994, *U.S. News & World Report.*)

2100, and that without phosphate fertilizers the Earth can support only one to two billion people.

Not only are we very quickly depleting resources, but we are also destroying ecosystems (as exemplified by deforestation and desertification), causing massive species extinctions, and irretrievably altering our environment by dumping greenhouse gases into the atmosphere (Chapter 18) and destroying the Earth's ozone layer. Later chapters will examine the consequences of these actions in detail.

Such ecological damage is not solely a function of more people. Given the discrepancies in affluence and technology among the Earth's peoples, not everyone impacts equally on the environment (remember the equation I = PT from Chapter 1). Persons in rich, industrialized countries (the MDCs) typically cause much more ecosystem damage per capita than persons in poor, nonindustrialized countries (LDCs). Based on such considerations, Paul Ehrlich has suggested that one new American baby and 250 new Bangladeshi babies pose an equal threat to the environment. The United States contains less than 5% of the world's population, yet consumes approximately 25% of the world's energy resources and produces about the same percentage of the world's pollution. Likewise, U.S. citizens consume approximately 12 times as much energy per capita as the average citizen in a developing country.

Generally, a country's quality of life decreases as its birth rate increases. Overpopulated countries and nations with quickly expanding populations tend to be characterized by low gross national product (GNP) per capita and high infant mortality rates. The poorest nations tend to have the highest population growth rates, but are least equipped to deal with increasing numbers of people. For example, a nation with a population growth rate of 3% (typical of some LDCs) will double its numbers in about 24 years. Simply to maintain the meager standard of living of its citizens, such a country must double its physical in-

frastructure (buildings, factories, roads, sewers, energy grids, and so on), as well as its production, agricultural output, medical and social services, and employment opportunities within the same amount of time. That would be a very difficult task for a rich nation, much less for an LDC. The inevitable result is that as the population increases, the per capita standard of living is lowered.

How does one measure quality of life? Widely applied criteria include single statistics such as the GNP per capita and the infant mortality rate. Other indices include the **Physical Quality of Life Index (PQLI)** and the **Human Suffering Index (HSI)**.

The PQLI, which was developed by the Overseas Development Council in the late 1970s, rates a country on the basis of the average life expectancy, infant mortality, and literacy rates of its citizens. Countries with low birth rates tended to have high PQLI rankings, whereas countries with high birth rates typically fell low on the PQLI scale.

More comprehensive is the HSI developed by the Population Crisis Committee in the 1980s. This index is the summation of a number of different ratings, such as the GNP per capita, food sufficiency, inflation, accessibility of clean drinking water, literacy, energy consumption, growth of the labor force, urbanization, and political freedom. The HSI scale ranges from 0 to 100, such that a rating of 0 to 25 is the minimal "human suffering" range, 25 to 50 indicates moderate suffering, 50 to 75 high suffering, and 75 to 100 indicates extreme suffering. Figure 5–9 shows the HSI for various nations; note that the higher the annual population increase, the higher the HSI. It is important to note that approximately 70% of the world's population lives in countries in Asia, Africa, or Latin America with suffering indices of 50 or higher and average annual population increases of 2.8%.

Rapid population growth and overpopulation lead to increased urbanization, increased unem-

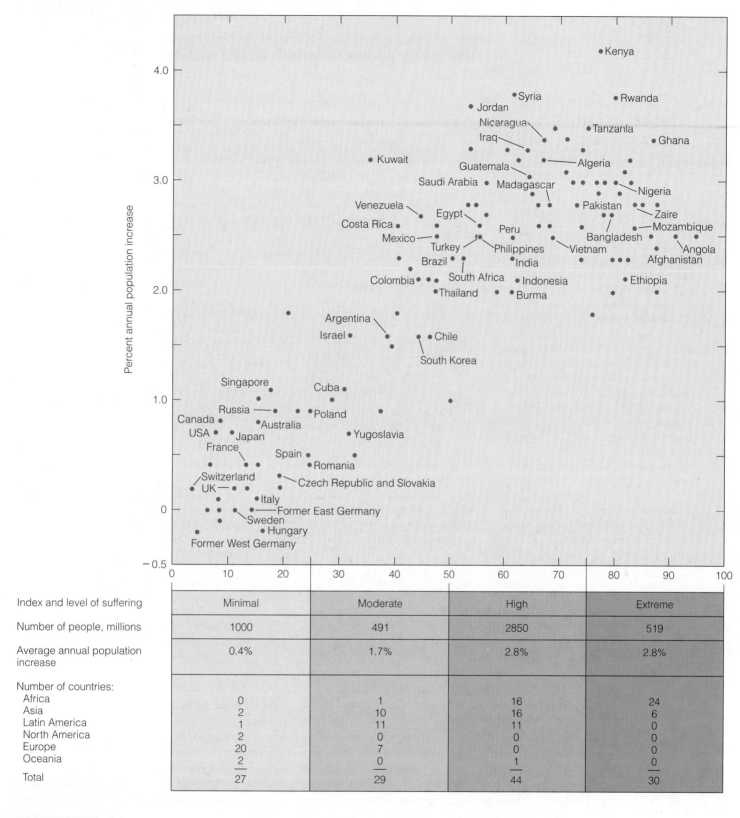

| Index and level of suffering | Minimal | Moderate | High | Extreme |
|---|---|---|---|---|
| Number of people, millions | 1000 | 491 | 2850 | 519 |
| Average annual population increase | 0.4% | 1.7% | 2.8% | 2.8% |
| Number of countries: | | | | |
| Africa | 0 | 1 | 16 | 24 |
| Asia | 2 | 10 | 16 | 6 |
| Latin America | 1 | 11 | 11 | 0 |
| North America | 2 | 0 | 0 | 0 |
| Europe | 20 | 7 | 0 | 0 |
| Oceania | 2 | 0 | 1 | 0 |
| Total | 27 | 29 | 44 | 30 |

### ▀ FIGURE 5–9

Population growth and human suffering. There is a strong correlation between the level of human suffering and the rate of population growth. Unfortunately, over half of the world's people live in countries characterized by high or extreme human suffering. (*Source:* S. L. Camp and J. J. Speidel, *The International Human Suffering Index* [Washington, D.C.: Population Crisis Committee, 1987]. Reprinted with the permission of Population Action International [formerly Population Crisis Committee].)

# *Urbanization*

The last two hundred years have seen a strong global trend toward **urbanization**. In about 1800, only 3% of humanity could be classified as urban. By 1950 this number had risen to approximately 30%, and in 1990, 43% of all people lived in cities. Some commentators refer to this movement from country to city as the "urban revolution." In some developed nations, almost everyone can be classified as "urban." In the former West Germany in 1990, for example, the urban portion of the population constituted 94% of the total. Although the majority of the world's people are still rural dwellers, if present trends continue, soon the urbanites will overtake the ruralists; it is projected that in 2025 the urban population will amount to 60% of the world's total population.

Although the first genuine cities arose about 8000 to 6000 years ago and some ancient cities such as Rome at its height had populations as large as a million, large cities were rare until the twentieth century. Even as late as the year 1900, only 13 cities had populations of over one million (Chicago, Philadelphia, New York, London, Paris, Berlin, Vienna, St. Petersburg, Moscow, Beijing, Shanghai, Calcutta, and Tokyo; see ▬ Fig. 1). Today over two hundred cities contain more

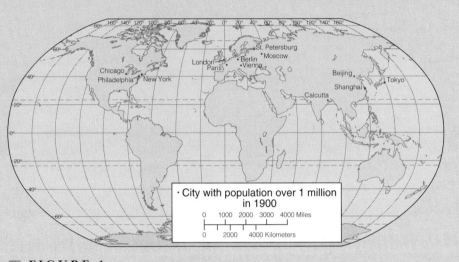

▬ **FIGURE 1**
Major cities with populations over 1 million in 1900.

than a million people ( ▬ Fig. 2), and by the end of the century, more than two dozen are expected to exceed 10 million. One of the largest is Mexico City with a 1990 population of over 20 million and a projected population of nearly 28 million for the year 2000.

The **megacity** with a population of more than 10 million people is a twentieth-century creation. As a city's population grows, it spreads out along the edges into the surrounding countryside,

giving rise to **suburban** sprawl. Lower land prices on the edge of the city may attract commuters who still go into the city center daily for employment. Slowly, residential suburbs push further and further away from the city center, and shopping centers and malls, theaters, and medical facilities, not to mention schools, churches, and post offices, are built to service the suburban residents. Soon people living in the suburbs may rarely venture into the heart of the city at all; they can find every-

ployment, and spreading poverty. Projections indicate that 60% of the world's population will live in urban areas by 2025 (see Issues in Perspective 5–4). In the developing world, many cities are growing at phenomenal rates and to phenomenal sizes (● Table 5–2, page 130), but much of the growth is in the form of slums, shanty towns, and squatter settlements that lack such necessities as adequate housing, safe drinking water, and proper sanitation systems.

Increasing population pressures lead to political instability and political and civil rights abuses. Population growth leads invariably to competi-

tion for limited resources, often culminating in outright armed conflict. This may take the form of increasing local crime and violence, particularly among various ethnic and racial groups, some of whom may have voluntarily migrated or been forcefully displaced due to increasing population pressures. Sometimes the conflict escalates to actual warfare, primarily domestic civil wars. There have been more than 20 million war-related deaths in the world since 1945, and over 75% of these came in domestic civil wars. The majority of these deaths have occurred in highly populated countries. Bangladesh, with one of the highest

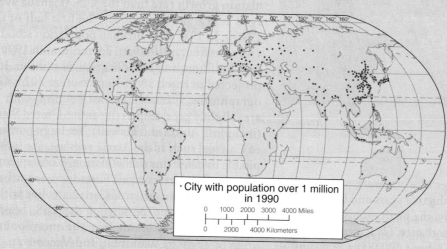

**FIGURE 2**

Major cities with populations over 1 million in 1990.

reach international status. An example is Rome, which since its humble origins nealy three thousand years ago has exerted a major influence on much of Western history as both the capital of the Roman Empire and the city that houses the Vatican (an independent city-state within the city of Rome), home of the head of the Roman Catholic church. For two thousand years, Rome has been a major center of culture and learning. Other major cities have been planned virtually from scratch and therefore never went through the stages of village, town, and small city. An example is Canberra, the capital of Australia. Its outlines were designed by the American Walter Burley Griffin (1888–1937) as a "garden city" emphasizing public open space. Although officially inaugurated in 1911, much of Canberra was not constructed until the 1950s and later.

City centers may decline as the suburbs develop and expand. As the population moves away from the center, the core of the city may deteriorate until eventually low land prices attract businesses and developers once again. A large city may go through stages of growth, stagnation, and rejuvenation.

thing they need without leaving suburbia. As the suburbs of large cities expand outward, adjacent cities and their suburbs may meet and begin to merge, forming a vast network of adjacent urban and suburban communities (sometimes referred to as a conurbation), until they become a single vast urban area, the **megalopolis**. The term *megalopolis* was first coined to describe the almost continuous urban and suburban sprawl in the northeastern United States from Boston, through New York City and Philadelphia, down to Washington, D.C. Examples of megalopolises can now be found throughout the world; for instance, in the Netherlands, Amsterdam, Leiden, The Hague, Rotterdam, and Dordrecht all run together, and in Japan the Tokyo-Yokohama complex forms a megalopolis.

Cities may rise and fall. Some cities grow slowly, progressing from the village stage, to the town stage, to the small city stage, and gradually grow larger until they

population densities in the world, accounts for 1.5 million of these deaths. Likewise, since 1994, hundreds of thousands of people have died as a result of civil strife in Rwanda.

# THE POPULATION OF THE UNITED STATES AND CANADA

The current population of the United States is approximately 270 million, just under 5% of the world's population. Although the total fertility rate is currently about 2.1 (as described in Issues in Perspective 5–2, 2.1 is generally accepted as **replacement level** fertility) and the average completed family size is 1.9 children, the population is still growing by approximately 2.5 million every year, in part due to **immigration**. During the first half of the 1990s the U.S. annual growth rate averaged slightly over 1%, faster than that of most industrialized countries. In fact, the most recent data indicate that the United States may be undergoing a small baby "boomlet."

The continued growth of the U.S. population is primarily attributable to two factors: (1) The current age structure of the population is such oping countries view family planning as genocide, for the developed, industrialized nations are encouraging the undeveloped and developing nations to curtail their populations. Many African governments have traditionally opposed family planning in the belief that curtailing population growth would hurt them economically; without people, leaders of these countries felt they could not reach their full economic potential. But this view is changing.

## Birth Control Methods

● Table 5–3 summarizes the estimated use of effective birth control methods worldwide, including abortion as a separate category (after-the-fact birth control). Here effective refers to methods that, when used properly and regularly,

have a high chance of successfully avoiding an unwanted pregnancy.

Notice that female sterilization is extremely common in developing countries; IUDs are also used extensively, especially in China. In contrast, condoms and oral contraceptives, followed by abortion, are among the most popular forms of birth control in the industrialized nations. As these data illustrate, different types of contraceptives are suited to different cultures. Use of oral contraceptives is difficult, for instance, in a society that lacks good distribution networks for medicines.

The birth control methods that are probably best suited to the needs of developing countries include injectable contraceptives that can last for one to several months and hormonal implants that can help a woman avoid pregnancy for several years. Although many such methods are still in the laboratory stage, the hormonal implant NORPLANT shows potential. NORPLANT, which was approved for use in the United States in 1990, consists of small rods containing time-released hormones that are planted under the skin of the upper arm; they will protect the woman from unwanted pregnancy for up to five years. At any time the implant can be removed and the fertility of the woman restored. NORPLANT has no proven serious side effects (there have been complaints of headaches, weight gain, anemia, and other symptoms).

## Problems with Contraceptive Use

Worldwide only 55% of couples at risk of pregnancy use contraceptives. Although some couples are not practicing birth control because they desire to have children, many simply are not informed about modern birth control methods and/or have limited or no access to contraceptives.

A major problem is that modern contraceptives are too expensive for many couples to afford. According to a 1991 study by the Population Crisis Committee, in about three-fourths of the developing nations, the average family cannot afford modern birth control methods. In some countries, the relative cost of birth control is exorbitant: 30% of the average annual income for a year's supply of birth contol pills or condoms in Ethiopia, or 7% of the average annual income for condoms and 37% for birth control pills in Kenya. This means that from a practical standpoint, contraceptives must be regarded as a "luxury" to be indulged in only after such basic needs as food, clothing, and shelter are satisfied—unless they are supplied free or at reduced cost by

---

**TABLE 5–3** *Estimated Use of Effective Birth Control Methods*

The estimates in the table are only approximate and are based on late 1980s data. It is very difficult to acquire and compile reliable statistics on contraceptive use and abortions, but the numbers presented here are representative.

| Birth Control Method[a] | China | Other Developing Countries | Industrial Countries | World |
|---|---|---|---|---|
| | (million) | | | |
| Female sterilization | 53 | 45 | 15 | 113 |
| Intrauterine devices | 59 | 13 | 11 | 83 |
| Oral contraceptives | 9 | 28 | 27 | 64 |
| Condoms | 5 | 12 | 28 | 45 |
| Male sterilization | 17 | 18 | 8 | 43 |
| Other effective methods[b] | 3 | 8 | 13 | 24 |
| | | | | |
| Total Users | 146 | 124 | 102 | 372 |
| Total Couples at Risk[c] | 200 | 463 | 197 | 860 |
| | (percent) | | | |
| Contraceptive prevalence (users as share of those at risk) | 73 | 27 | 52 | 43 |
| | (million) | | | |
| Abortions | 12 | 16 | 26 | 54 |

[a]Effective or modern methods exclude natural family planning (rhythm), withdrawal, abstinence, and breastfeeding.
[b]Includes diaphragms, sponges, injectables, and implants.
[c]Number of married couples of reproductive age at risk of pregnancy; does not include those currently pregnant or sterile for other than contraceptive reasons.

(*Source*: J. Jacobson, "Planning the Global Family," in L. R. Brown *et al.*, *State of the World 1988* [New York: W. W. Norton, 1988], p. 161. Reprinted with permission of Worldwatch Institute, Washington, D.C., Copyright © 1988.)

# PROBLEMS OF RESOURCE DEPLETION

*Once we see our place, our part of the world, as surrounding us, we have already made a profound division between it and ourselves. We have given up the understanding. . . that we and our country create one another, depend on one another, are literally part of one another; that our land passes in and out of our bodies just as our bodies pass in and out of our land. . . It is for this reason that none of our basic problems is ever solved.* WENDELL BERRY, poet, essayist, and social commentator

PHOTO    *Offshore oil platform near Louisiana at sunset.* (*Source:* Bob Thomason/Tony Stone Images.)

# PRINCIPLES OF RESOURCE MANAGEMENT

## PROLOGUE   *A Town that Pioneers Sustainability*

Arcata, California (population 16,000), which was founded in the mid-1800s, began in the usual way: an economy based on rapid exploitation of local resources. Gold fields in nearby mountains and lumber camps in the surrounding forests provided jobs and money for residents. For many decades, these and other natural resources were extracted, processed, and sold to the outside world. Often such rich natural bounty is eventually used up, and logging towns like Arcata

PHOTO   *Recycling is a labor-intensive job that can potentially employ many more people than mining or extracting resources.* (*Source:* Phil Degginger/Tony Stone Images.)

tend to disintegrate like the mining "ghost towns" of the Old West. But Arcata continues to thrive today because it has broken the traditional cycle of dependence on virgin natural resources. Instead of extracting and processing only virgin materials, many local businesses are generating sizable profits and many jobs by reprocessing used and discarded materials. Cascade Forest Products, for example, employs about 35 people to make soil additives such as compost from discarded wood from local sawmills; Cascade's 1993 sales totaled $3.3 million. Another company, Fire & Light Originals, turns recycled glass cullet collected by Arcata Community Recycling Center into decorative tiles. Along with increased efficiency, this switch to manufacturing with recycled materials is one of the foundations of a sustainable economy and society. Instead of depleting the natural resources of future generations, the economy prospers by recycling materials that have already been extracted. Arcata illustrates how environmental concern can promote economic as well as ecological health.

# $\mathcal{I}$NTRODUCTION

In this chapter, we take an overview of the nature of resources and how to better manage them. As Figure 6–1 shows, many natural resources, from all four spheres, suffer from depletion. Depletion occurs when a resource is utilized faster than it is replaced by natural processes. An oil deposit that took millions of years to form, for example, may be extracted and burned in just a few years, or a species that took many thousands of years to evolve may be driven to extinction in a few years.

The ideal goal of much resource management is sustainable resource use, which seeks to "conserve" or *slow down* the rate of resource exploitation to the point where the resource can be replaced by nature. Tree harvesting and ocean fishing are examples. In other cases, if the resource is in immediate threat of disappearing, sustainable management must go farther and actually "preserve" the resource by *stopping* its current exploitation. Endangered species and endangered ecosystems, for instance, must often be preserved immediately, or they will disappear in a few years.

Recall (Chapter 1) that stopping or slowing down the rate of resource use not only slows depletion but usually has the added benefit of reducing pollution. A sustainable society would have "throughput" reduced to the point where exploited resources (inputs) are being renewed by natural processes and pollution (outputs) can be safely absorbed by natural processes. Historically, resource management has *not* achieved this goal of sustainable use because of social, economic, and

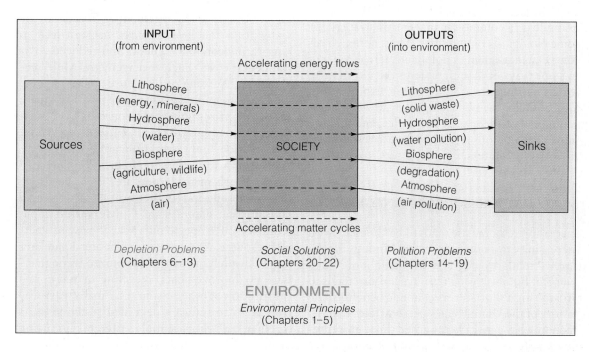

**FIGURE 6–1**
A major environmental problem with natural resources is their rapid depletion. This occurs when the movement of matter and energy through society is accelerated.

political pressures that emphasize rapid exploitation of resources.

## THE NEED TO MANAGE RESOURCES

To some people, the concept of resource management reflects human arrogance. They argue that viewing the natural environment as a "resource" is a very narrow anthropocentric (human-centered) approach to nature. Another objection is that the concept assumes that humans not only should manage environmental resources but are able to manage them effectively. Both of these are very questionable assumptions. Many debates in environmental ethics revolve around whether humans have a right to "tamper" with nature, and if so, how much tampering is justified. Ethics aside, the assumption that humans are able, as a practical reality, to effectively manage nature is not shown in human history. Recall (Chapter 1) that David Ehrenfeld (in his book *The Arrogance of Humanism*) and many others have argued that humans have never effectively managed anything for very long.

In spite of these valid concerns, the need for resource management is inescapable. As human populations and technologies grow, inevitably pressures to exploit the environment will increase. Proper management can help minimize environmental damage. Careful planning of water use, for instance, could spare water for native ecosystems that would have been used for agriculture. Furthermore, management can help undo past damage. Elimination of alien (introduced) species, for example, is a common management strategy for some biological communities. Thus, although resource management is not an attractive concept in some ways, it is preferable to the alternative, which is uncontrolled resource exploitation. Global society will be facing many difficult environmental challenges in the future, and making informed decisions about how to use resources is essential for success.

## WHAT IS RESOURCE MANAGEMENT?

Increasing resource use tends to be "bought" with increasing environmental costs. Mining, for example, tends to degrade the land more than tourism. But increasing resource use also tends to provide high short-term economic benefits. The history of the United States demonstrates that the economy has generally rewarded those entrepreneurs who most rapidly exploited natural resources. This process seemed justified to most people because modern society has traditionally ignored most environmental costs (Chapter 1). For instance, **benefit-cost analysis (BCA)** is a method of comparing the benefits of an activity to its cost. When the benefits (calculated in a dollar amount) are greater than the costs (calculated in a dollar amount), there is said to be a net benefit to society. If you ignore most environmental costs, any short-term economic benefits of resource use will seem worthwhile: when environmental costs are very low (artificially), the benefit will be greater than the costs. For example, clear-cutting a virgin forest could yield enormous profits (benefits) in the short term.

A more realistic way to analyze resource use is to include the long-term economic benefits of not using them. When this is done, less resource use often translates to greater economic benefits. The total economic value of a rainforest, for instance, is usually greater if the forest is utilized over a long time span for tourism, pharmaceuticals, native foods, and other uses then if it is cut down for a one-time short-term gain in lumber that leaves the forest unusable for decades or centuries. The total value of the rainforest is enhanced even more if extremely long-term environmental benefits are included, such as the value of the forest to future generations (Chapter 1).

## RESOURCE MANAGEMENT: PRESERVATION, CONSERVATION, AND RESTORATION

Proper resource management is based on the recognition that less resource use can lead to long-term economic benefits and reduced environmental costs. Such management, while recognizing that some resource use is unavoidable, thus seeks to minimize use where possible. There are three basic options that resource management can apply to minimize resource use: preservation, conservation, and restoration.

**Preservation** refers to nonuse. A "preserve," national park, or wilderness area is an ecosystem that is set aside and (in theory at least) protected in its pristine, natural state. **Conservation** (input reduction) attempts to minimize the use of a natural resource. As discussed in Chapter 1 and later in this chapter, use can be minimized through efficiency improvements, recycling or reuse, and substitution of other resources. Finally, **restoration** seeks to return a degraded resource to its original state. For example, attempts are being made to redirect the Kissimmee River of Florida into the original path that is followed before it was altered by humans. The rapidly growing field of restoration ecology is attempting to return many ecosystems, such as tall-grass prairies and wetlands, to their original state.

## A Brief History of Preservation, Conservation, and Restoration

When the national parks and national forests were being established in the early 1900s under Theodore Roosevelt, there was a lively debate over how much public land should be allotted to preservation and how much to conservation. By prohibiting most forms of resource use except tourism, national parks are an example of preservation ( Fig. 6–2). In contrast, national forests (and most other federal lands) permit timber cutting, mining, grazing, and other uses. The promoters of conservation won the debate, and most federal land has permitted these resource uses. In theory, such uses represent "conservation" because the resources are supposed to be closely managed in a way that minimizes damage to the land. This is rarely realized in practice, however, and many federal and state public lands have suffered extensive damage from overuse. As a result, many environmental groups have argued for setting aside more land as "designated wilderness" and other areas of preservation. Others, especially the Nature Conservancy, buy such land and set it aside as private preserves.

Restoration, the newest type of resource manage-ment, has become much more common in the 1990s. Aquifers, ecosystems, lakes, soils, and many other environments are being restored by a growing number of restoration specialists. Preservation and conservation are more cost-effective than restoration, which can be extremely expensive. Nevertheless, because so many environments are highly degraded from past abuses, restoration will undoubtedly become increasingly common.

Restoration is most effective at the *landscape level*. It does little good to restore a lake acidified from mining runoff to its normal chemistry unless the surrounding land is treated to help reduce acidic runoff. Similarly, reintroducing wolves into a small forest is unlikely to be successful unless the natural ecosystem for the entire region is prepared to support them. A small forest is not large enough for a self-sustaining wolf population (Chapter 12).

## WHO CARES? THE MANY VALUES OF NATURAL RESOURCES

Up to this point, we have talked about the value of resources in economic terms. But as Figure 6–3 shows, people can place at least five values, sometimes called the **five e's**, on natural resources. One of the e's, ethical value, is what philosophers call an **intrinsic value**.

 **FIGURE 6–2**
The U.S. national park system represents an attempt to preserve nature. This scene shows the pristine beauty of Grand Teton National Park. (*Source:* Steve Bly/Tony Stone Images.)

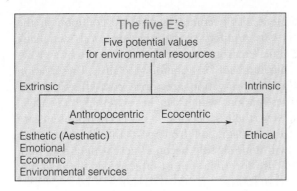

This is the value of a resource unto itself, regardless of its value to humans. Does a mountain have as much right to exist as you do? Does a worm? If you say "yes," then you place a high intrinsic value on these natural resources (Chapter 21). Intrinsic values are "ecocentric" (environment-oriented).

The other four e's are what philosophers call **extrinsic values** (Fig. 6–3). These are values that are external to a resource's own right to exist, referring instead to the resource's ability to provide something for humans. Such values are "anthropocentric" (human-oriented). Extrinsic values are more utilitarian, or practical, than intrinsic values and therefore tend to be more widely discussed in political and economic debates on resource management. Esthetic (aesthetic) value is the value of a resource in making the world more beautiful, more appealing to the senses, and generally more pleasant. The value you place on a mountain hike in the cool morning air might be an example. Some people place no value on this and would pay nothing for it. Others find it indispensable. Emotional values include the value of a resource beyond sensory enjoyment. Some people, for example, develop very strong emotional bonds to certain natural areas or certain plant or animal species. This is sometimes called a "sense of place." Many psychologists consider nature to be important for mental health, especially in children.

Economic values are directly involved with tangible products that can be bought or sold: food, timber, energy, and so on. As we previously discussed, society needs to focus more on long-term economic values, which actually provide more income over the long run. The value of resources for tourism, native fruits, or other sustainable products is ultimately much greater than the value of their destructive uses. Environmental service values are the value of resources in providing intangible "services" that allow humans (and other life) to exist on Earth. Plants help pu-rify air and produce oxygen, and plant roots and soil microbes purify water; ultimately, all food relies on a variety of environmental services.

Some people place all five values on all environmental resources. How many values would you place on the forest shown in Figure 6–4? How many on a beach? Many people would place only economic values on such resources. Logging, mining, and other types of harvesting that destroy the resources are called **direct values**. Most environmental problems arise when resources are appreciated for only their direct value. Placing only "direct," short-term economic value on natural resources artificially "discounts" their true value to society and to future generations. For example, four of the five e's—esthetic, emotional, environmental services, and ethical values—are not direct values. They represent what economists call **indirect values**, meaning that they are valued in ways that do not involve direct mining, harvesting or other destruction of the resources. If resource prices incorporated both indirect values and long-term direct values, the prices would reflect the resources' true environmental cost. Consider the following comparison:

| SHORT-TERM VALUE | LONG-TERM VALUES |
|---|---|
| Short-term economic value | Long-term economic value |
| | + Esthetic value |
| | + Emotional value |
| | + Ethical value |
| | + Environmental service value |

While the short-term economic value of resources provides immediate financial rewards, harvesting the short-term value often destroys (1) the long-term economic value and (2) many or all of the indirect values. If society included all the values in the right hand column in its calculations of the value of existing natural resources, it would encourage less destructive harvesting of them. A major problem is that such values are subjective and very difficult to calculate, but estimates can be made (Chapter 20). Including these long-term values would motivate society to preserve resources and conserve them. More sustainable uses of resources, such as extractive forestry and ecotourism, will be encouraged and rewarded. As long as only short-term values are considered, overuse and exploitation will be encouraged and rewarded.

# KINDS OF RESOURCES

A **resource** is a source of raw materials used by society. These materials include all types of matter and energy that are used to build and run society. Minerals, trees, soil, water, coal, and all other naturally occurring materials are resources. **Reserves** are the subset of resources that have been located and can be profitably extracted at the current market price. Raw materials that have been located but cannot be profitably extracted at the present time are simply called resources, as are those raw materials that have not been discovered.

**Renewable resources** can be replaced within a few human generations. Examples include timber, food, and many alternative fuels such as solar power, biomass, and hydropower. **Nonrenewable resources** cannot be replaced within a few human generations. Examples include **fossil fuels**, such as oil and coal, and ore deposits of metals. The phrase a "few human generations" is necessary because some resources are replaceable on very long, geologic time scales. Oil, coal, soils, and some metallic mineral deposits may form again if we wait for thousands to hundreds of millions of years. However, these rates of renewal are so many thousands of times slower than the rates of use that, for all intents, they are nonrenewable on a human scale. In contrast, solar energy is actually supplied faster than we can use it.

The concept of renewability is sometimes blurred. Very old groundwater in deserts may take centuries or even many thousands of years to replace, while groundwater in rainy tropical areas may be replaced in a few days. Thus, deep groundwater in deserts, sometimes called "fossil groundwater," is essentially a nonrenewable resource. Although nonrenewable resources cannot be replaced through natural processes on a human time scale, some (such as certain metals) can be recycled many times.

# PATTERNS OF RESOURCE DEPLETION

Recall from Chapter 4 that there are two basic inputs from the environment, matter and energy. Matter constantly cycles through society and the environment whereas energy primarily has a one-way flow. Because of this difference, matter and energy are depleted differently.

## How Matter Resources Are Depleted

Matter resources are depleted by being "lost" or dispersed. Ore deposits are unusually concentrated deposits of minerals that are normally

■ **FIGURE 6–4**
What is the monetary value of a forest? Is it worthless? Is it priceless? The answer varies greatly from person to person. (*Source:* Michael Busselle/Tony Stone Images.)

found in more dilute form in the Earth's crust. When we mine and process the ore into metals to build cars and other refined products, the atoms may be eventually dispersed (such as when gears wear down grinding against one another) or lost to further human use when we dispose of the products in landfills and elsewhere (of course, the "urban ore" of a landfill may later be mined for its metal content). Similarly, rapid erosion depletes soil not because the nutrients and minerals in the soil are destroyed, but because the soil is dispersed, ultimately into the oceans.

These examples are nonrenewable matter; when dispersed, molecules of metals and soils will stay dispersed unless we spend much energy and money to reconcentrate them. In the case of re-

# How to Exceed Maximum Sustainable Yield: Overfishing in New England

In 1981, the United States declared a 200-mile (322 km) boundary around its shores, banning most foreign trawlers that had fished U.S. waters. The ban was an attempt to save the beleaguered New England fishing industry. The measure worked until Americans themselves began overfishing. Encouraged in part by a federal loan program, they began building more boats, equipping them with powerful fish-finding electronics. They lobbied to remove quotas on catches. And, for a while, they caught a lot more fish. But the trawler catch in New England peaked in 1983 and has since fallen sharply ( Fig. 1). Stocks of flounder and haddock are near record lows. The cod population is down. Bluefin tuna and swordfish have been depleted. There have been booms and busts before, but scientists say that this time is different. The fleets are so big and the technology so advanced that fish no longer have anywhere to hide.

In 1983, the trawler catch reached 410 million pounds (186 million kg), up 66% from 1976. In 1990, the haul had declined to 282 million pounds (128 million kg). Although this was up from the low of 234 million pounds (105 million kg) in 1989, marine scientists say the increase was achieved by catching huge numbers of juvenile fish that had just reached the minimum size. Many of

**FIGURE 1**
New England fishermen are struggling to make a living because of the decline of many species. (*Source:* Tom Stewart/The Stock Market.)

the fish hadn't had a chance to spawn. They are being fished out faster than they are reproducing.

Some people in the fishing industry say they can't back off. They have to keep the boats going nonstop to make enough to survive. But others and conservationists insist that current measures, such as minimum net mesh sizes and occasional closures of overfished waters, simply are not enough. Strict catch quotas, trip limits, even moratoria on new boats are needed, or more people will be forced out of the business in the long run. Legislation has been introduced to reduce the size of the New England fleet by buying out vessels with money from a tax on the diesel fuel the fishing boats use. Some have suggested that the government should subsidize the fleets by meeting mortgages for those who do not fish a certain number of days. And severe restrictions are being placed on fishing in some areas, such as the once-fertile Georges Bank ecosystem off the coast of Massachusetts. Some way of rationally allocating fishery resources is needed to guarantee that the industry remains intact.

This is a classic example of the "tragedy of the commons." The oceans are used by many individuals and nations. Thus, many nations must agree on laws that govern access to ocean resources, and, perhaps more difficult, these laws must be enforced in ways that prevent overfishing.

---

ciency and reuse/recycling of wastewater are common.

### Efficiency Improvements

Efficiency improvements occur when the same task is accomplished with fewer resources (Chapter 1). An example would be lighter, more fuel-

efficient cars to conserve fuel and building materials. Between 1973 and 1992, the average efficiency of cars made in the United States doubled from 14 to 28 miles per gallon (6 to 12 km per liter). Such cars perform the same tasks as less fuel-efficient cars but use fewer resources in doing so. As another example, about two-thirds of the water used in irrigation is lost to evapora-